NAMIBIA

A visual tour through its regions

THOMAS DRESSLER

NAMIBIA

A visual tour through its regions

SUNBIRD PUBLISHERS

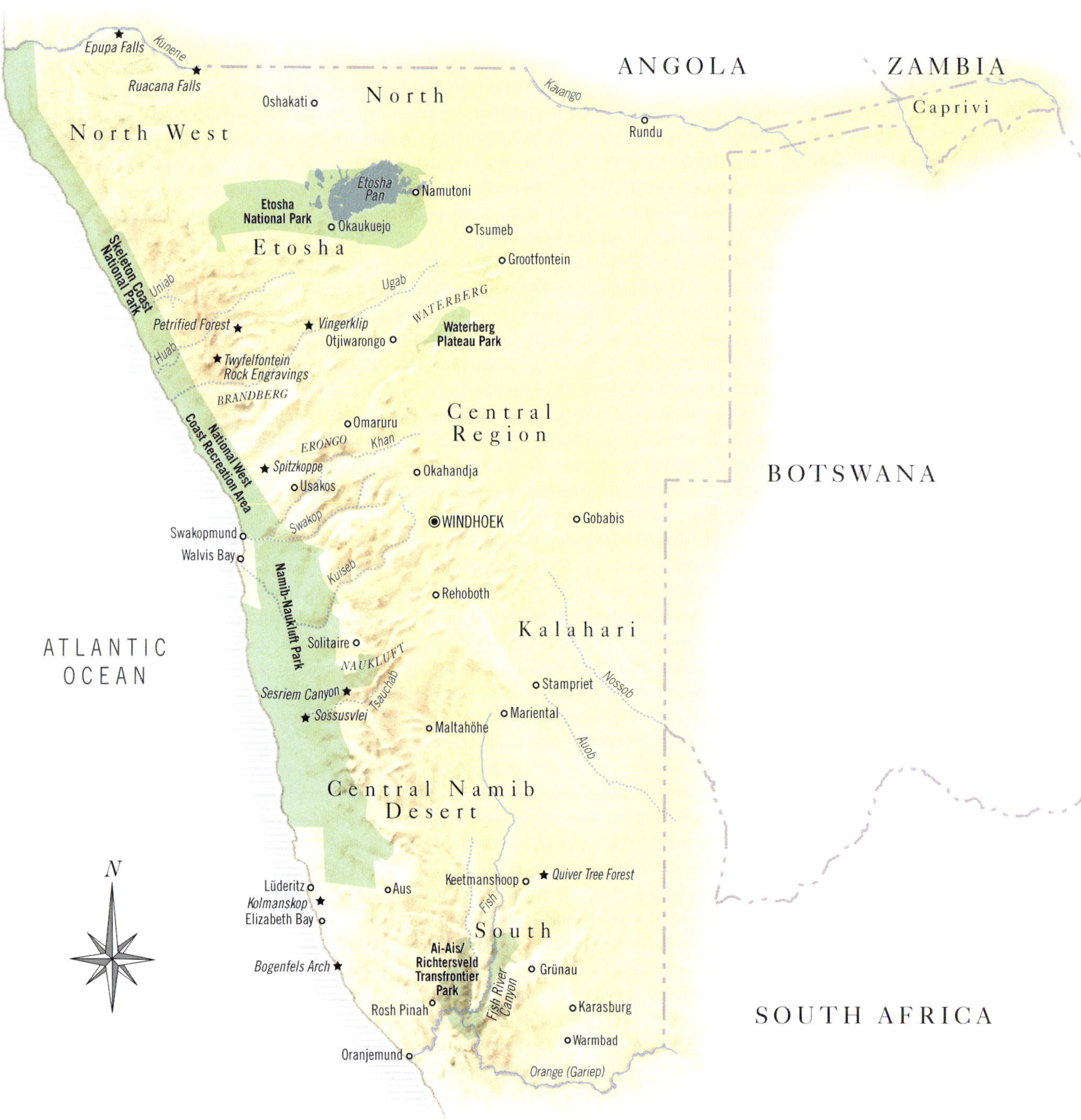

Epupa Falls
Kunene
Ruacana Falls
ANGOLA
ZAMBIA
Oshakati
North
Kavango
Caprivi
Rundu
North West
Etosha Pan
Namutoni
Etosha National Park
Okaukuejo
Tsumeb
Etosha
Grootfontein
Skeleton Coast National Park
Uniab
Ugab
WATERBERG
Petrified Forest
Vingerklip
Waterberg Plateau Park
Otjiwarongo
Huab
Twyfelfontein Rock Engravings
BRANDBERG
Central Region
Omaruru
ERONGO
Khan
National West Coast Recreation Area
Spitzkoppe
Okahandja
BOTSWANA
Usakos
WINDHOEK
Gobabis
Swakop
Swakopmund
Walvis Bay
Kuiseb
Namib-Naukluft Park
Rehoboth
Kalahari
ATLANTIC OCEAN
Solitaire
NAUKLUFT
Stampriet
Nossob
Tsauchab
Sesriem Canyon
Mariental
Sossusvlei
Maltahöhe
Auob
Central Namib Desert
N
Keetmanshoop
Quiver Tree Forest
Lüderitz
Aus
Kolmanskop
Fish
Elizabeth Bay
South
Ai-Ais/ Richtersveld Transfrontier Park
Grünau
Bogenfels Arch
Fish River Canyon
Karasburg
Rosh Pinah
SOUTH AFRICA
Warmbad
Oranjemund
Orange (Gariep)

Contents

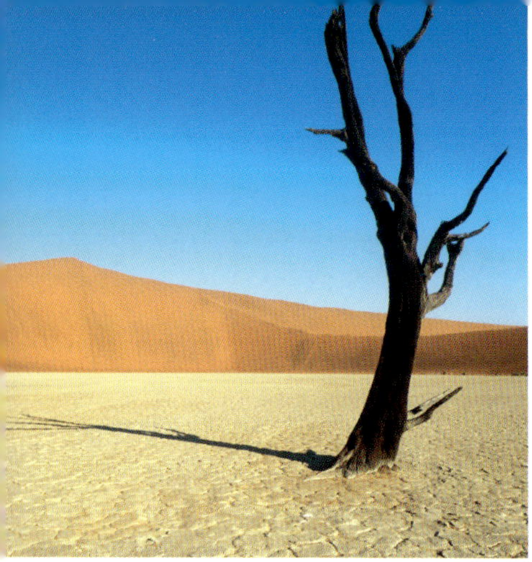
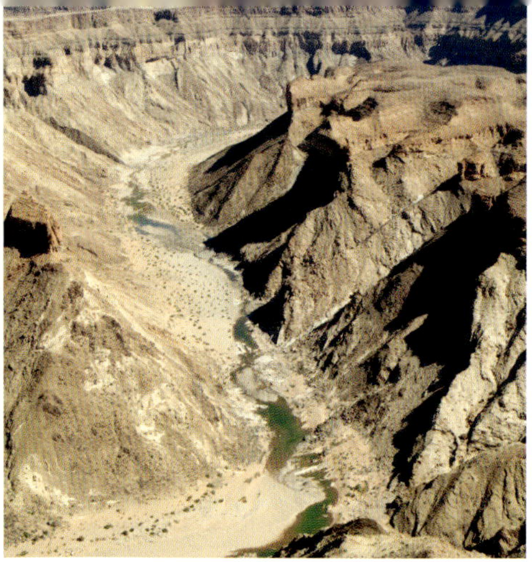
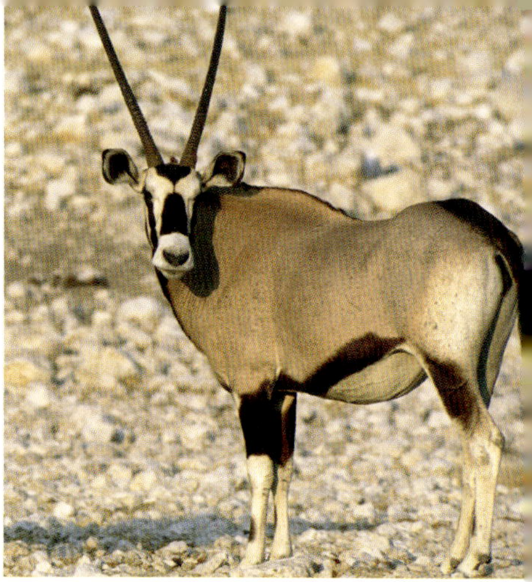
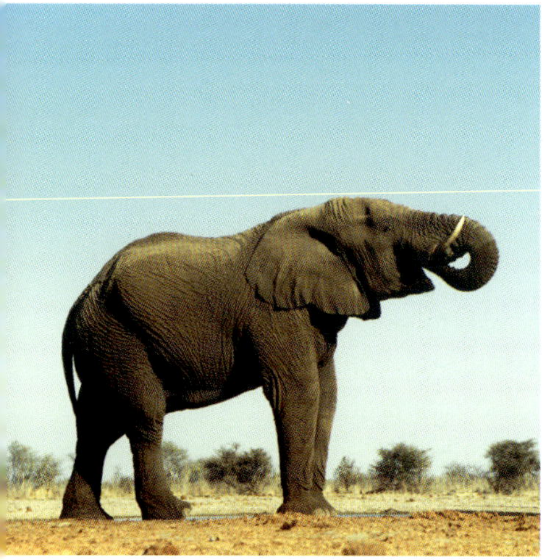
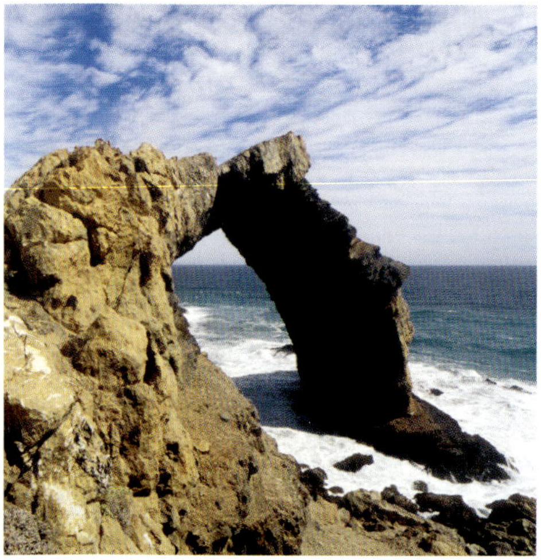
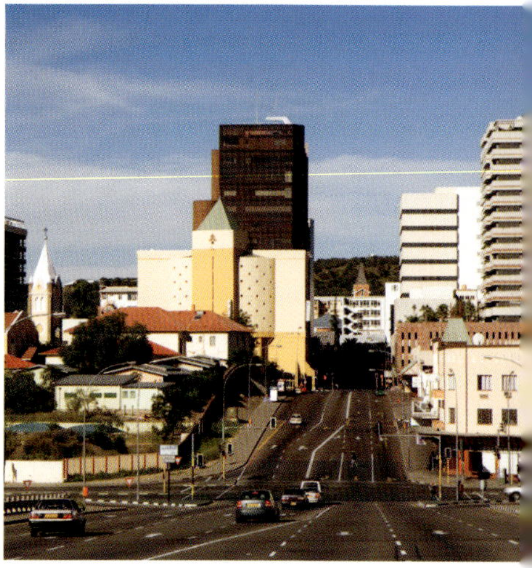
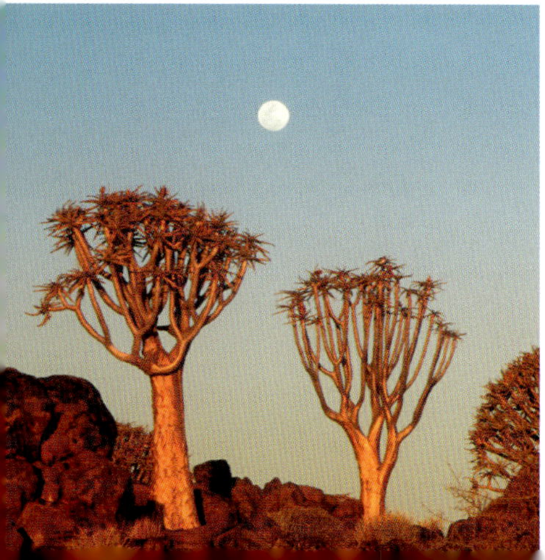
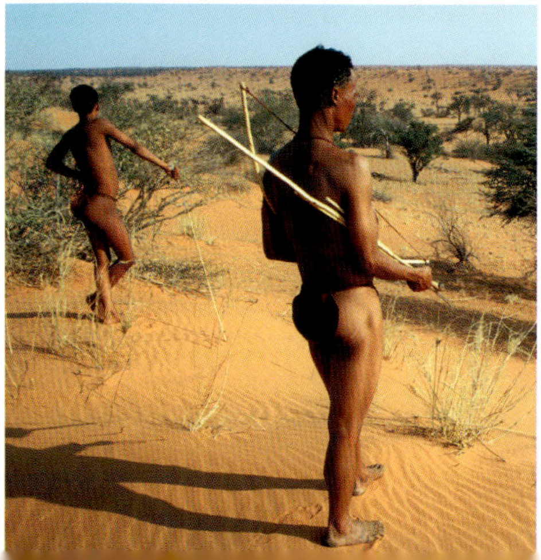
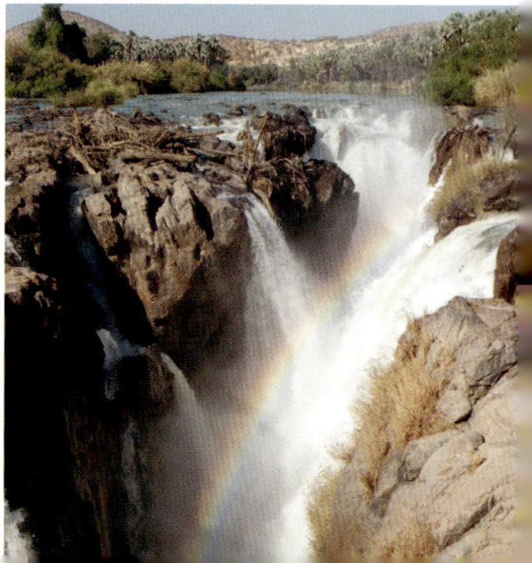

Namibia

The Namibian landscape is hauntingly beautiful. Some would call it austere. Others stark. And yet, once the first rains have fallen and life has been restored to its parched lands, it is a country teeming with life – its wildlife congregating in large herds or small family groups, its sombre sands exploding with colour.

Bound by the icy waters of the Atlantic in the west, the searing sands of the Kalahari and Botswana in the east, Angola to the north and South Africa to the south, this is a country set apart from all else Africa has to offer. Relatively small pockets of urban settlements lie scattered across an arid expanse that stretches from the Skeleton Coast to the dunes of the Kalahari, which skirt Namibia's border with Botswana. Hedged between the two extremes is Namibia's heartland, where surprisingly abundant farmland continues its daily struggle to keep the desert sands at bay and creatures great and small have made their home in what otherwise may be considered a harsh and inhospitable landscape.

The land here – in places scorched and dry, in others lush and green – is the extraordinary result of the erosive power of wind and water, volcanic activity and glaciation over millennia. Many of Namibia's iconic landmarks – among them the Fish River Canyon and the Skeleton Coast, Vingerkop and the Spitzkoppe and the lunar landscapes that have erupted around the saltpans – consist of bizarre abstract forms, animated rock formations and natural oddities, and all are testimony to the incredible power of nature that typifies this corner of Africa.

While Namibia has earned international acclaim for its extraordinary landscapes and abundant wildlife, which draw

OPPOSITE FROM LEFT TO RIGHT:

- Skeletal silhouette of a camelthorn tree at Dead Vlei, Namib Desert.
- Craggy faces of the great Fish River Canyon, Ai-Ais/Richtersveld Transfrontier National Park.
- The iconic gemsbok (or oryx) in Etosha National Park in the northern reaches of Namibia.
- An African elephant bull at a water hole in Etosha National Park.
- The impressive arc of the Bogenfels Arch near Lüderitz on the southern coast.
- Contemporary cityscape of the Namibian capital, Windhoek, in the country's heartland.
- Quiver trees, of the aloe family, stand tall and proud in the 'forest' near Keetmanshoop.
- !Kung traditional hunter-gatherers who have made their home in the vast wasteland of the semi-arid Kalahari.
- The magnificent cascades of Epupa Falls on the Kunene River, which forms the border between Namibia and Angola.

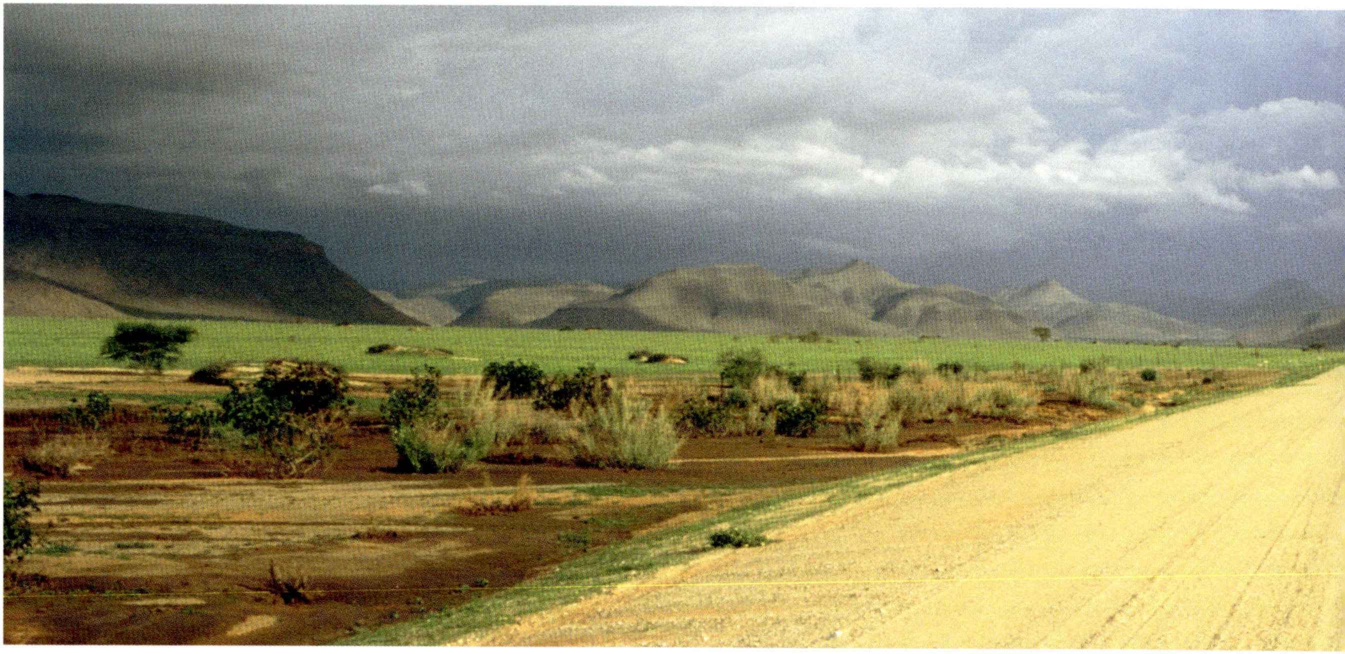

hundreds of thousands of visitors annually, it is also remarkably rich in diamonds and other minerals, which contribute no small percentage to the national economy and welfare of its people.

The nation of Namibia is a fascinating mix of indigenous groups who made their home here over hundreds if not thousands of years, including the San, Himba, Herero, Owambo and Damara people, as well as the descendants of British, Dutch and, most significantly, German colonists who made their way here to seek their fortune. Today the country, with a population of approximately two million, is one of the most sparsely populated in the world – said to be second only to Mongolia in density – and covers more than double the land space of highly populated nations such as the United Kingdom. Even Namibia's capital, Windhoek, has what is essentially a miniscule population of about 300 000.

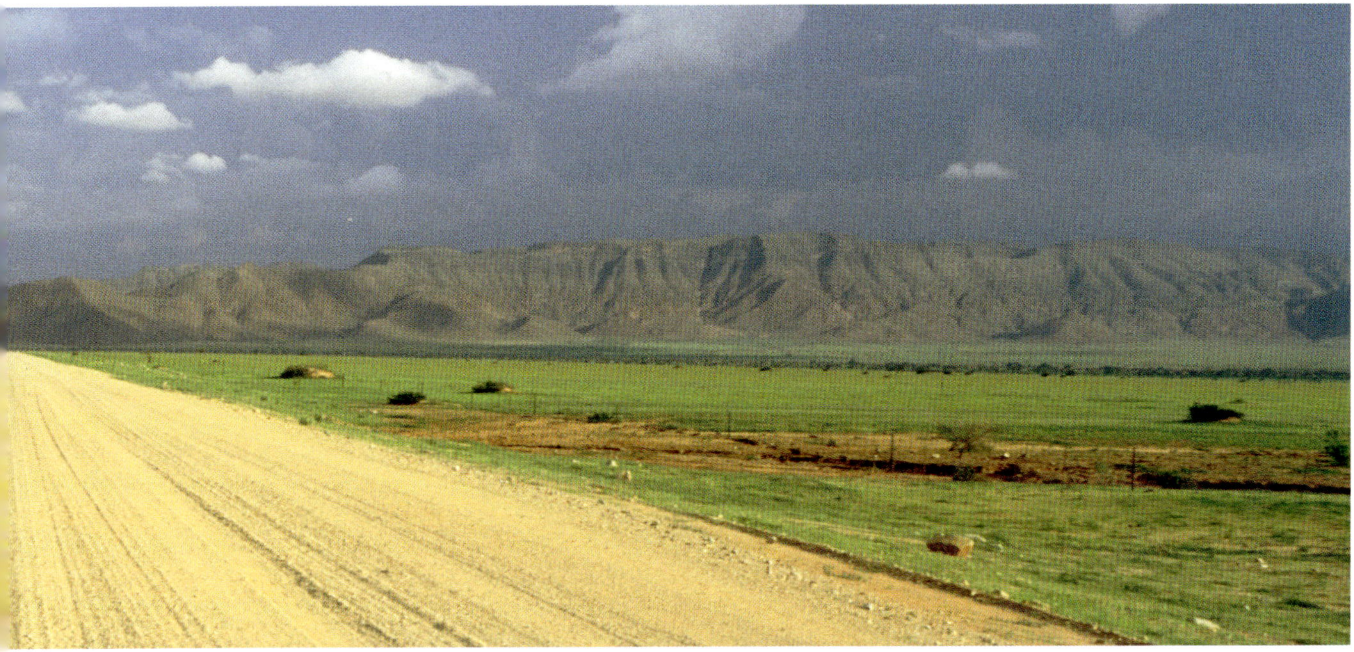

Namibia finally gained independence in March 1990: free from the colonial rule of Germany, and even South Africa, as well as from the protracted guerrilla warfare that threatened the stability of this developing nation. For more than 20 years, a Namibian government, led by the ruling party SWAPO, has steered a country that has since emerged as one of the jewels in Africa's crown. Its people are peaceful and its land well endowed: a haven for an extraordinary diversity of wildlife that ranges from the gemsbok and desert elephant to succulent plants and the peculiar welwitschia.

National treasures – apart from the architectural splendours of Windhoek and the cultural heritage of Swakopmund – include drawcards such as the Fish River Canyon, Skeleton Coast, and the Namib-Naukluft and Etosha national parks.

ABOVE: The Namibian countryside is usually dusty and dry, but after the rains it turns an astonishingly verdant green. While many roads are tarred, some – such as the seemingly endless stretch of the C14 between Solitaire and the Naukluft mountains – are simply gravel.

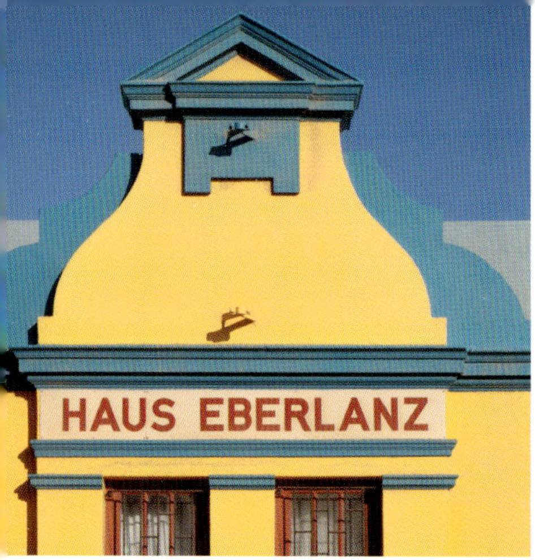
HAUS EBERLANZ
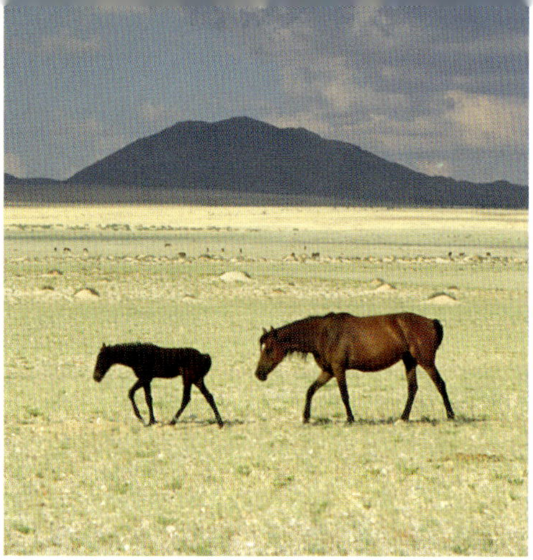
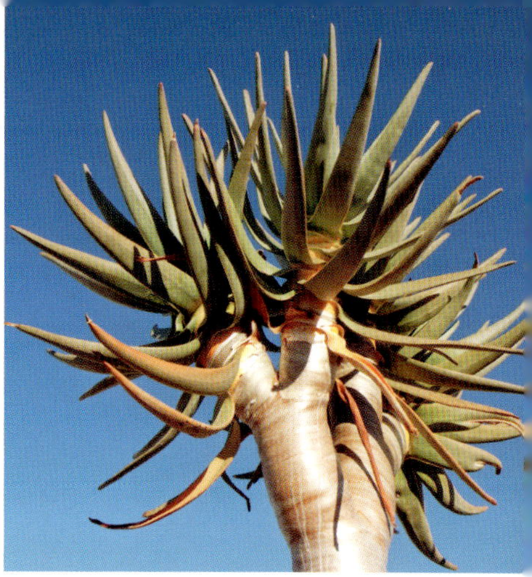
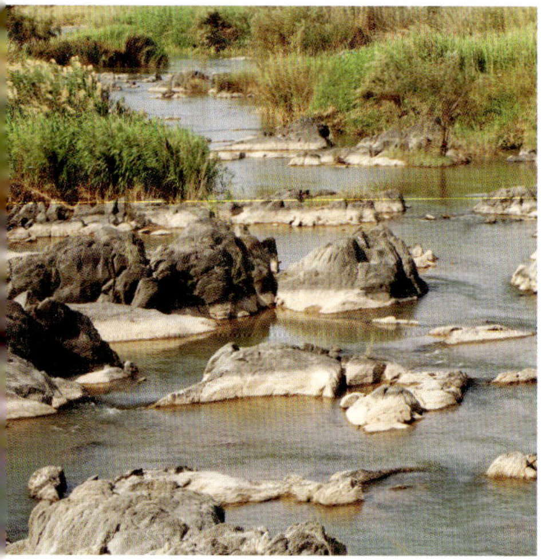
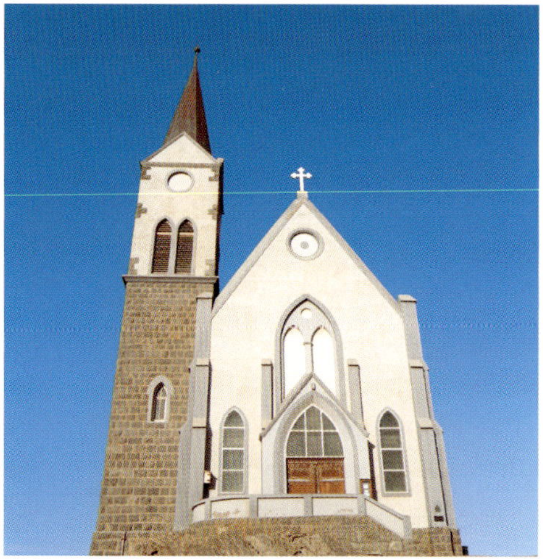
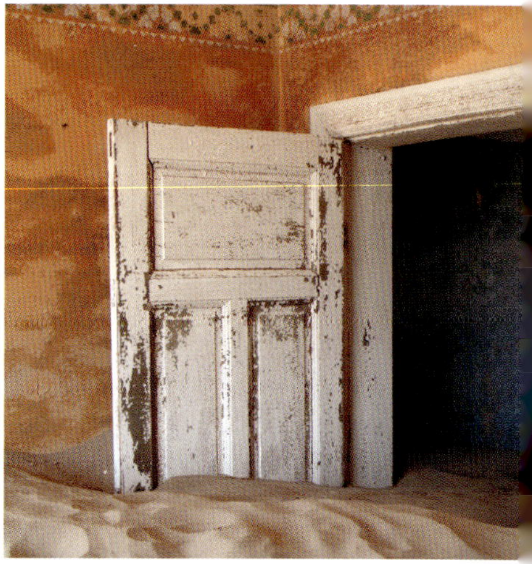
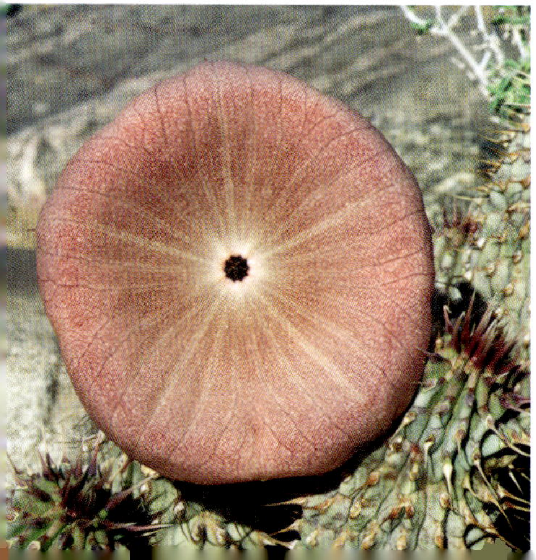
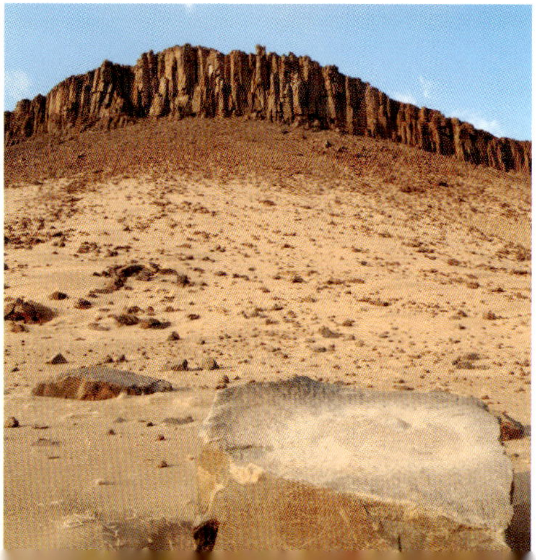
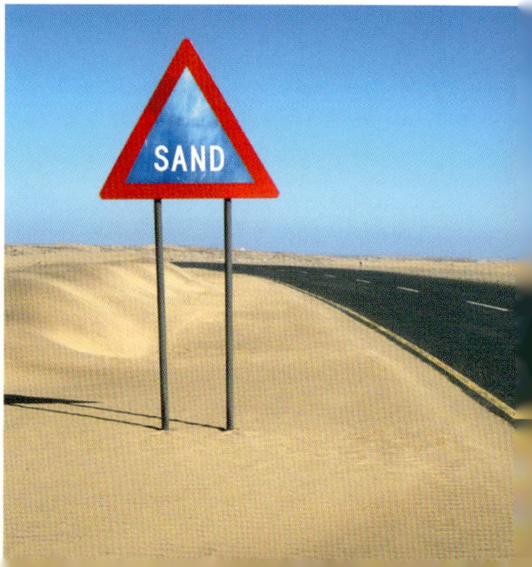
SAND

South

The far south of Namibia stretches from the country's border with South Africa north to about the B4 highway linking Keetmanshoop in the interior with the coastal town of Lüderitz, and is perhaps the most temperate region in the entire country. It is here that craggy rock faces and deep ravines are gently counterbalanced by sandy plains and the long, languid watercourses of the Fish River and its tributaries. It is here too that the Fish River carves its way deep into the rocky substrate as it winds its way to the ocean, through the iconic national treasure of the Fish River Canyon and beyond into the Ai-Ais/Richtersveld Transfrontier National Park before it finally merges with the Orange River and spills into the Atlantic at Oranjemund.

Tucked away in the sparse hinterland is Keetmanshoop, a quiet, laid-back town established in 1866 as a German mission station to convert the local Nama people to Christianity. On the outskirts of Keetmanshoop are two of the region's most recognisable landmarks: the impressive stands of quiver trees so iconic of the region and the scattering of bizarre rock formations that make up Giant's Playground. This arid landscape of shrubs and succulents is scattered with camelthorn trees, providing a haven for an assortment of wildlife.

The cultural and socio-political centre of the Karas region is the harbour town of Lüderitz on the rocky Atlantic seaboard. Although still relatively small, this port town has developed considerably since its inception as a colonial trading post in the 1880s, mostly as a result of the discovery of diamonds nearby in the early 1900s.

OPPOSITE FROM LEFT TO RIGHT:

- Historic buildings in colonial style punctuate the skyline of the southern coastal town of Lüderitz.
- Wild horses roam the Garub plains to the west of the desert village of Aus.
- Local hunter-gatherers once used the hollowed branches of the quiver tree to hold their arrows.
- Rocky river bed of the Orange River, marking the southern boundary of Namibia.
- Façade of the Evangelical Lutheran Church, known locally as the Felsenkirche, in Lüderitz.
- Miner's house in the deserted settlement of Kolmanskop, abandoned after the diamond finds began to dwindle.
- Succulent hoodia plant, prized ingredient of herbal infusions concocted by local inhabitants.
- Ragged peaks line the banks of the mighty Orange River in the far south of Namibia.
- Roads through the desert are plagued by the often hazardous shifting sands of the Namib.

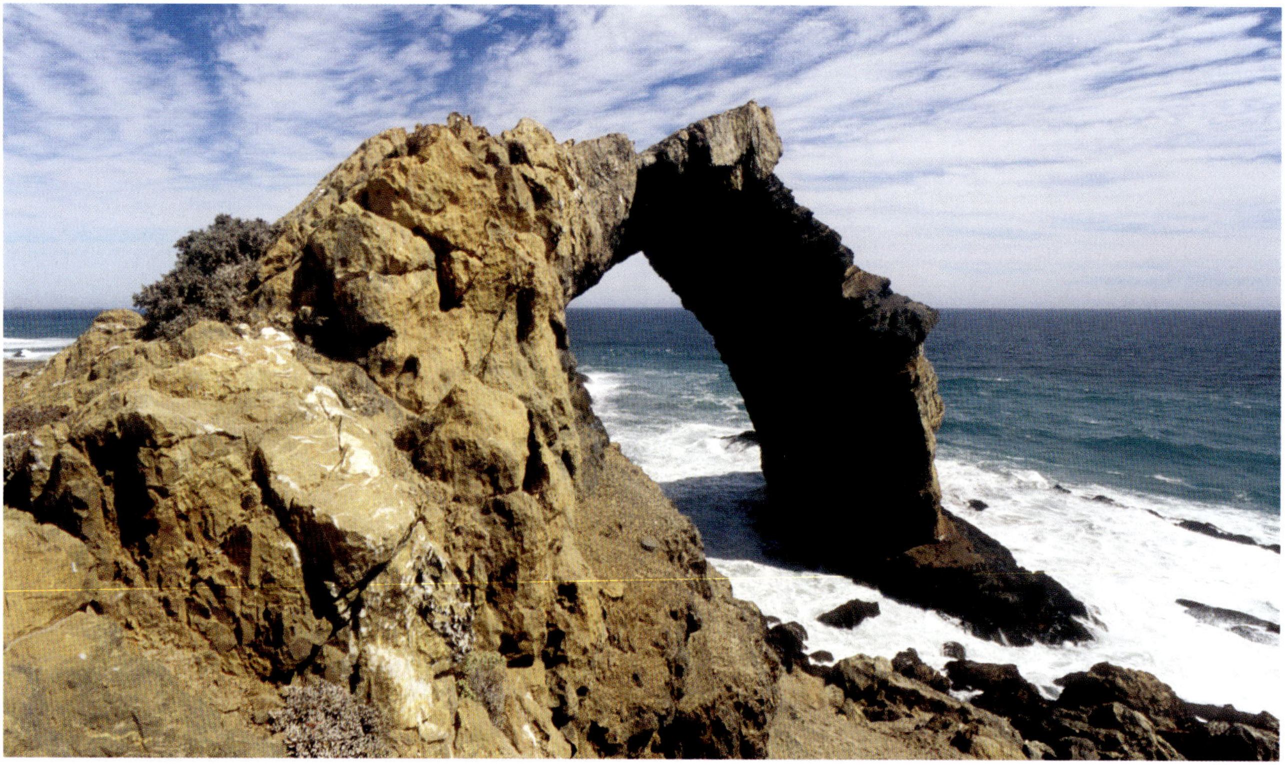

ABOVE: Raging seas and wind-borne particles of sand have sculpted the extraordinary Bogenfels Arch, a 55-metre natural rock formation that juts into the Atlantic Ocean just south of Lüderitz.

OPPOSITE: Buffeted by the same erosive activity that formed the Bogenfels Arch, man-made structures in abandoned Elizabeth Bay have suffered the same fate, the weathered bricks succumbing to salt-laden winds.

The seascape around Lüderitz is rugged and craggy, its cliffs and caverns chiselled by the ocean as it crashes and cuts into the rocky coast. Millennia of erosion have resulted in strange formations being carved out of the rock strata, none more spectacular than the Bogenfels Arch. The arch spans a particularly volatile stretch of the Atlantic coast south of Lüderitz and the neighbouring towns of Kolmanskop and Elizabeth Bay, long deserted since diamond finds began to dwindle in the mid-twentieth century. At their peak, towns spawned by Namibia's diamond fields were said to be the among the world's wealthiest. Today there is little left.

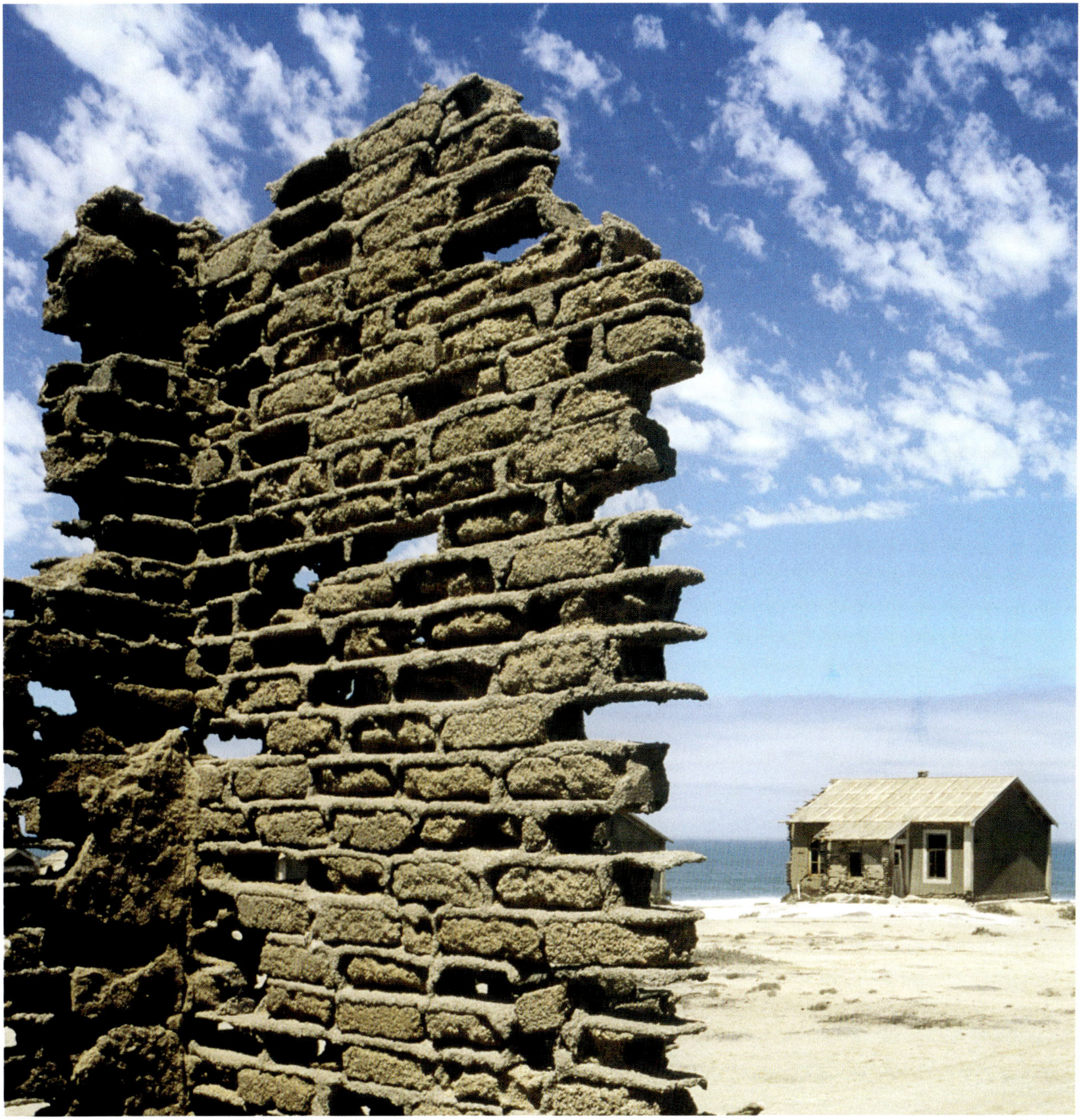

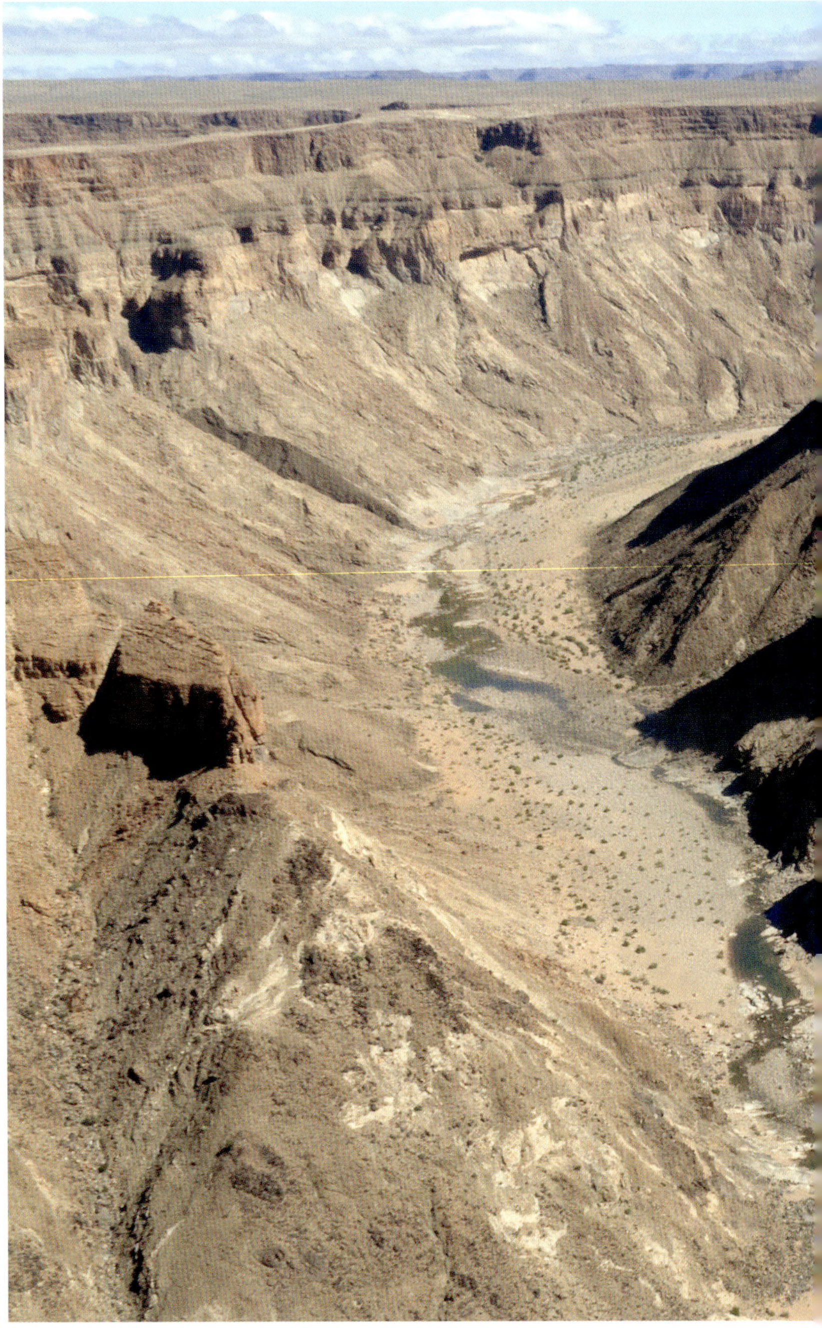

RIGHT: The awe-inspiring Fish River Canyon, with its deep ravines and towering rock faces, is – at 160 kilometres long, 25 kilometres wide and more than 500 metres deep in places – the largest in Africa, and said to be the second largest in the world after the Grand Canyon in Colorado, USA.

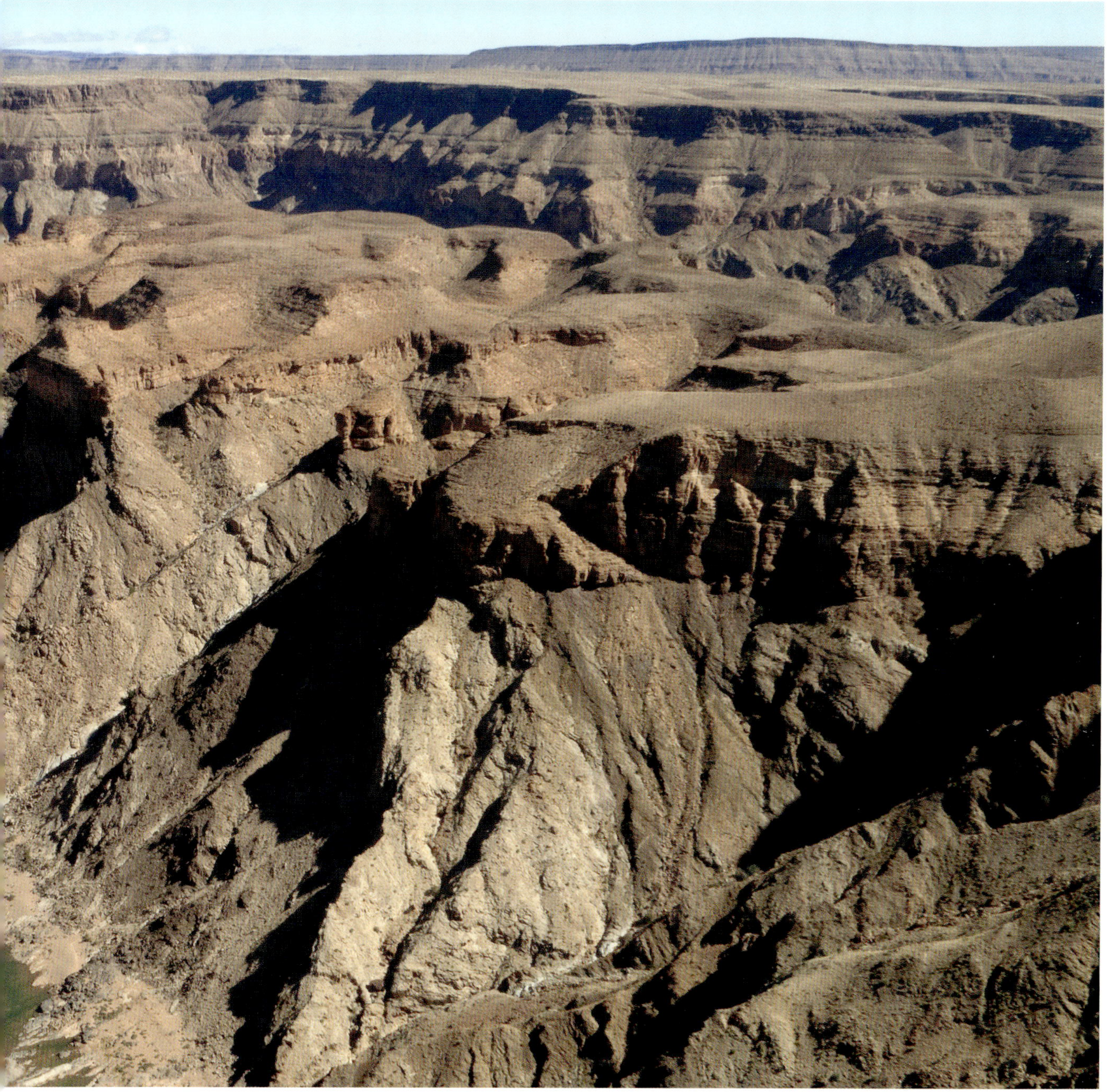

RIGHT: The famed Quiver Tree Forest on the Gariganus farm near Keetmanshoop is a stand of about 250 quiver trees indigenous to the southern African subcontinent. Also known as the *kokerboom*, quiver trees are of the aloe genus and are generally not found in such large groups.

OVERLEAF: Constant fluctuations in land temperatures sometimes mean oppressive heat and turbulent airflow over the desert, often resulting in spectacular lightning displays. Here the night skies over Keetmanshoop are illuminated by brilliant flashes of light.

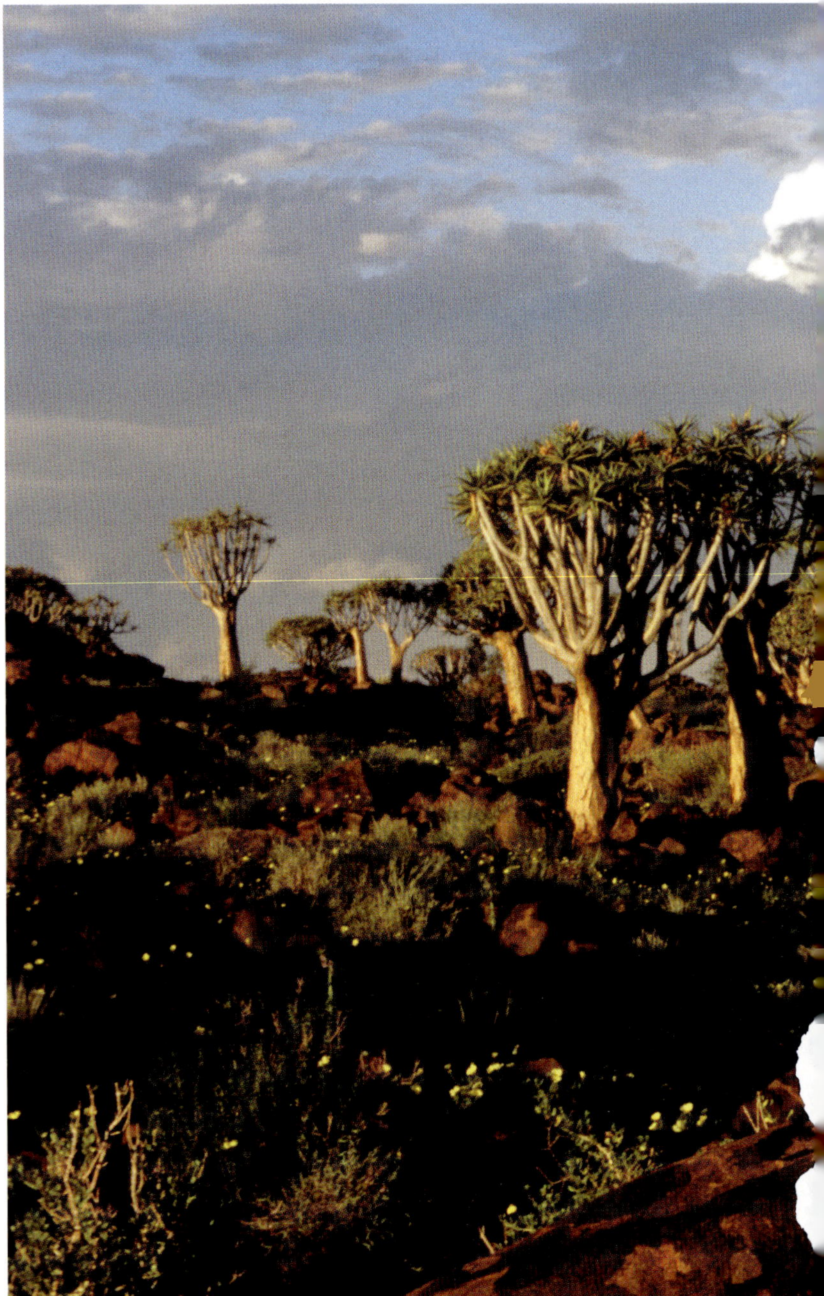

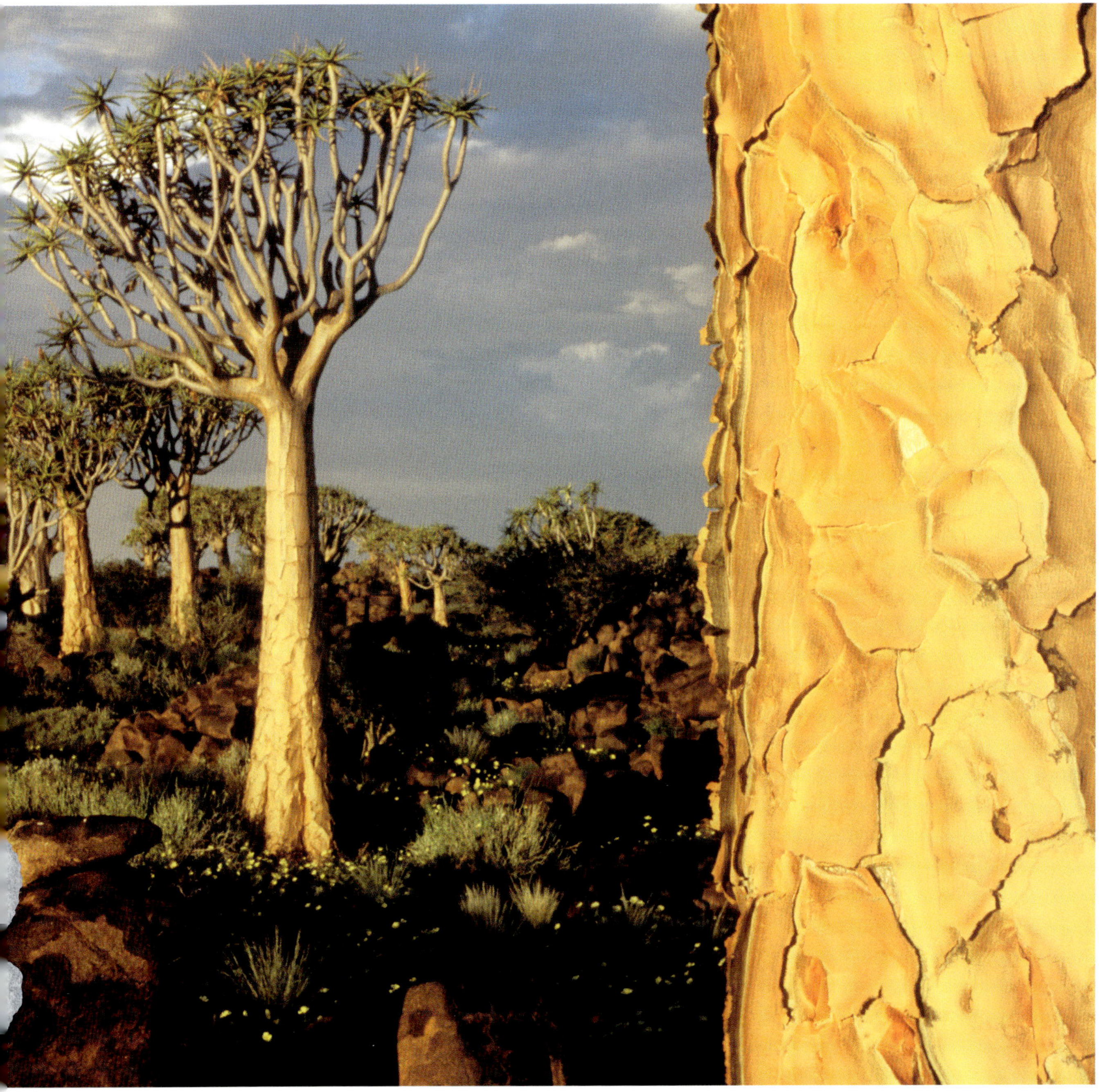

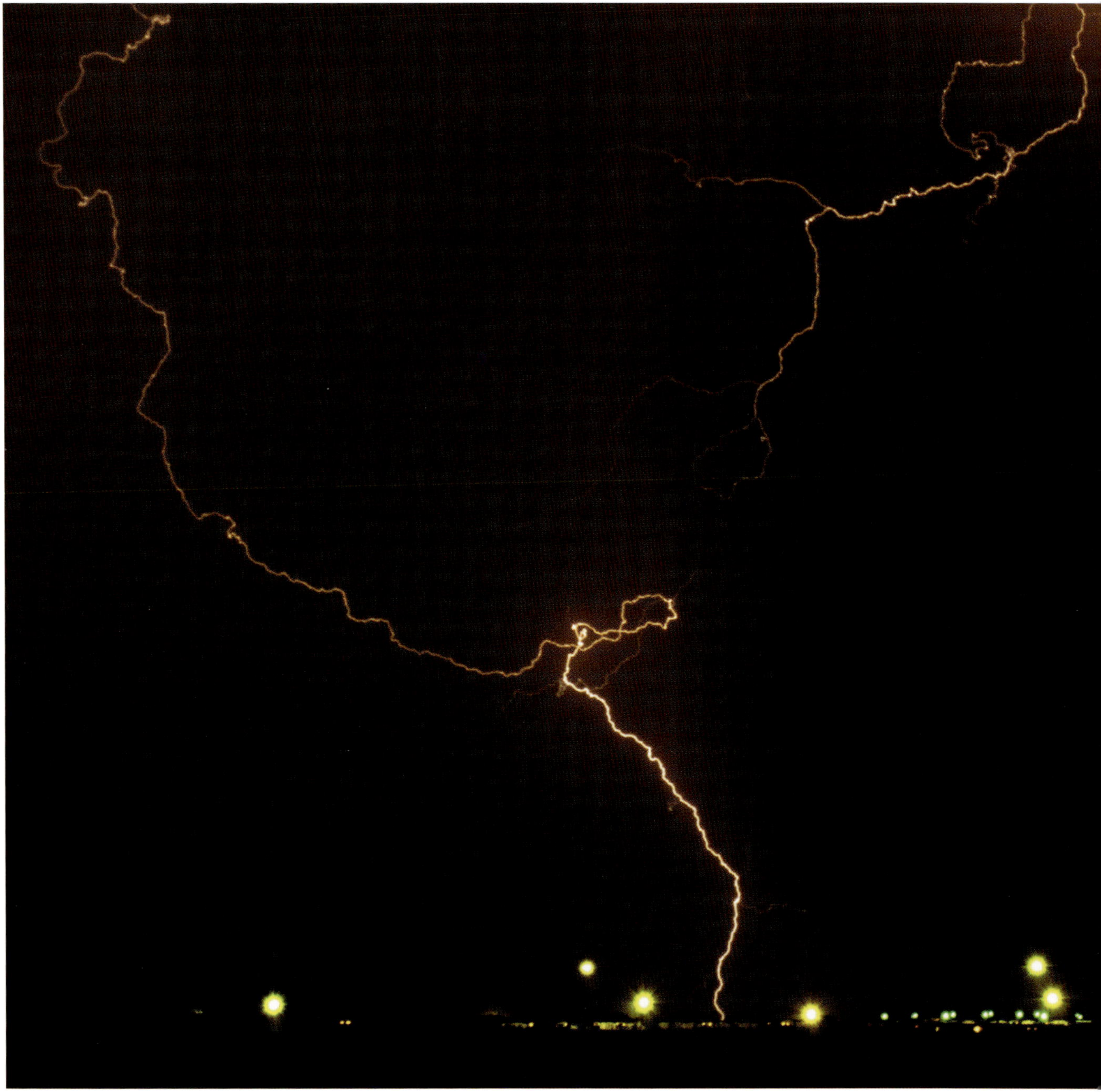

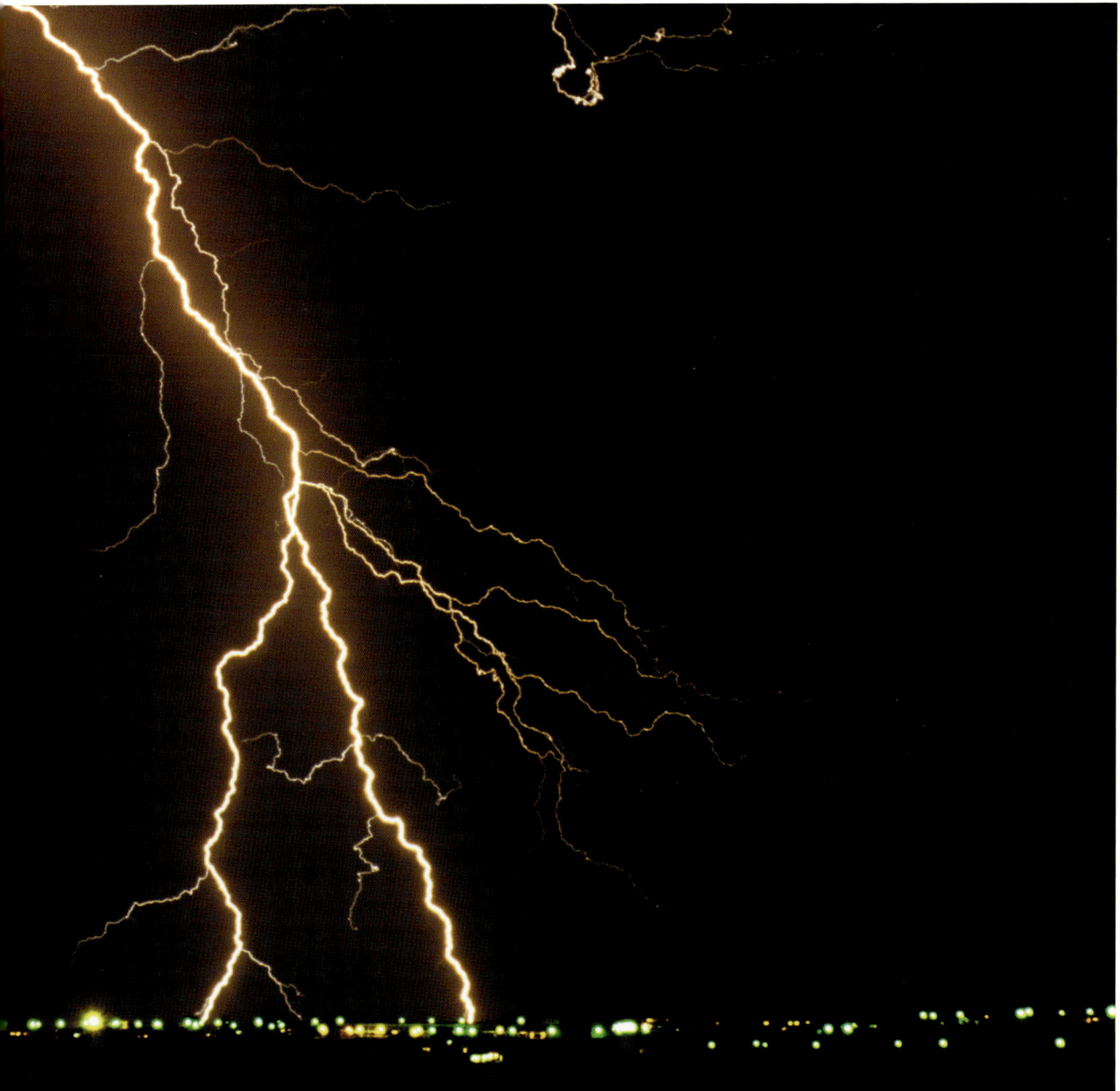

RIGHT: The irregular and unreliable rainfall associated with the desert climate means that rivers are intermittent, with many in Namibia flowing for only short periods during the year. As a result, plants and trees, such as the camelthorn, have to adapt or die.

OVERLEAF, LEFT: Searing heat and limited water mean that Namibia's plant life, including the many succulents that dot its rugged terrain, have to be hardy to survive on a negligible amount of water.

OVERLEAF, RIGHT: The Namaqua chameleon, a ground-dwelling member of the lizard family, has adapted well to life on the hot desert sands, and is able to hunt successfully on both sand and rock.

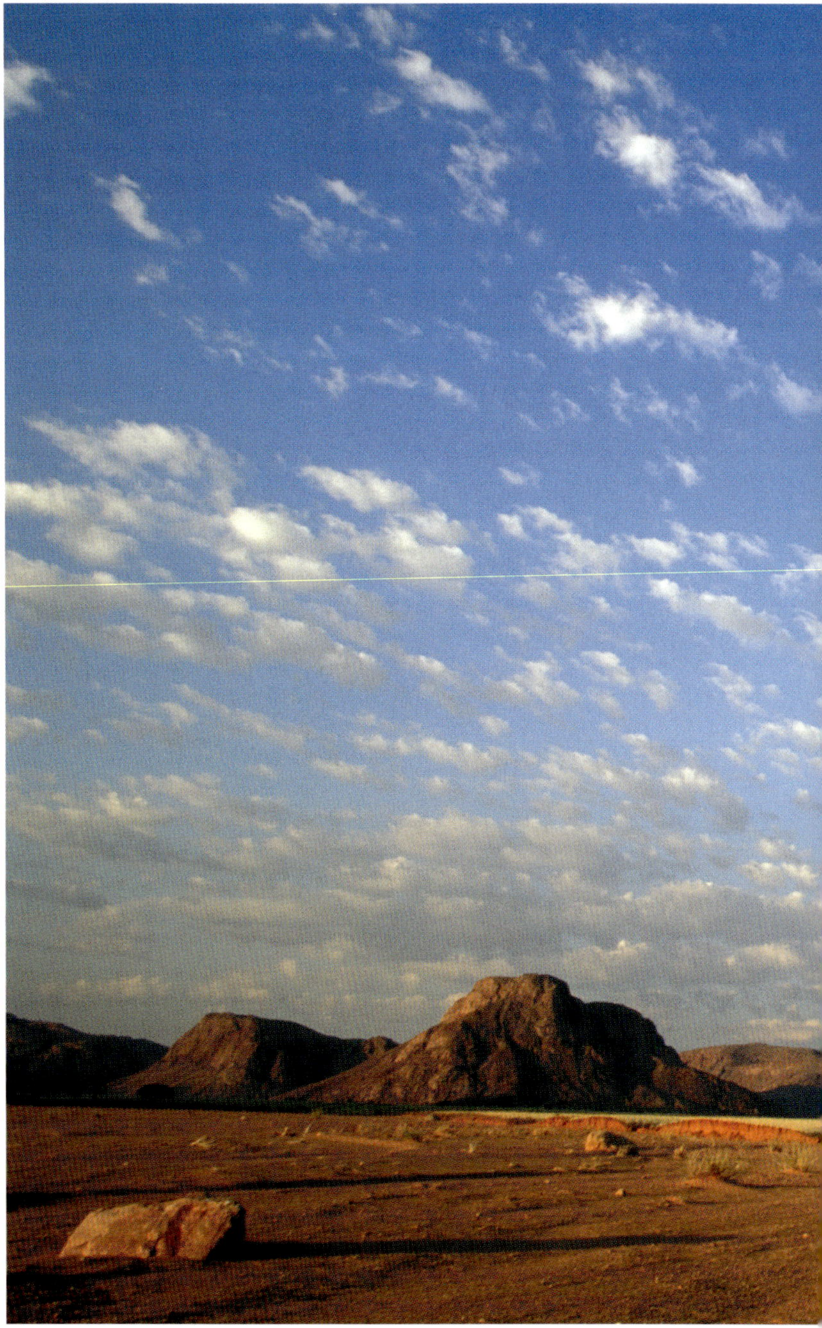

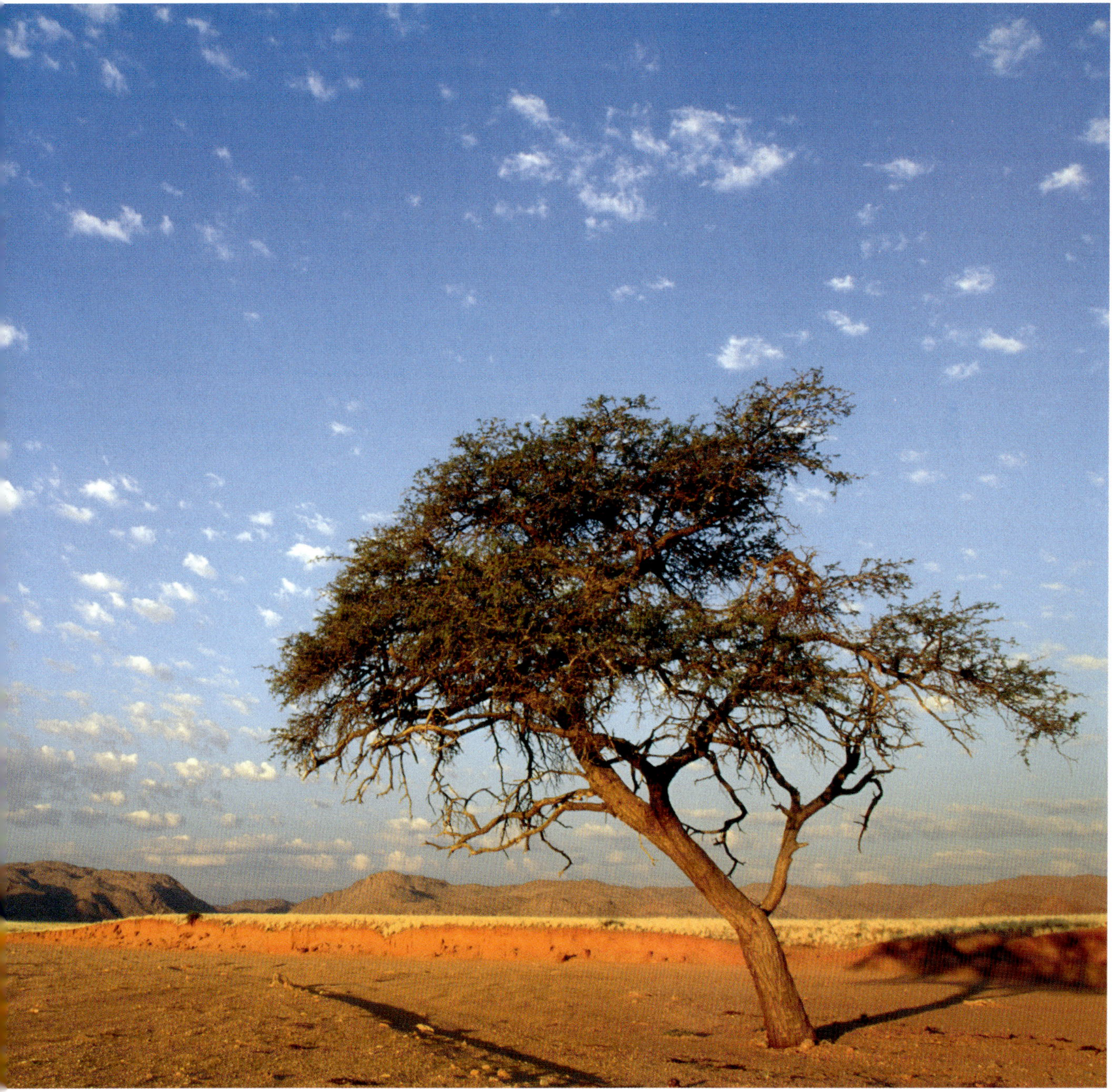

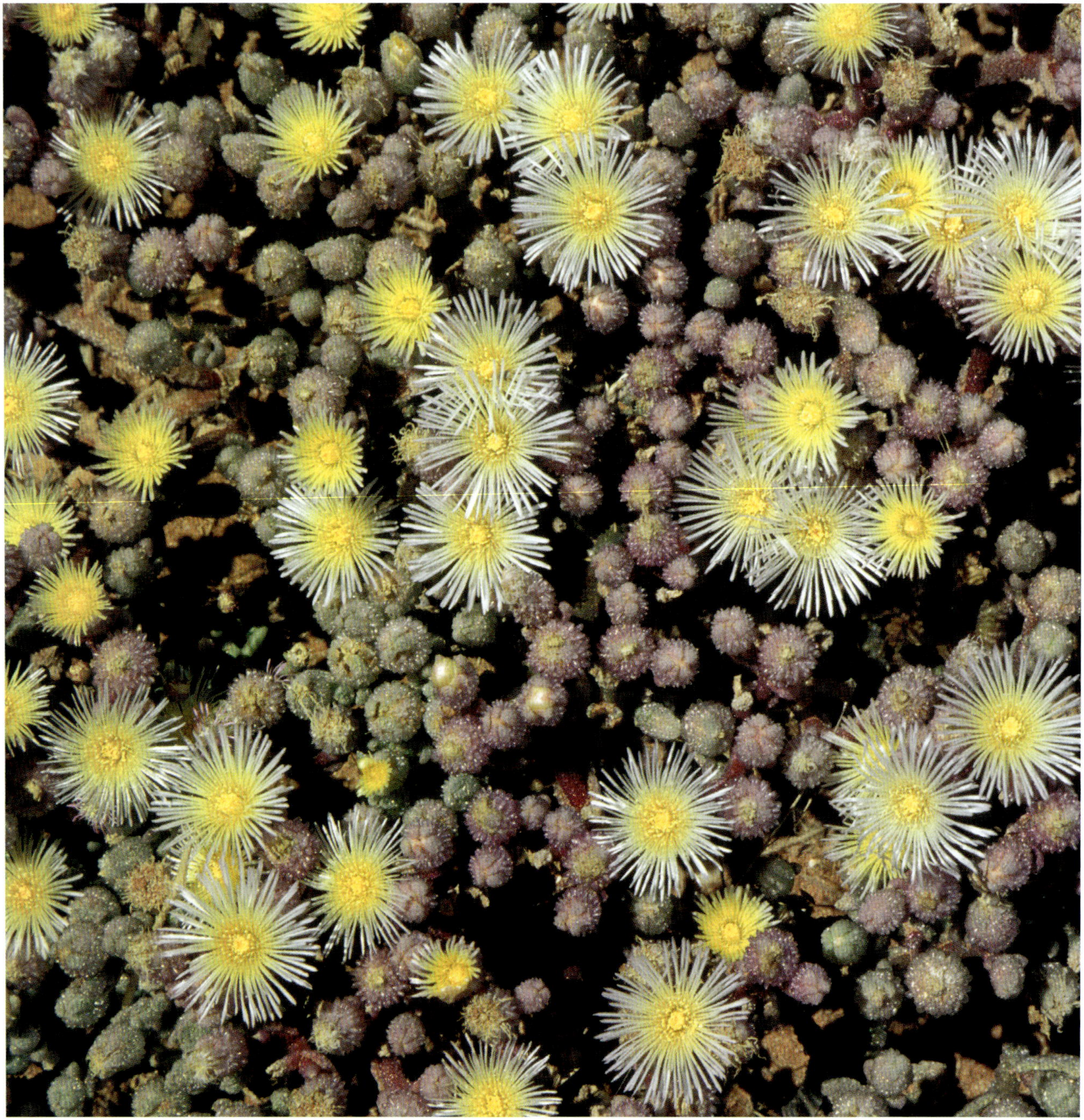

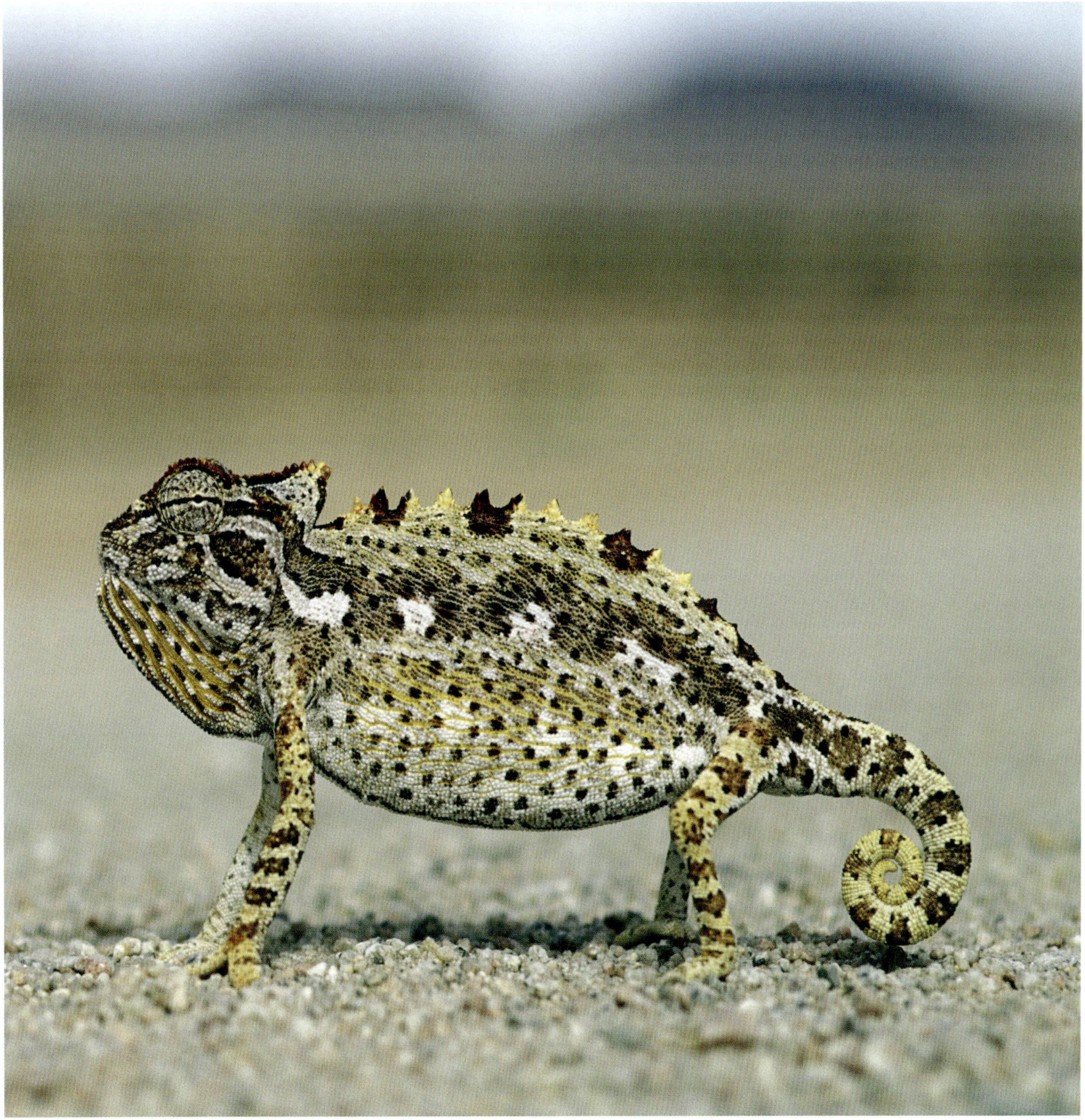

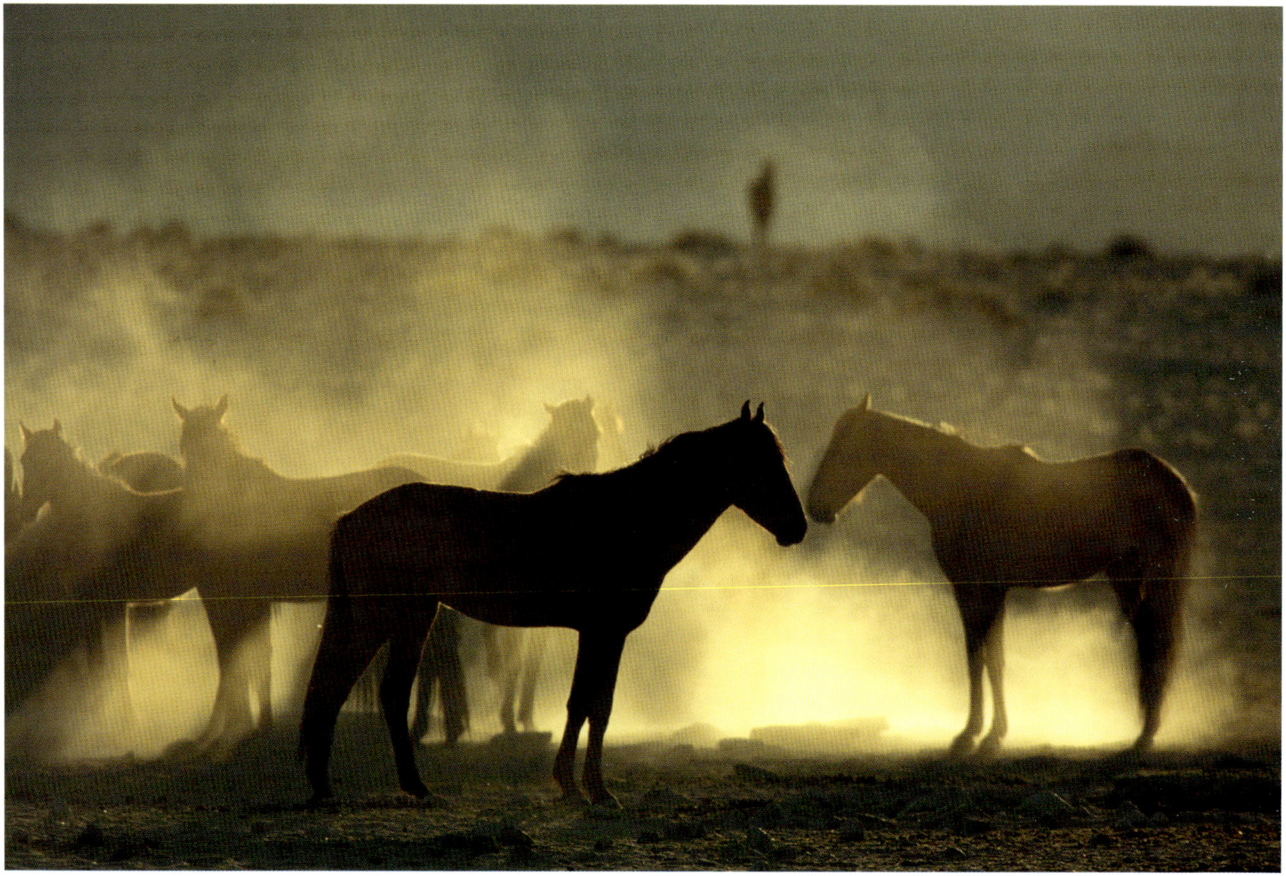

ABOVE AND RIGHT: Like so much of Namibia's wildlife, even the herds of wild horses of the Garub have adapted to tough desert life. The remarkable herds that roam these plains today are said to be descendants of those abandoned either by European settlers or German troops more than 100 years ago.

OVERLEAF: Nowhere is the power of the desert more evident than in the haunting relics of ghost towns such as Kolmanskop deep in the restricted Diamond Area east of Lüderitz.

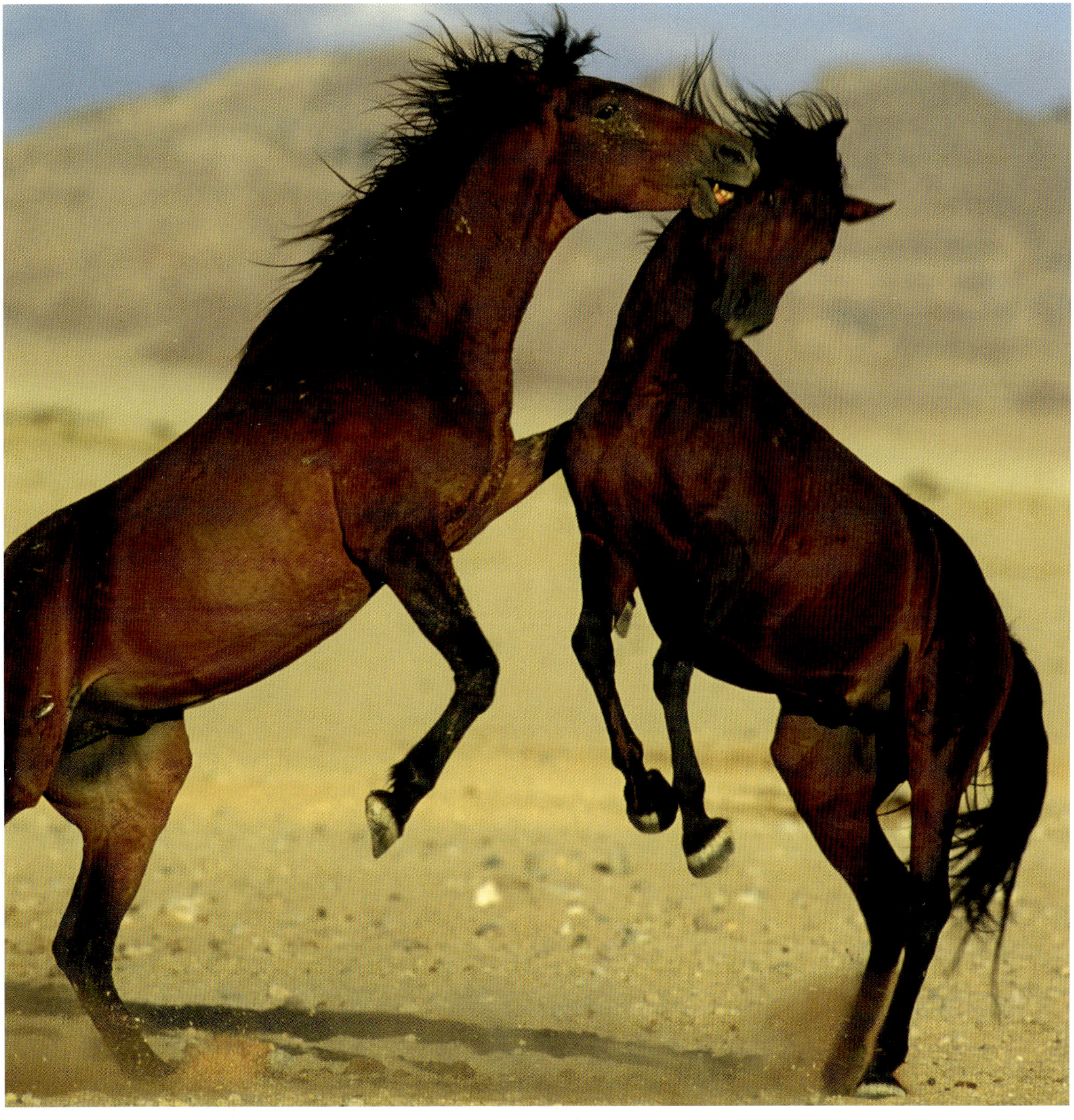

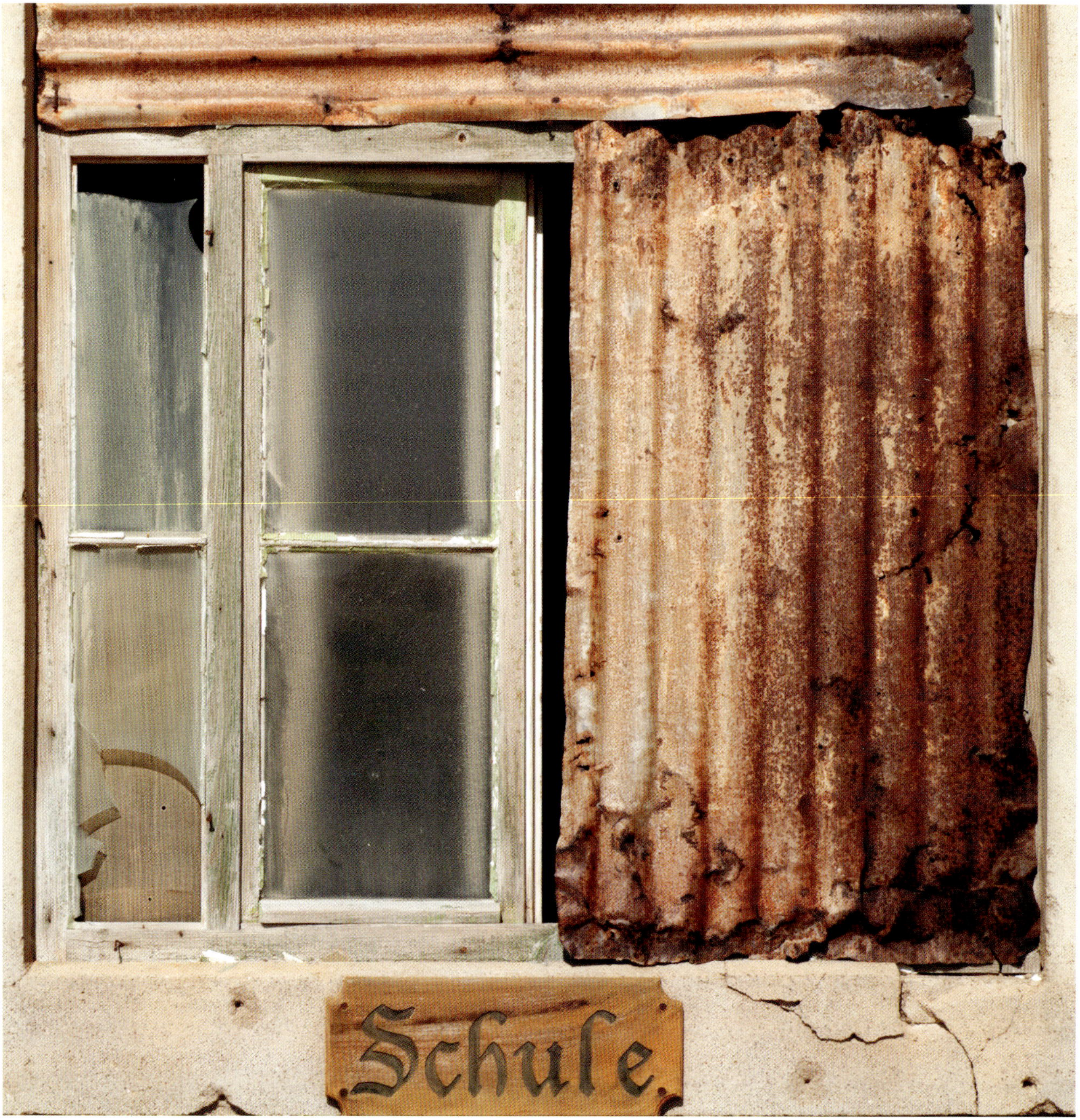
Schule

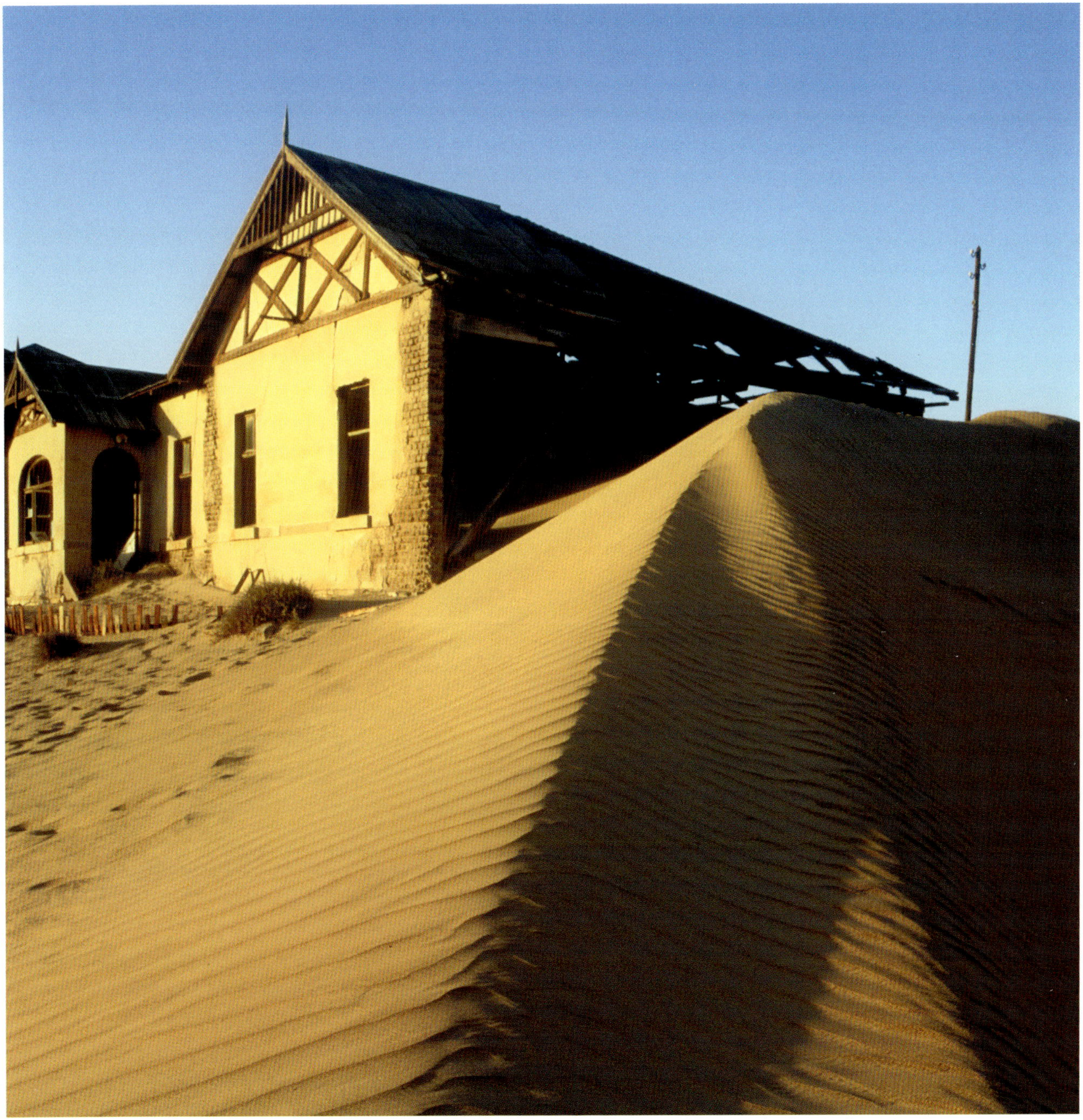

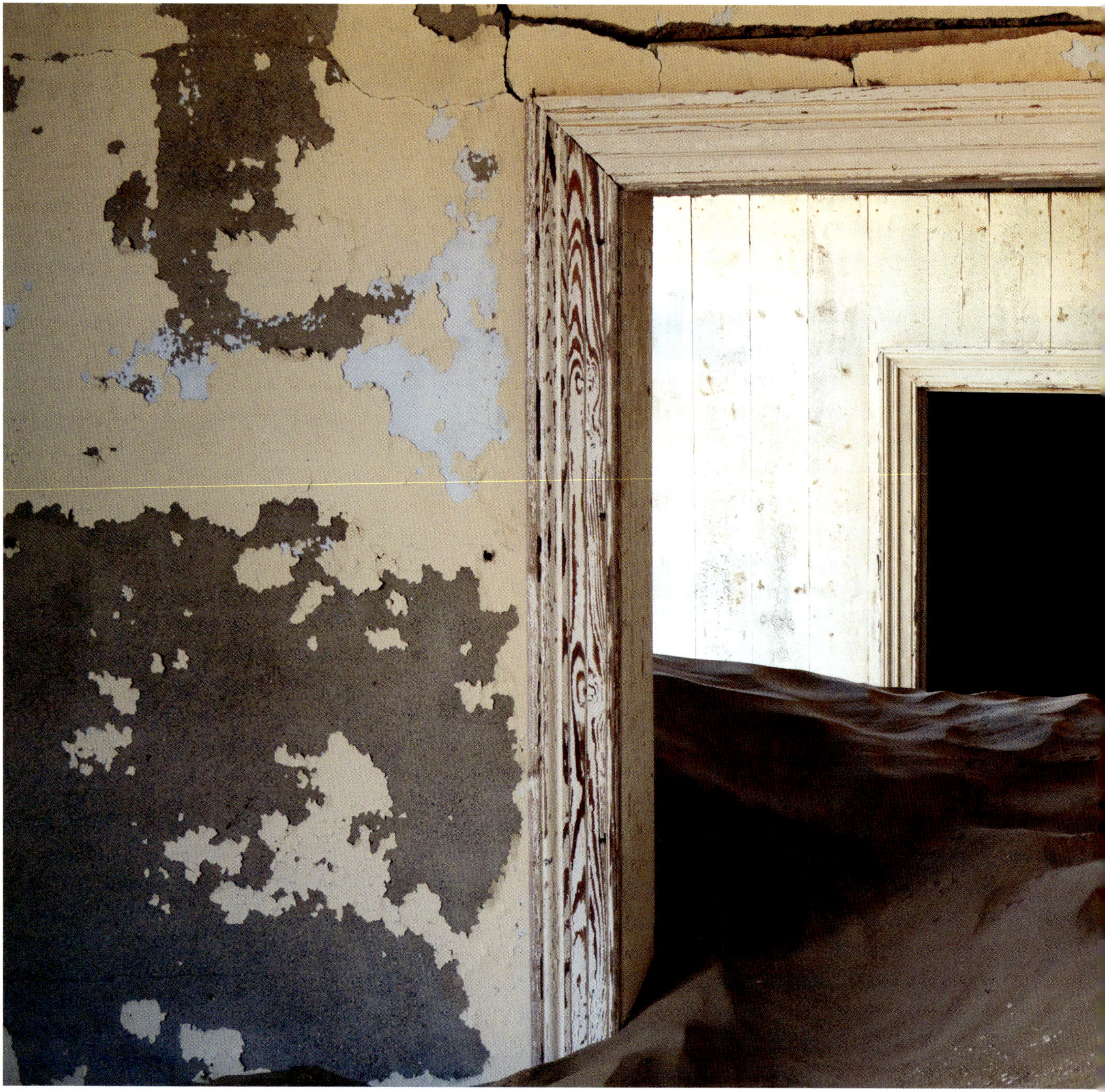

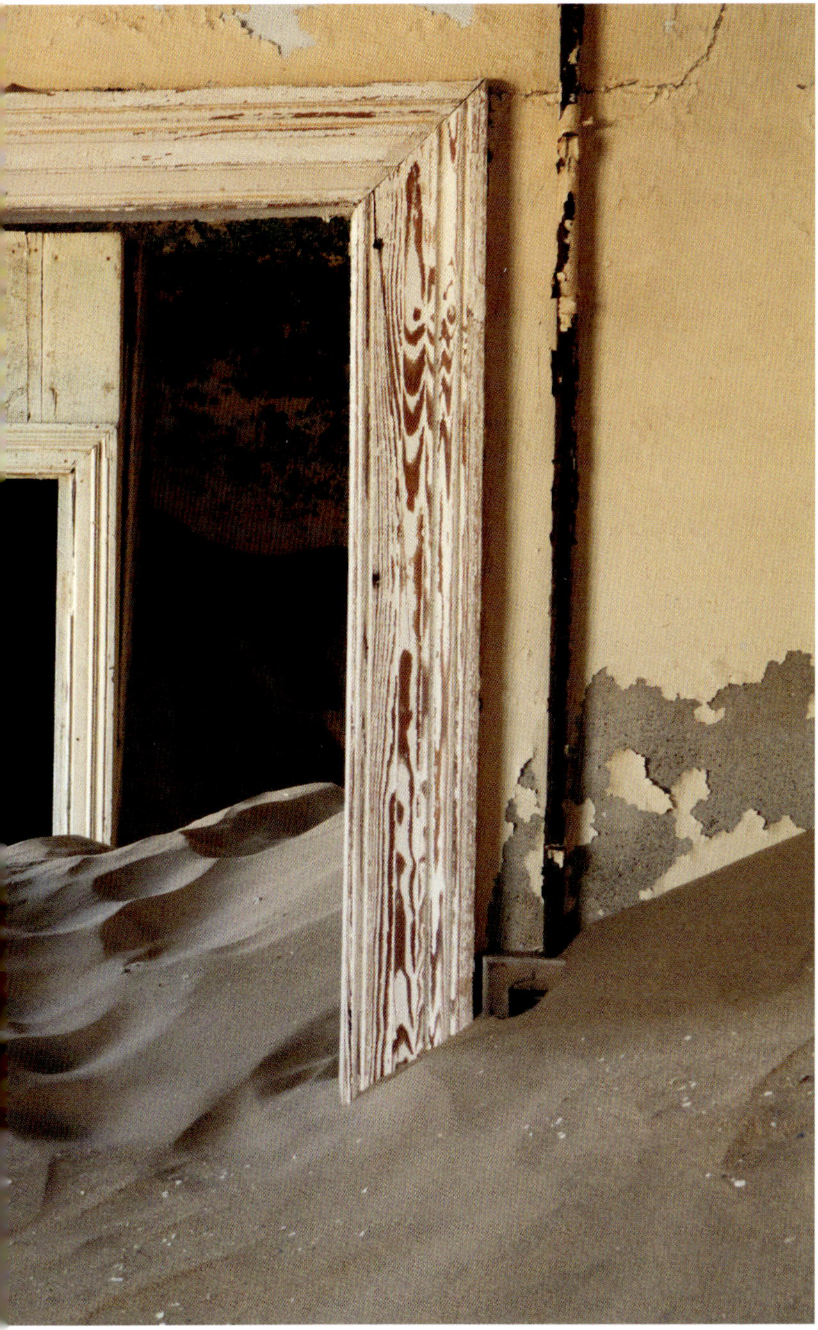

LEFT: At the peak of their diamond-mining days, small towns such as Kolmanskop were thriving centres of economic activity. Today, the buildings have been taken over by desert sands.

OVERLEAF: While early settlements in the Diamond Area may have succumbed to the creeping desert, towns such as Lüderitz have become significant social and commercial centres. The striking Felsenkirche was erected by the local Lutheran community in 1912 and remains an important landmark.

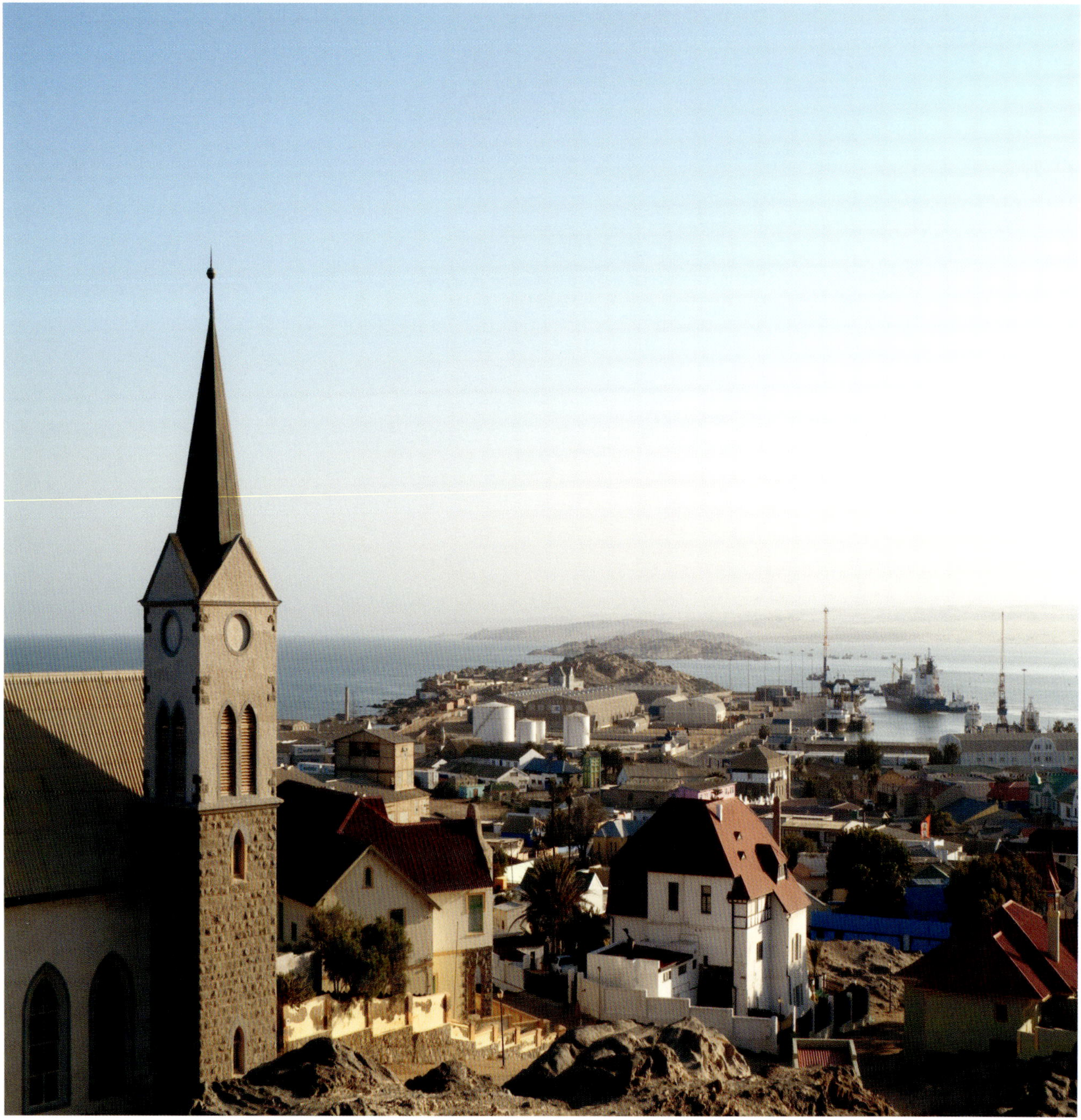

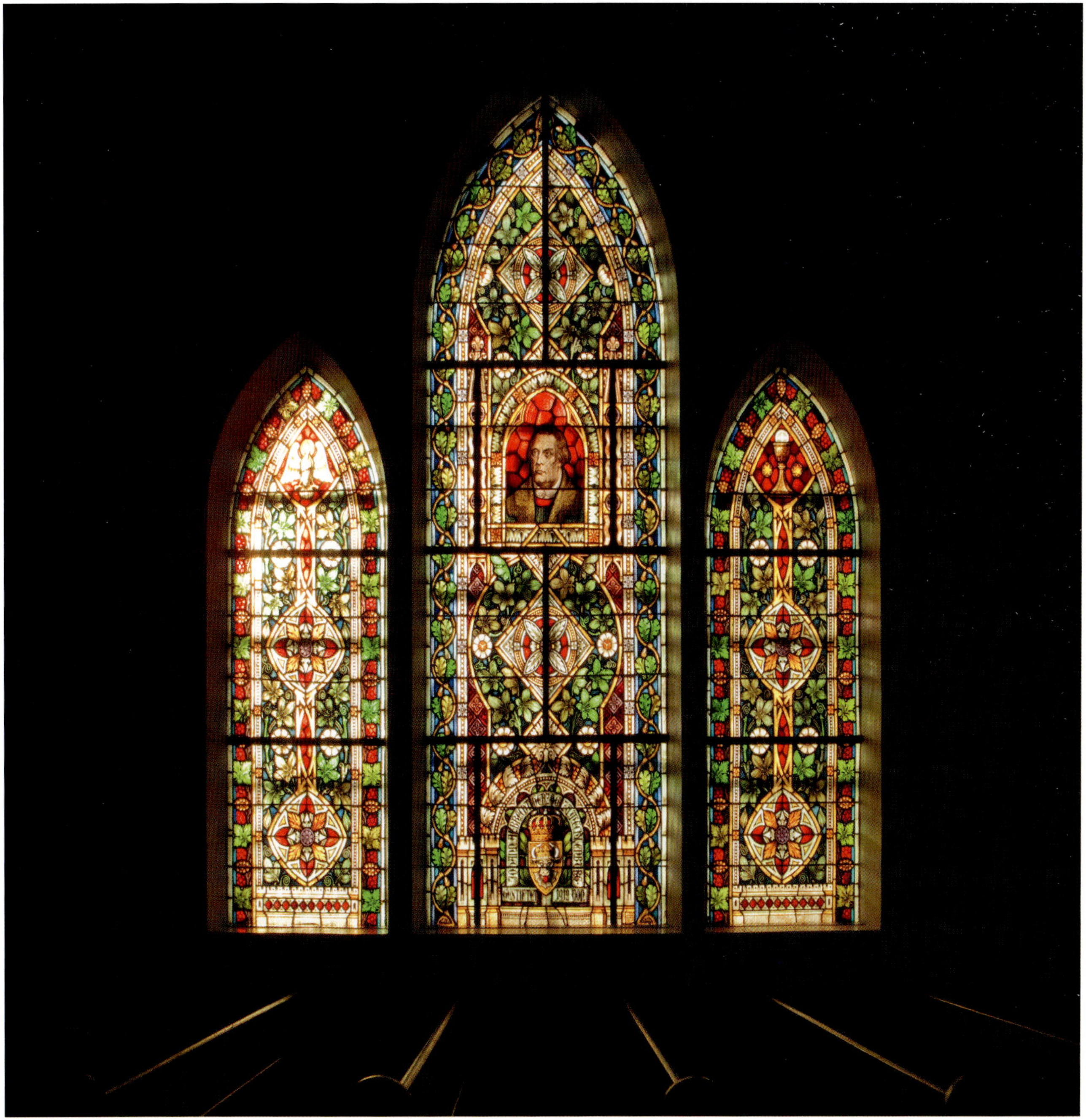

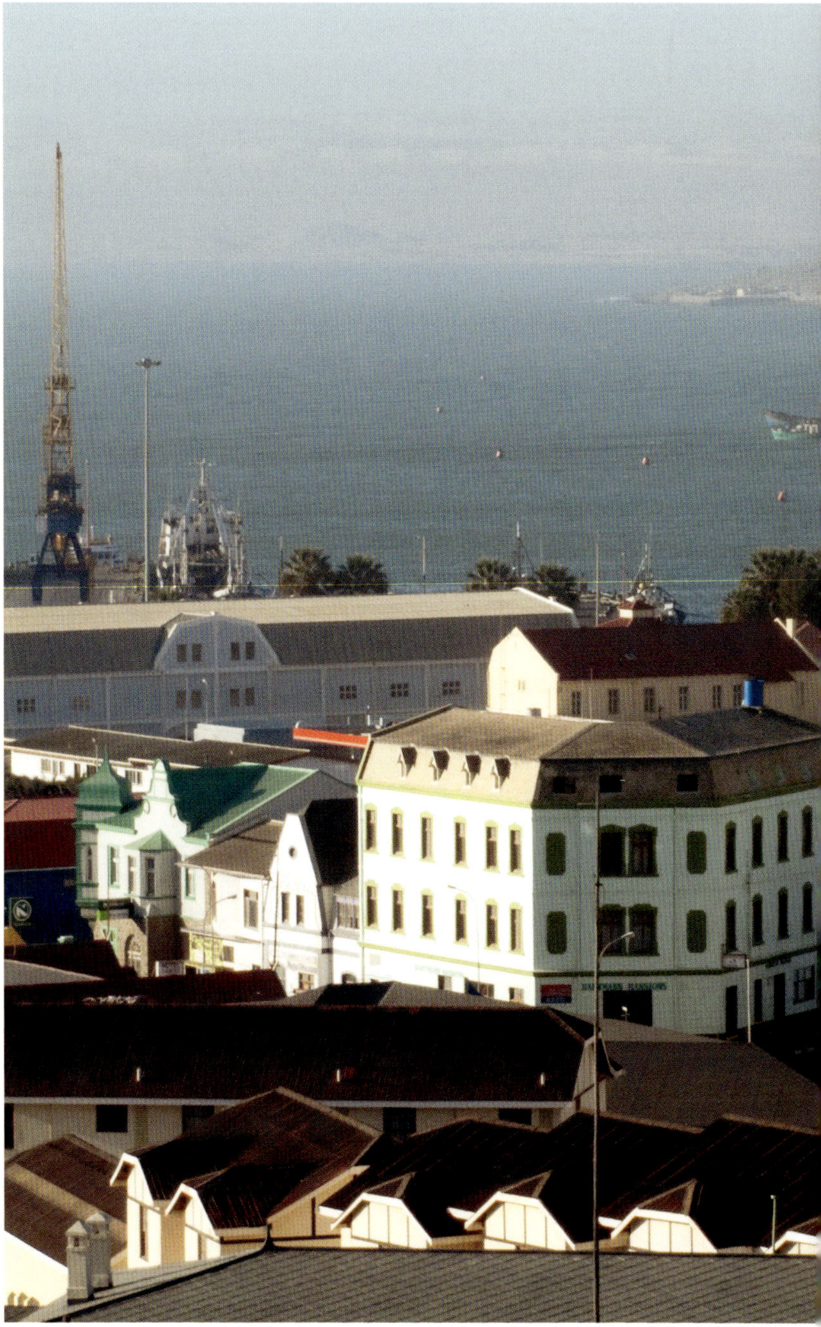

RIGHT: The harbour town of Lüderitz may be small, but it has maintained much of the charm and stature it has cultivated over the last century. Originally established in 1883 as a German trading post, it gradually developed into an important fishing hub and remains a significant tourism centre for southern Namibia.

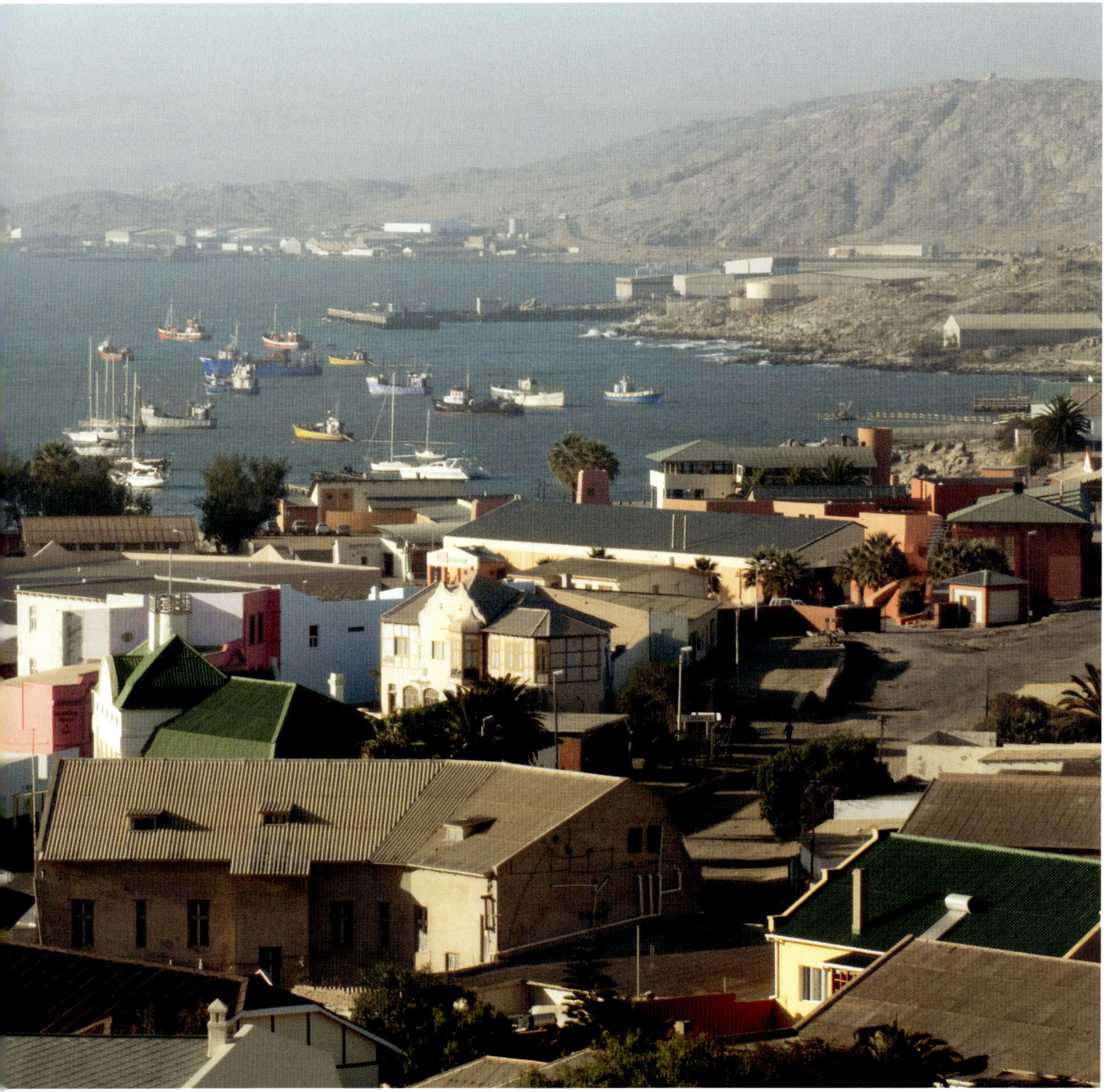

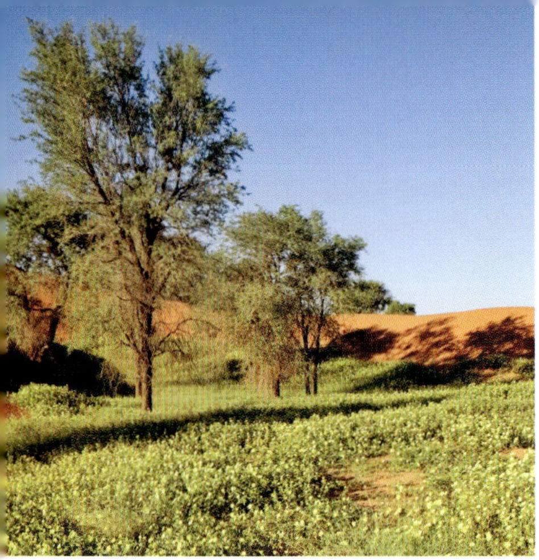
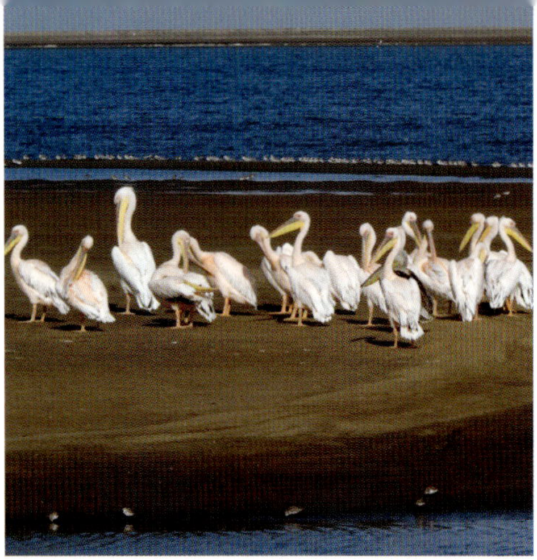
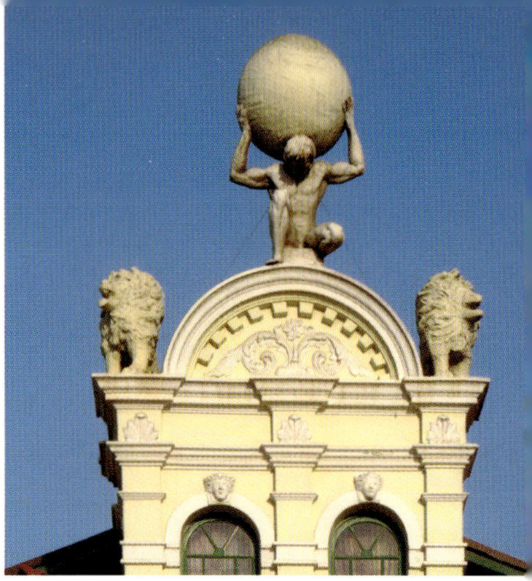
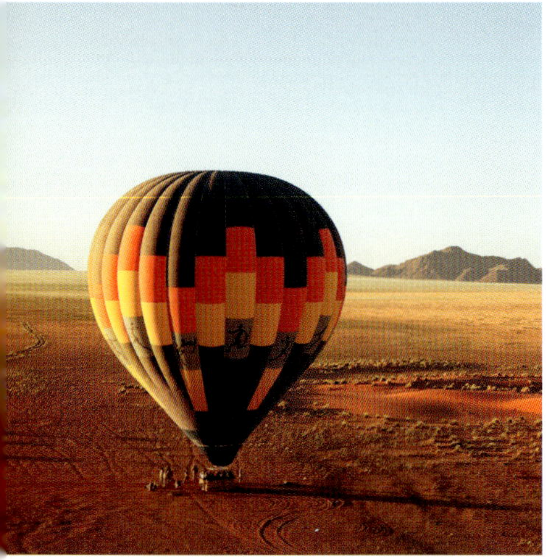
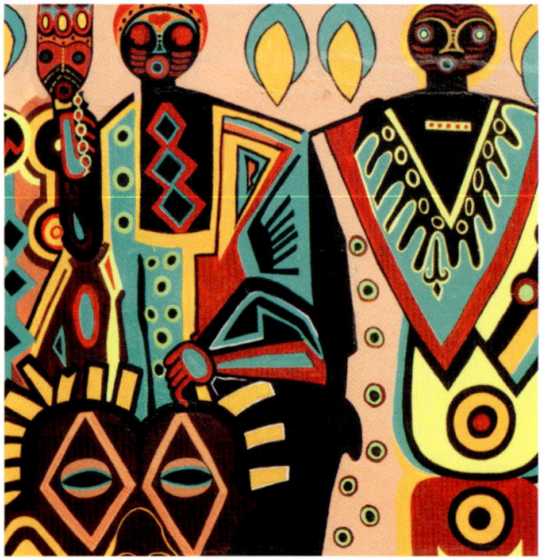
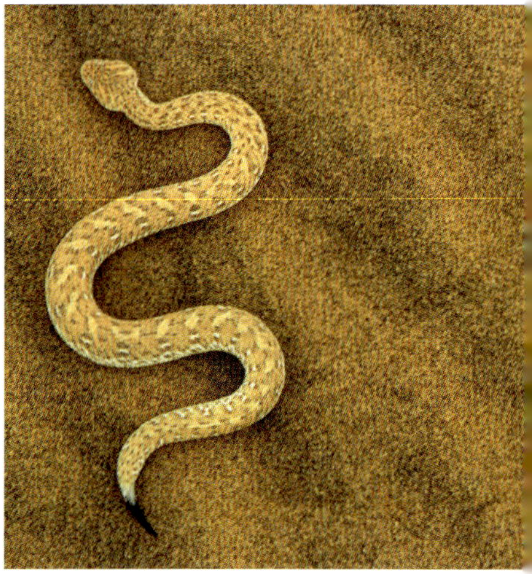
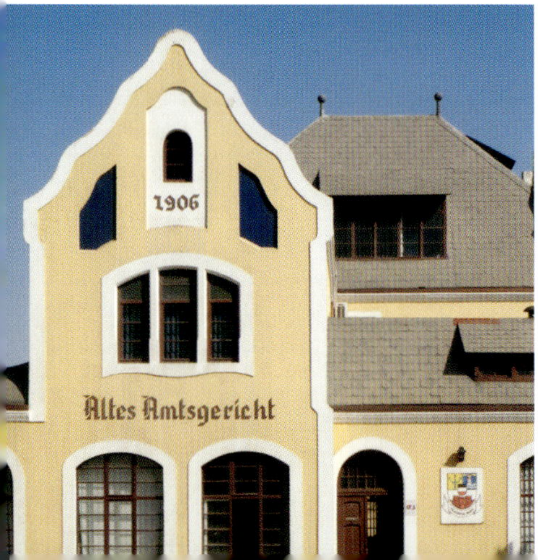
1906
Altes Amtsgericht
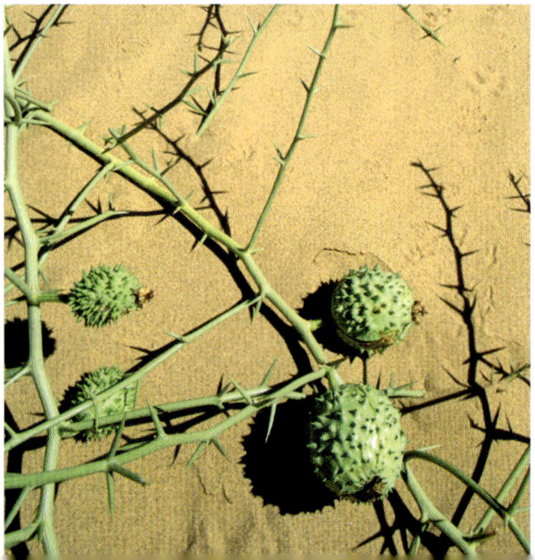
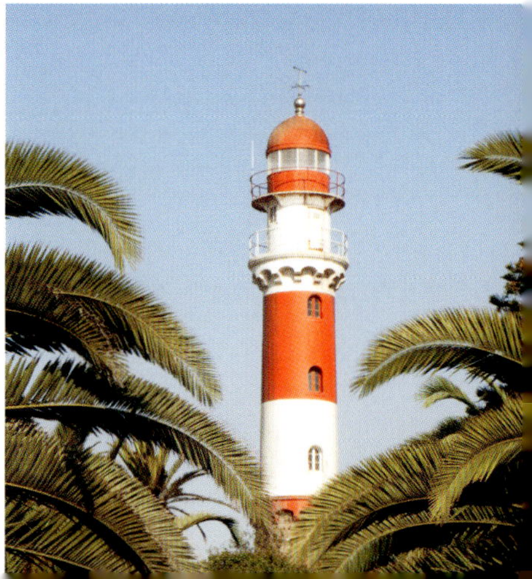

Central Namib Desert

The Namib Desert covers over six million hectares, some 15 percent of the country, so it is little wonder that its endless stretches of red sand dotted with oryx and sparse vegetation is the iconic image of Namibia. Included within its formal boundaries are the shores of the Skeleton Coast, the wilderness of the Namib-Naukluft National Park, as well as the NamibRand Nature Reserve and also a sweltering hinterland.

These vast, seemingly endless stretches of sand and gravel are hemmed in by constantly shifting and transforming dunes, ensuring that the landscape is not static. It is these undulating red-ochre dunes, combined with ghostly images of saltpans and lunar landscapes punctuated with welwitschias, that most visitors come to see. Many make their way up these dunes on foot to explore the sandy waves that make up the desert landscape, whilst others take to the skies to experience a bird's-eye view offered by a hot-air balloon ride. From the air, you witness an extraordinary world where desert sand meets ocean wave, where – when the rains do finally fall – the parched earth transforms into a patchwork of greens, especially in and around the urban settlements of Swakopmund and Walvis Bay.

Although the Namib comprises some of the southern hemisphere's driest and most inhospitable terrain, it remains a living desert hosting an astonishing range of flora and fauna including hundreds of succulent plants, the ubiquitous oryx (known locally as gemsbok), birds such as flamingos and pelicans, more than 20 endemic reptile species and nearly 200 vertebrates found nowhere else in the world.

OPPOSITE FROM LEFT TO RIGHT:

- After the rains, parts of the Namib are carpeted with Devil's Thorn.
- Great white pelicans congregate on the coastal waters at Walvis Bay on the edge of the desert.
- Baroque-style architecture of the Hohenzollern Building, Swakopmund, dating to 1906.
- Visitors experience a bird's-eye view of the scenic NamibRand Nature Reserve from a hot-air balloon.
- Vividly coloured façades of buildings hint at the rich cultural heritage of the seaside town of Swakopmund.
- Peringuey's adder is one of the most fascinating of the Namib's inhabitants, its side-winding action leaving characteristic tracks on the desert sands.
- The Old Magistrate's Building, a fine example of colonial architecture that survives in Swakopmund.
- Melon-like fruit of the nara bush provide food and an important source of water for indigenous wildlife.
- A prominent lighthouse marks the treacherous Atlantic coastline, Swakopmund.

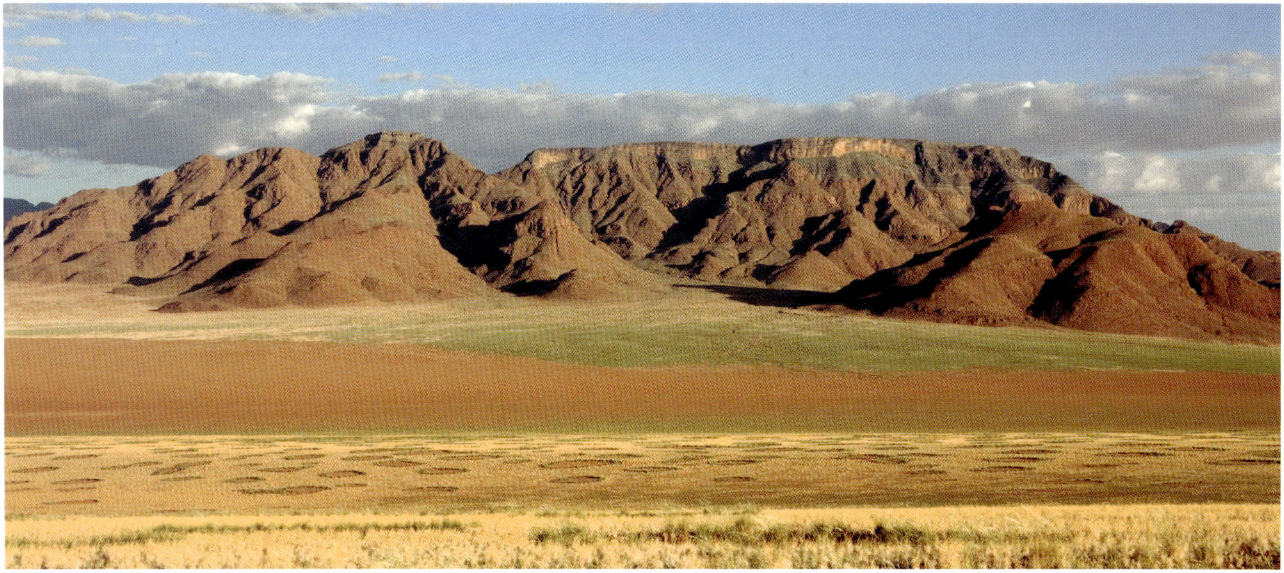

ABOVE: Established on the southwestern edge of the Namib, the privately owned NamibRand Nature Reserve – with its distant mountains and fascinating Fairy Circles – has rapidly become one of the region's most admired tourist attractions.

OPPOSITE: Guests at popular tourist stops such as the acclaimed Wolwedans Dunes Lodge and others in the region are drawn the area's diverse wildlife and extraordinary landscapes.

OVERLEAF: Hot-air balloons provide the perfect vantage point to view herds of oryx and other species that roam the land at the NamibRand Nature Reserve.

Of all the natural wonders with which Namibia has been blessed, one of the most scenic is the picturesque NamibRand Nature Reserve, established as recently as the 1990s and said to be Africa's largest private nature reserve. The landscape of this private conservation initiative is much like its surrounding terrain, consisting largely of dunes and mountains, sand and gravel plains. Dotting the foothills of the mountain ridges that skirt the desert sands and taking full advantage of the panoramas that frame this remarkable environment are some of the country's most popular resorts and lodges; some rustic and offering little more than basic amenities, others the epitome of luxury and indulgence, but all providing an extraordinary gateway to the NamibRand and its four distinct habitats: mountain slope, gravel plain, sand dune and the territory that is the interface between the latter two terrains.

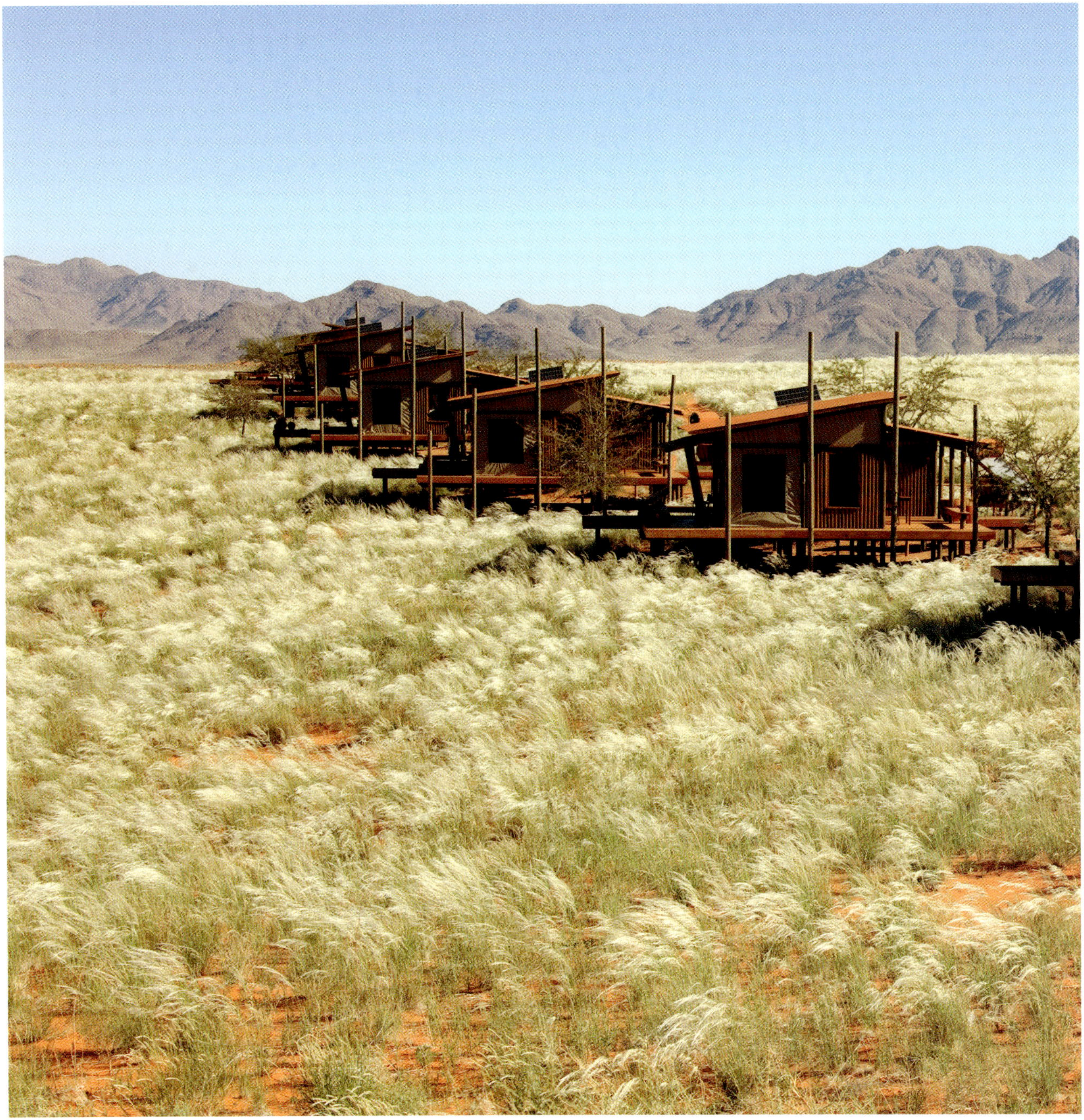

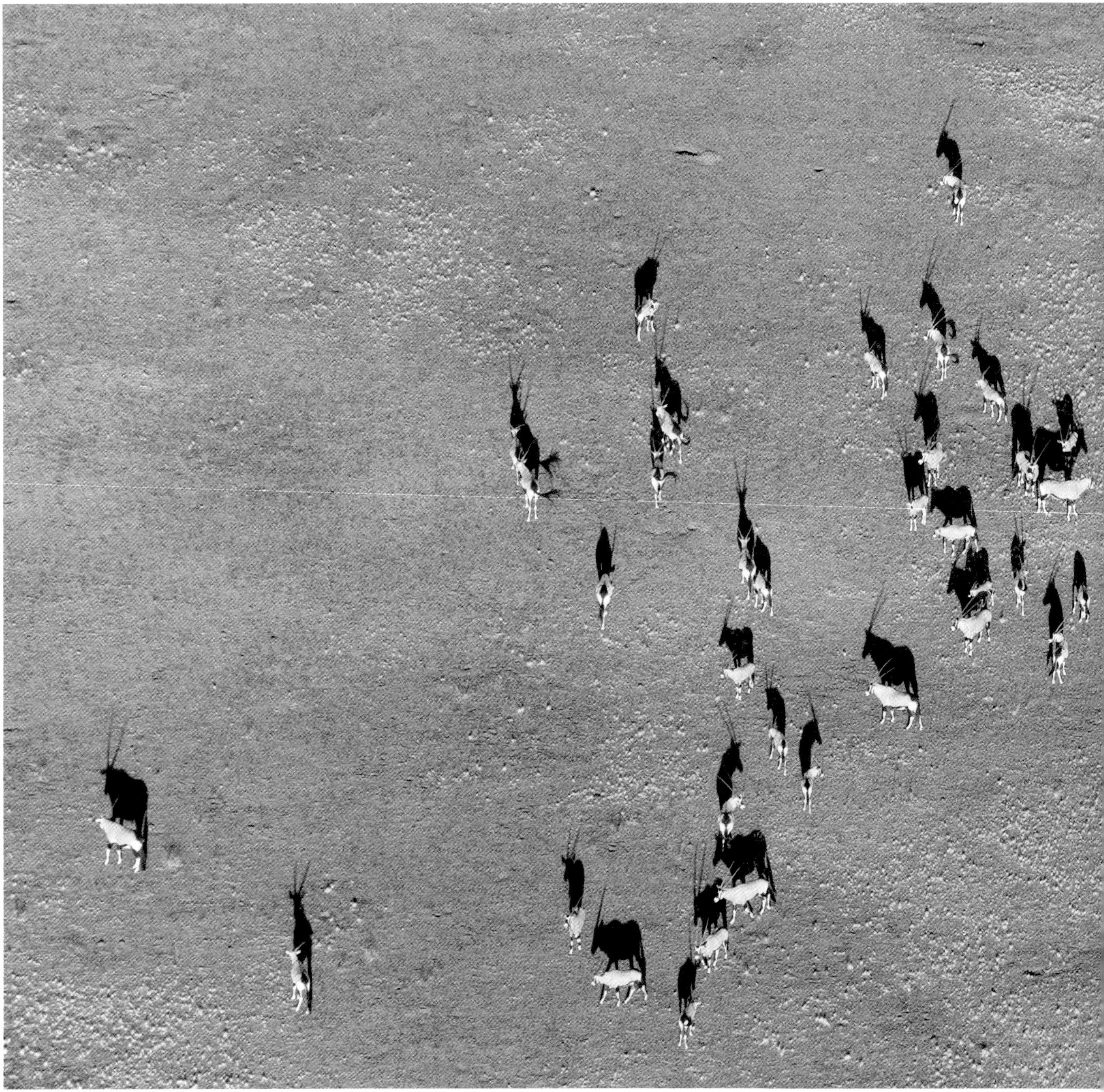

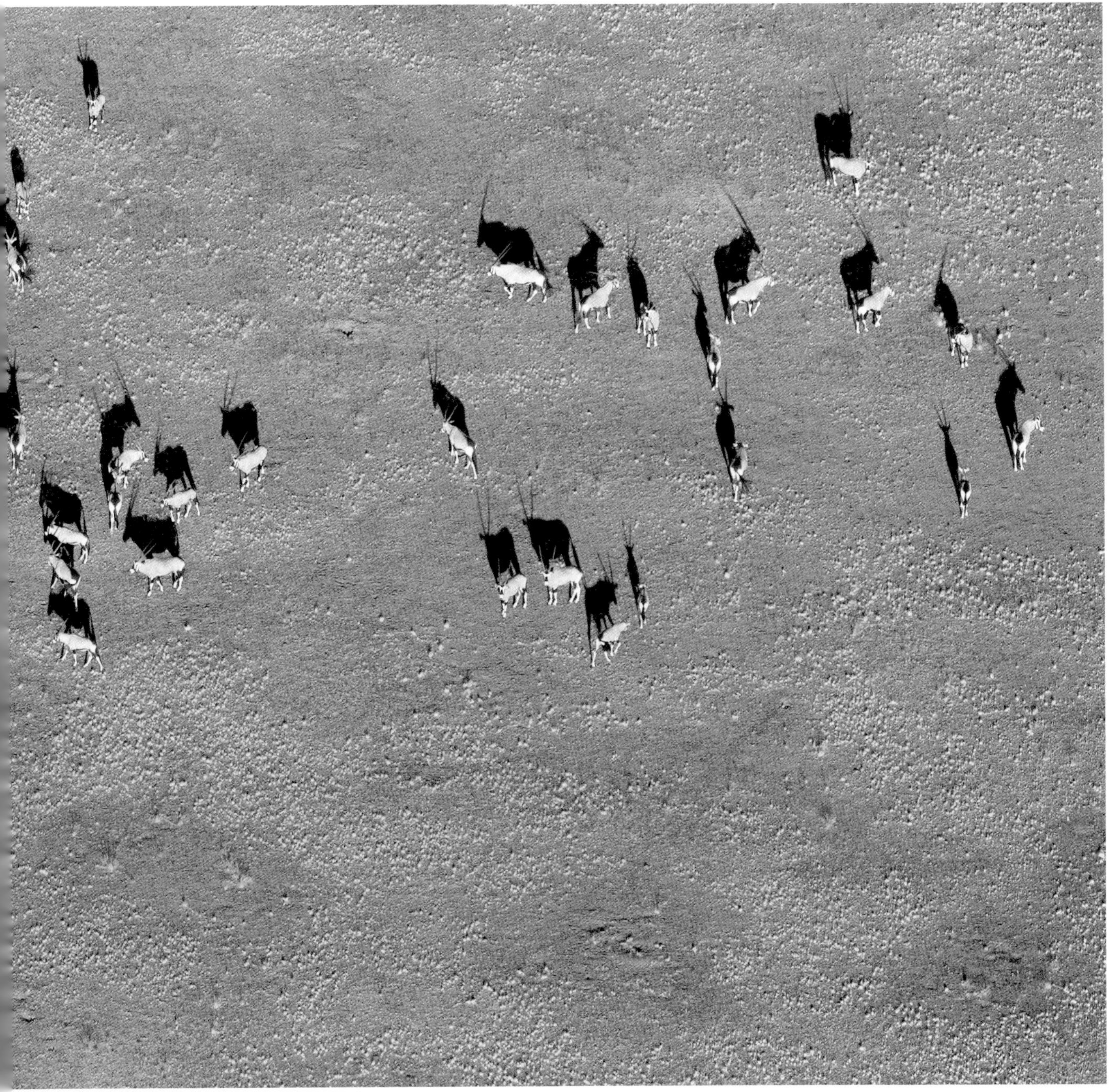

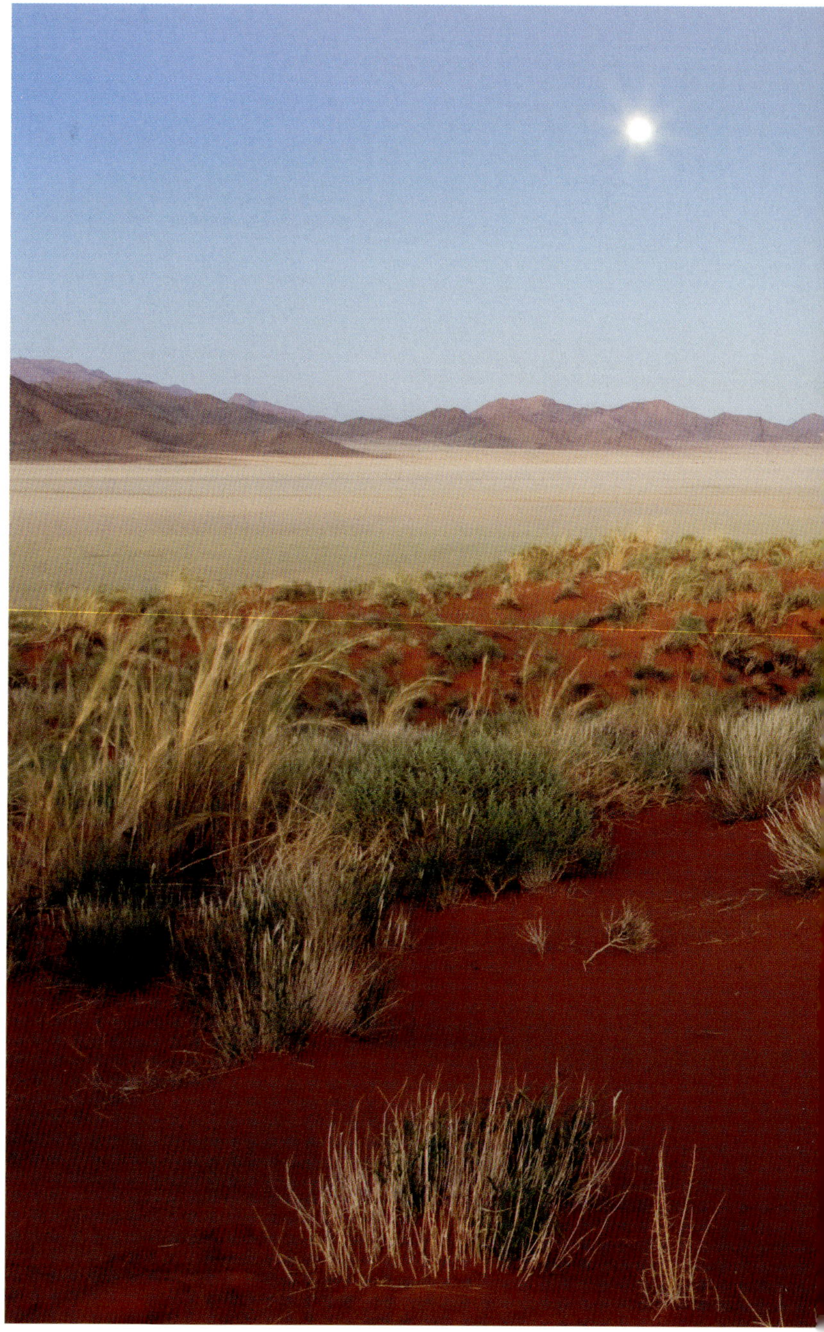

RIGHT: Despite the intense heat and oppressive conditions characteristic of the harsh Namib environment so nearby, the desert fringes offer some respite. Here much of the terrain is carpeted with vast stretches of bushman's grass that lends a gentle touch to an otherwise unforgiving hinterland.

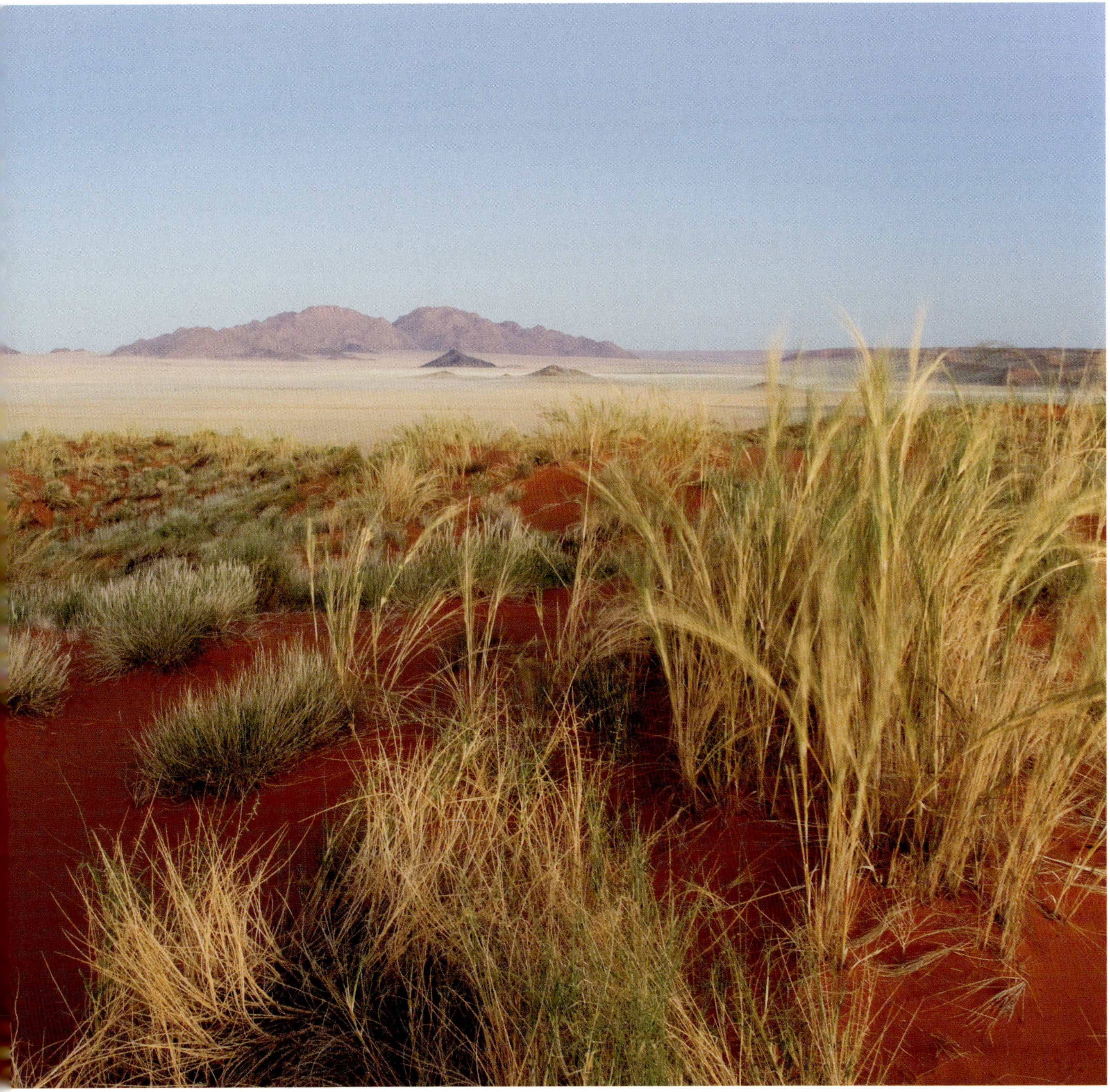

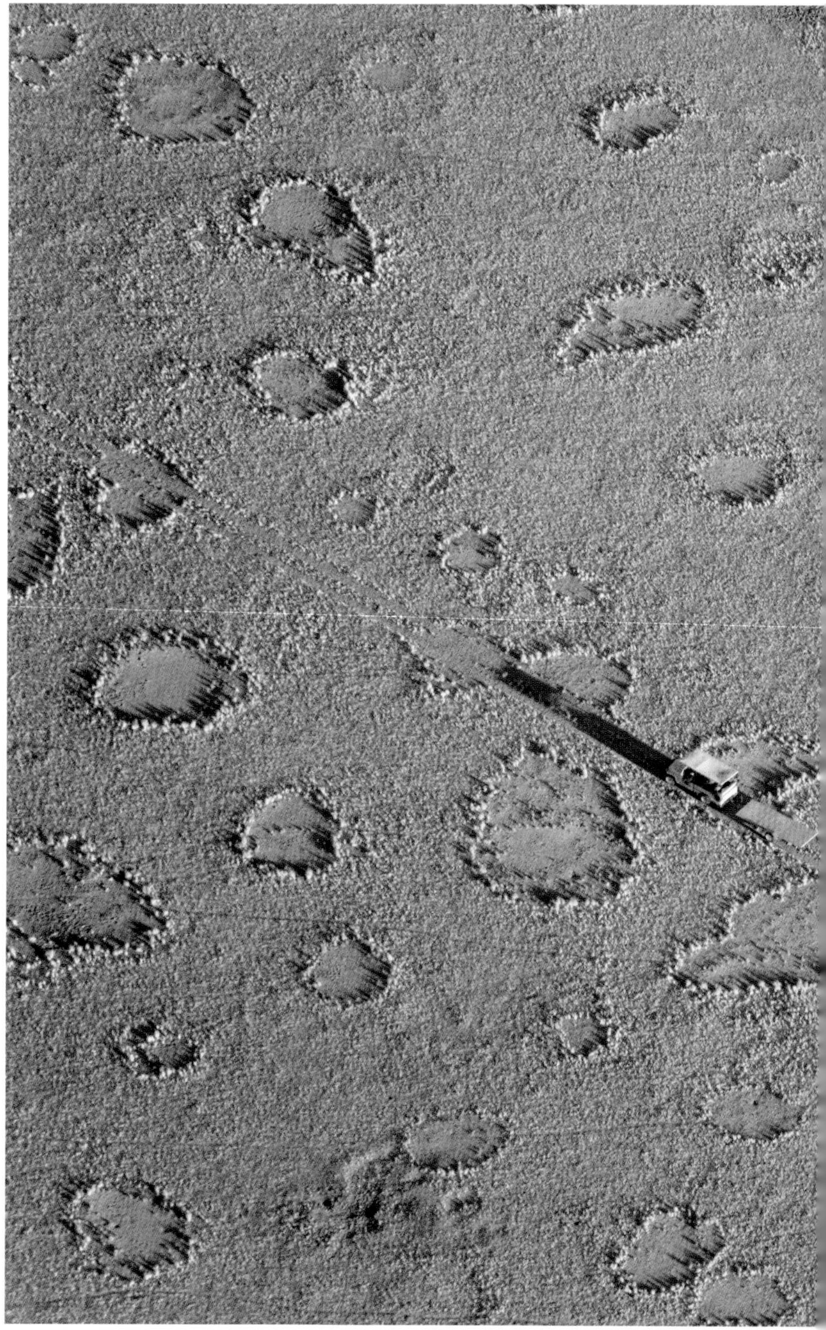

RIGHT: Resembling something straight from the realms of science fiction, parts of the NamibRand are pockmarked with a series of Fairy Circles. These natural phenomena arise from patches of vegetation denuded by the eating patterns of harvester termites.

OVERLEAF: From the air, the mountain ridges and craggy terrain of the Namib-Naukluft Park look something like a lunar landscape extending as far as the horizon and beyond.

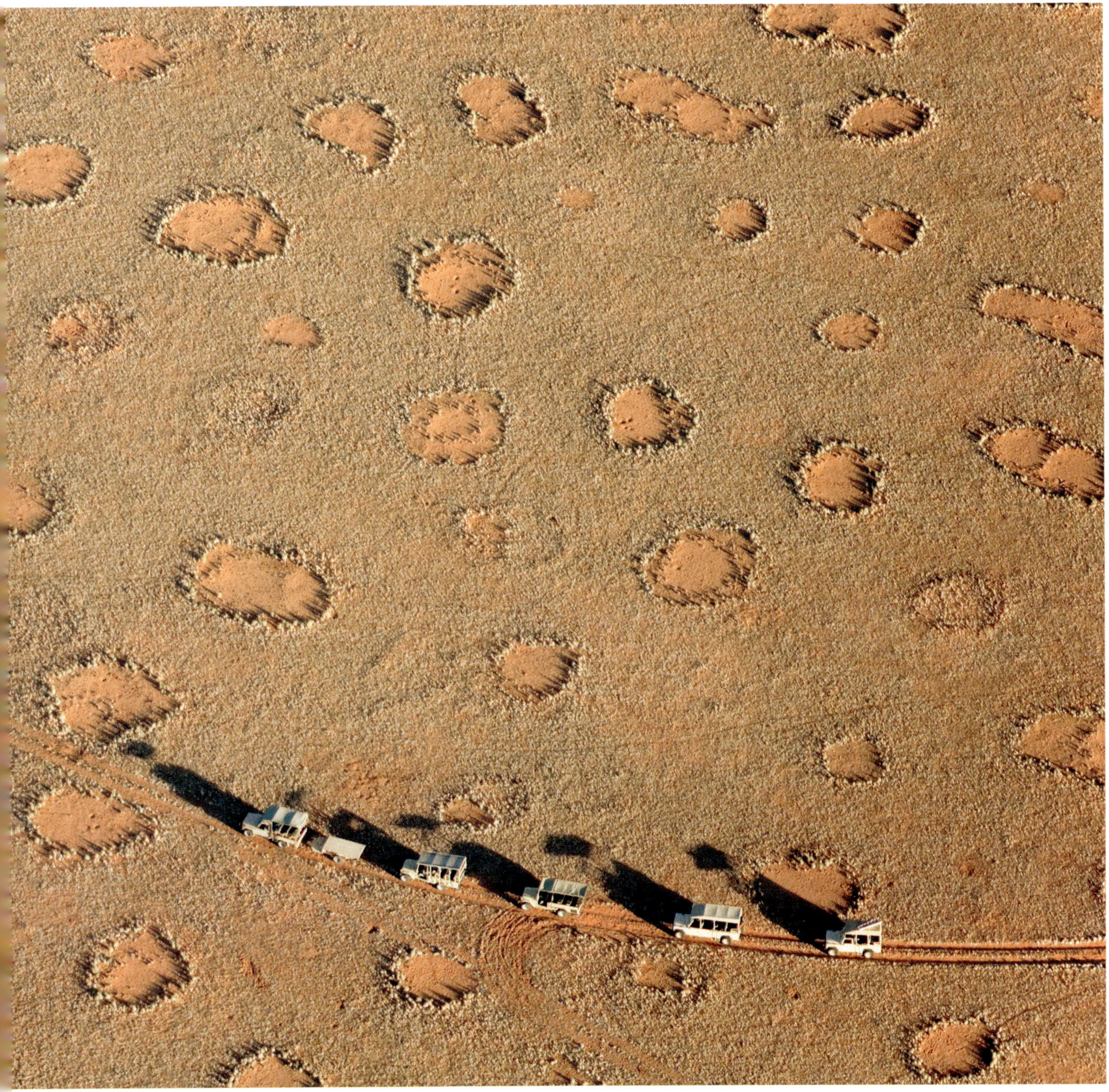

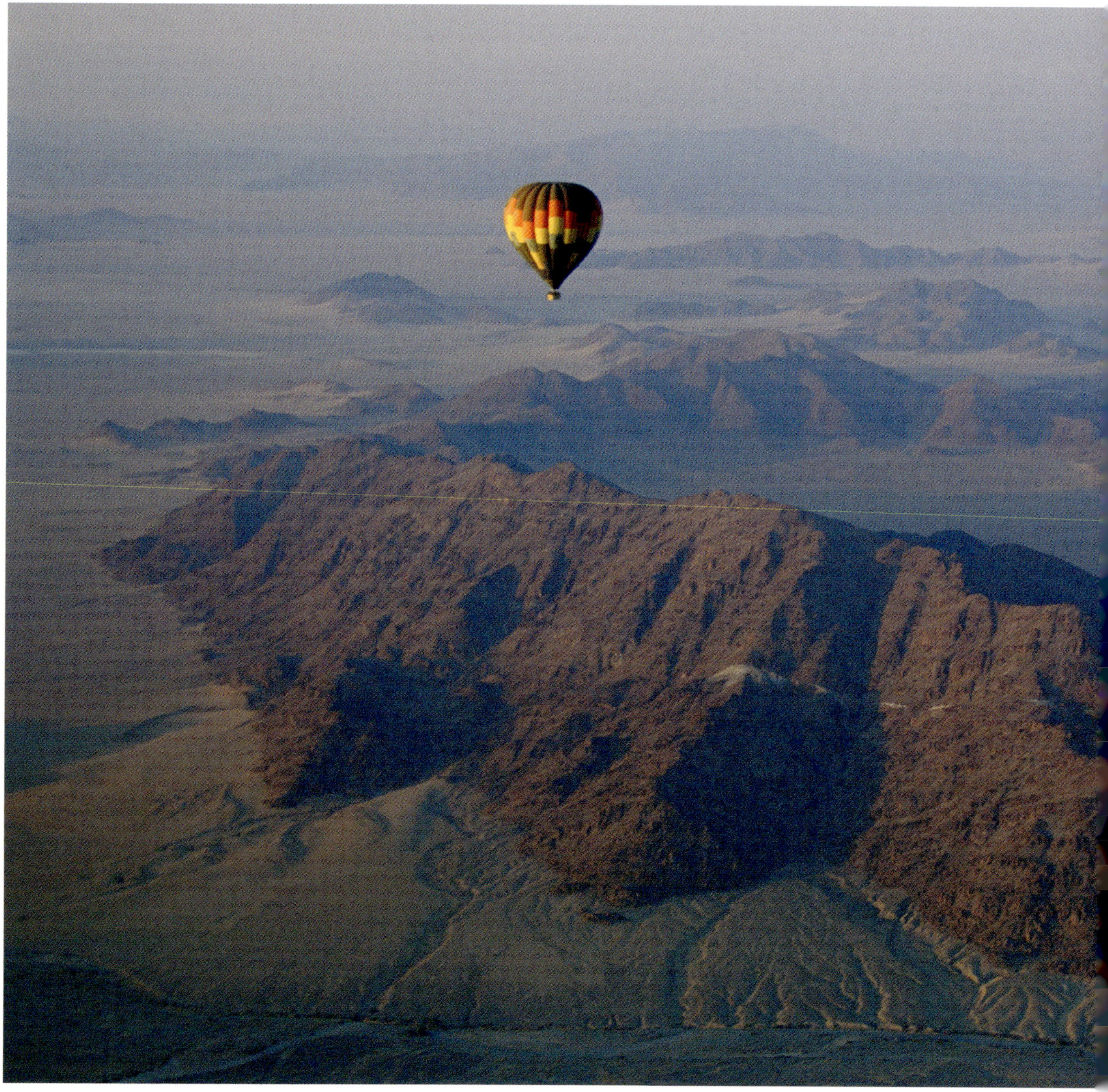

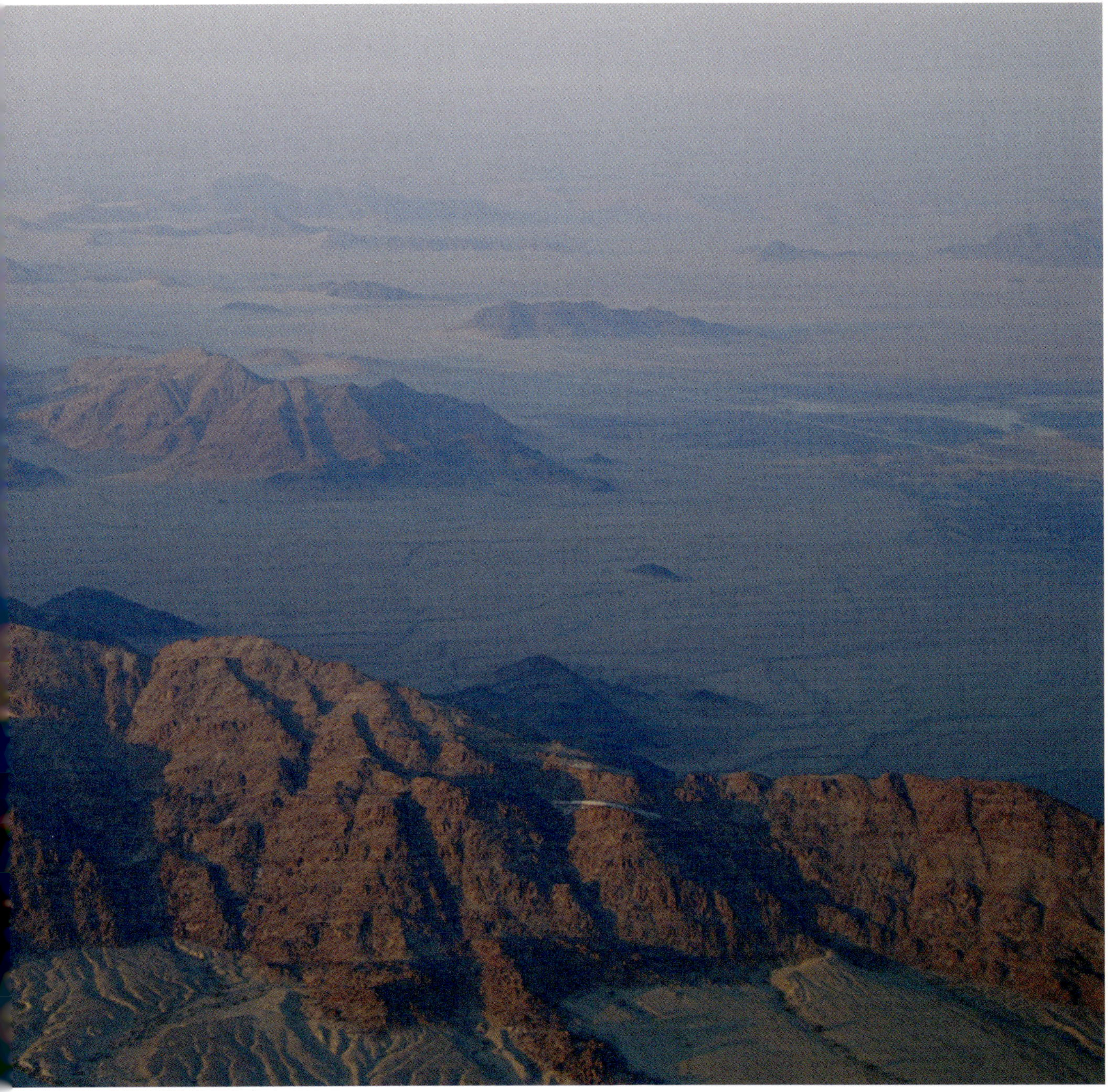

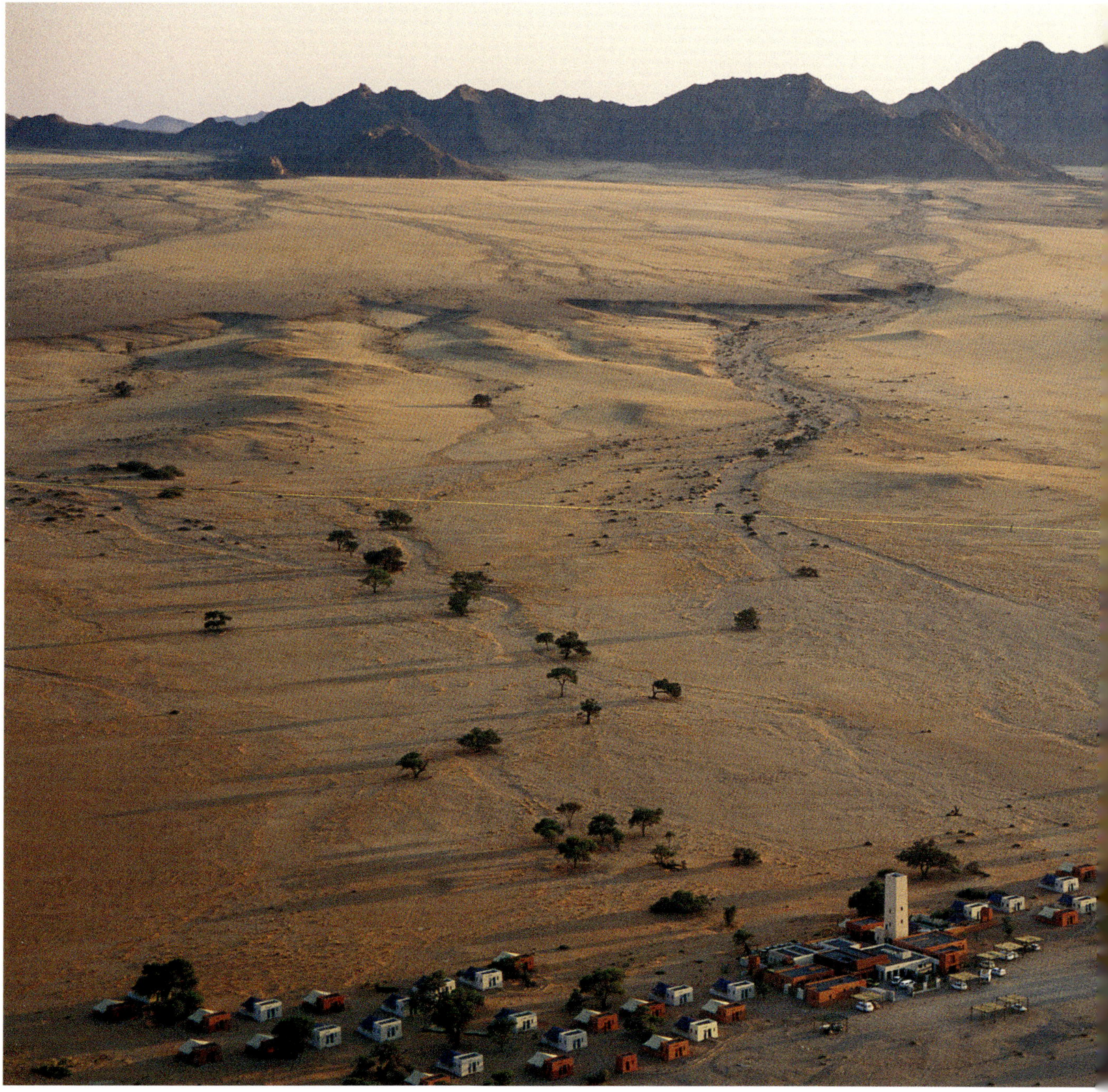

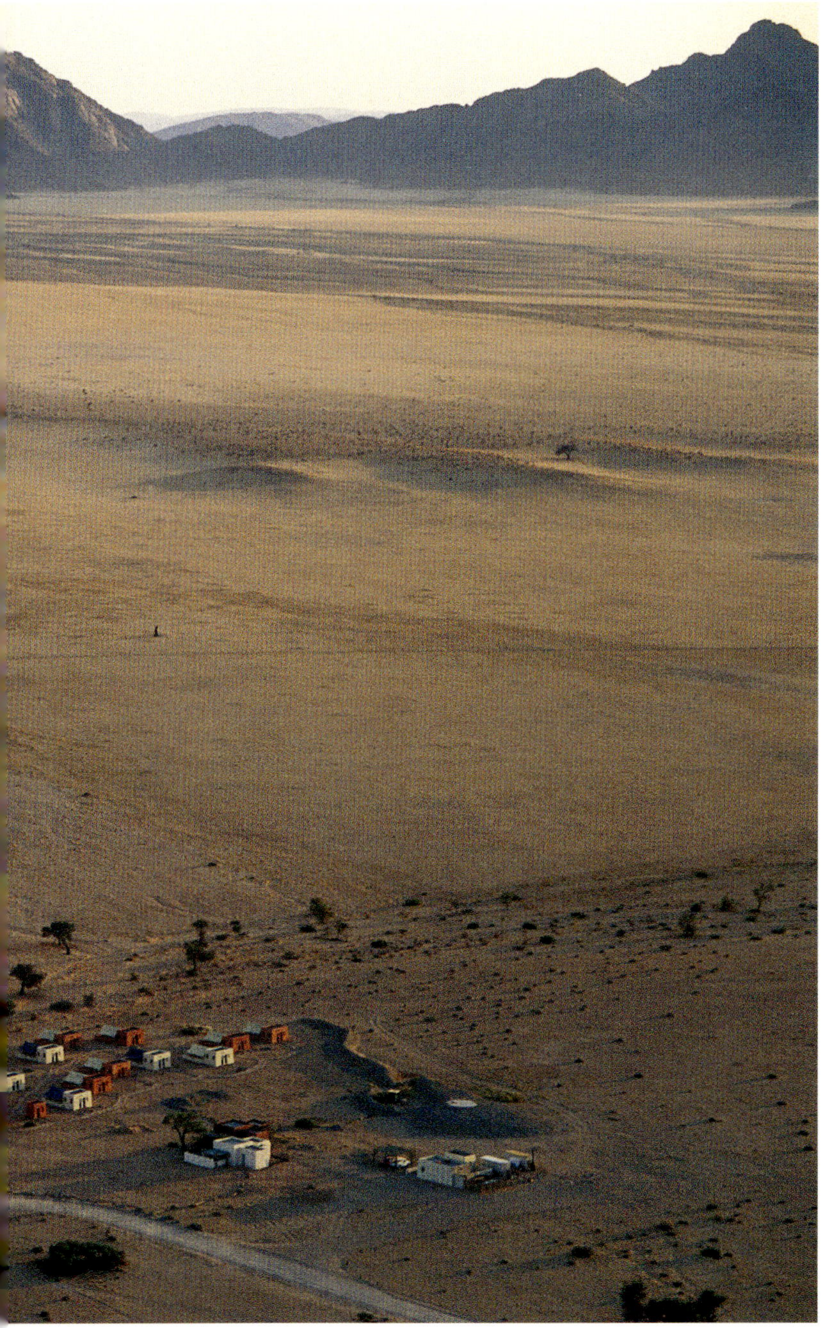

LEFT: The scenic Sossusvlei Lodge is framed by an apparently endless desert panorama. The lodge takes its name from the massive clay depression and salt pan in the centre of the desert that is fed during the rainy season by the flood waters of the Tsauchab River. For the rest of the year it is bone dry.

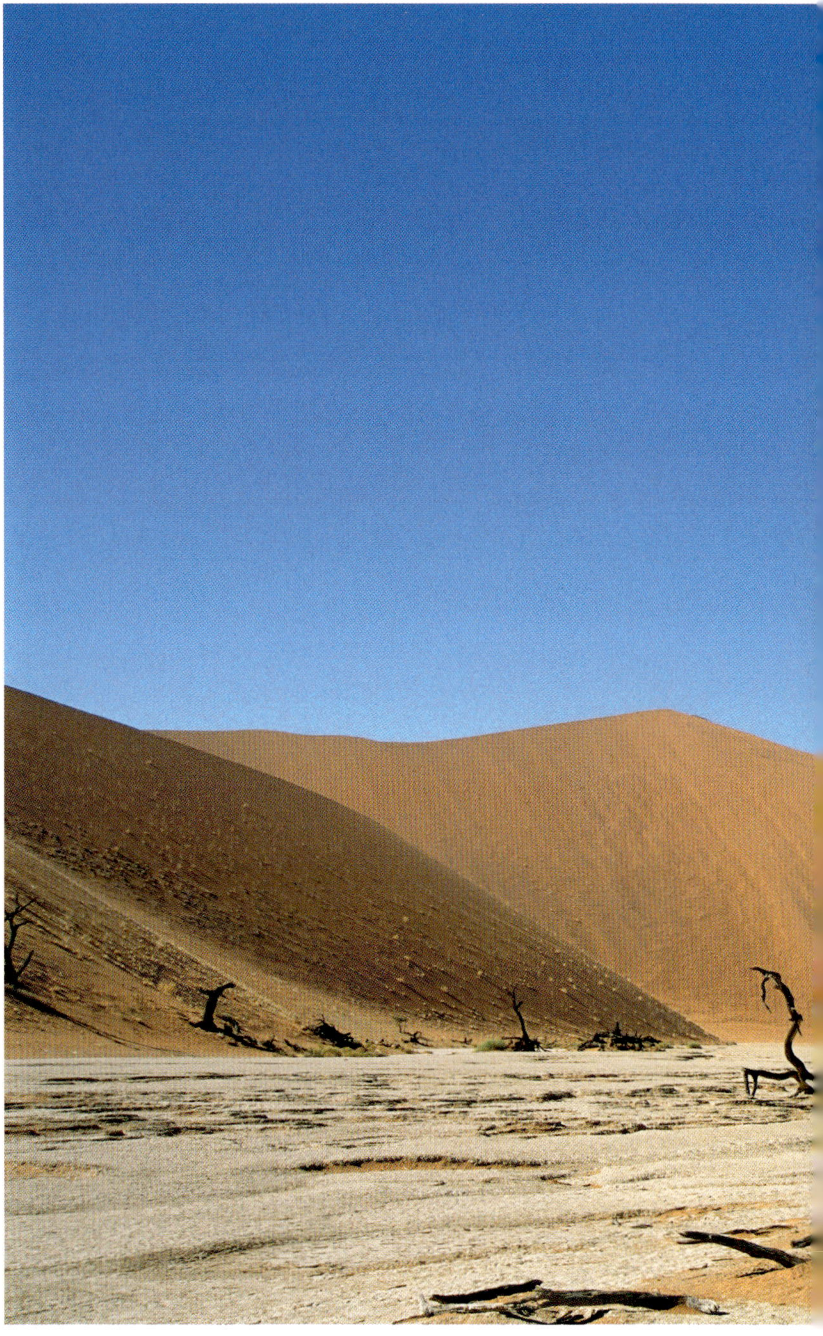

RIGHT: Despite the name – the word *vlei* is Afrikaans for 'lake' – Sossusvlei, Hidden Vlei and Dead Vlei (the latter pictured here) are, for much of the year, little more than massive hollows in the ground with no water whatsoever.

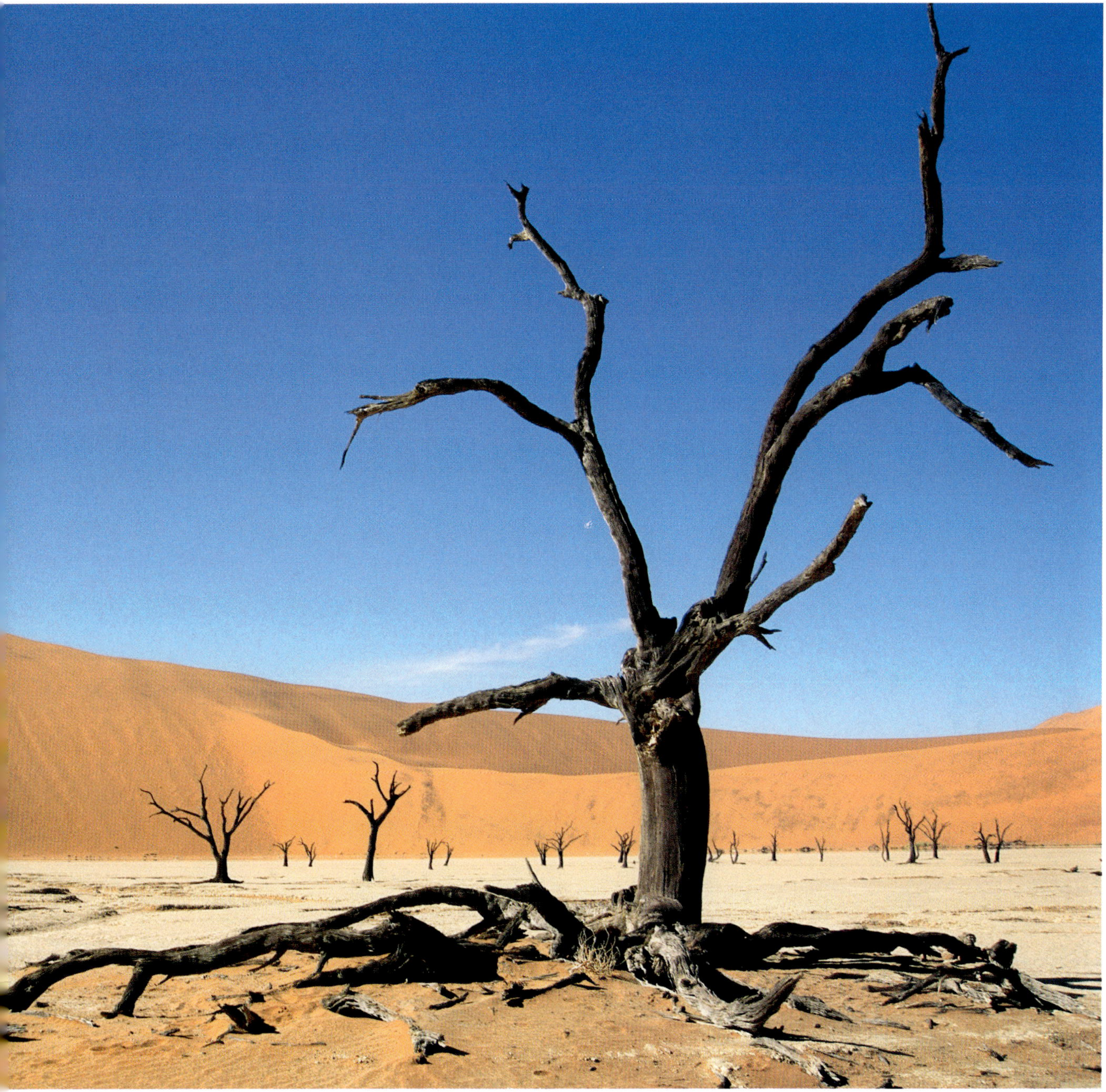

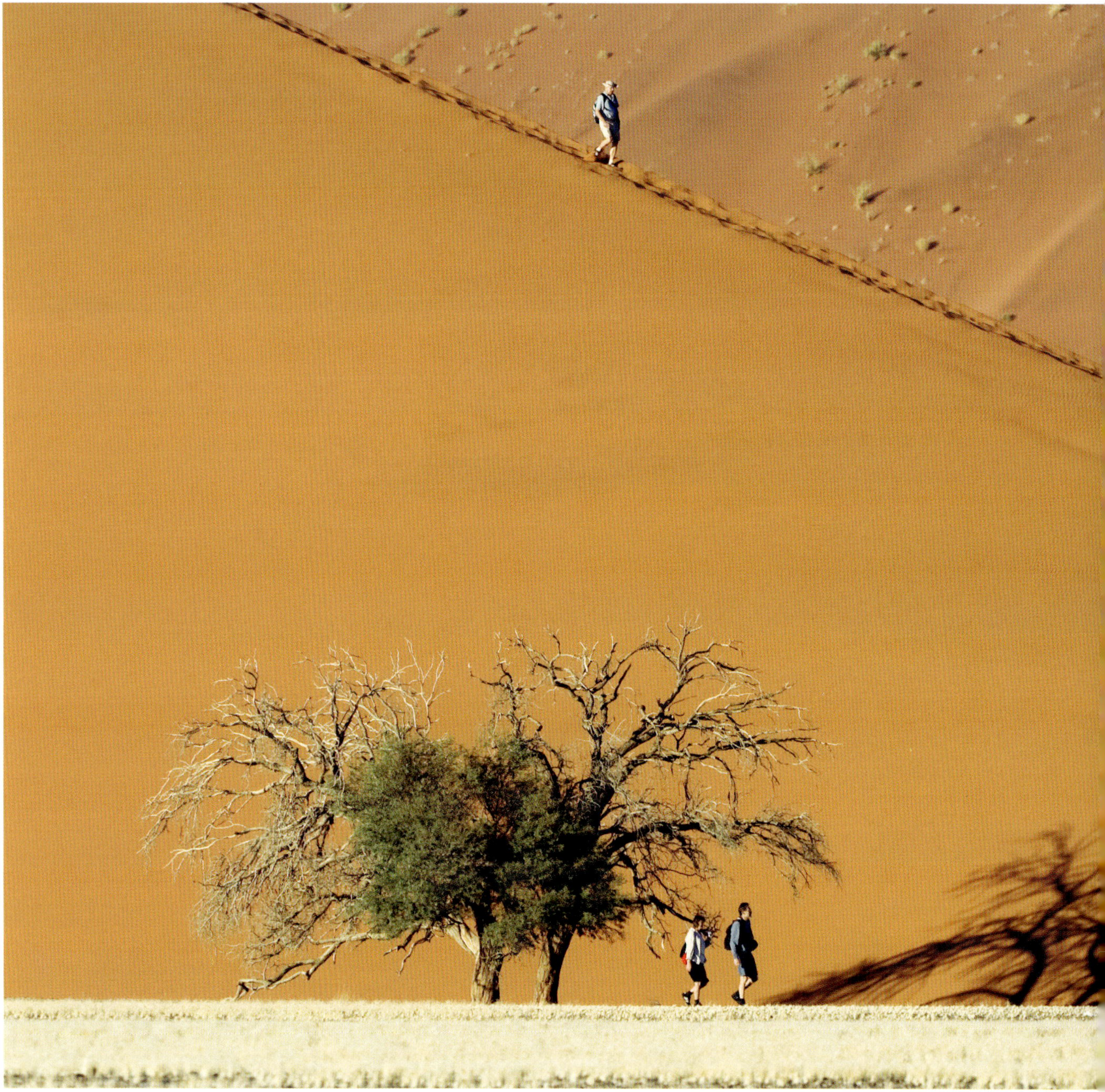

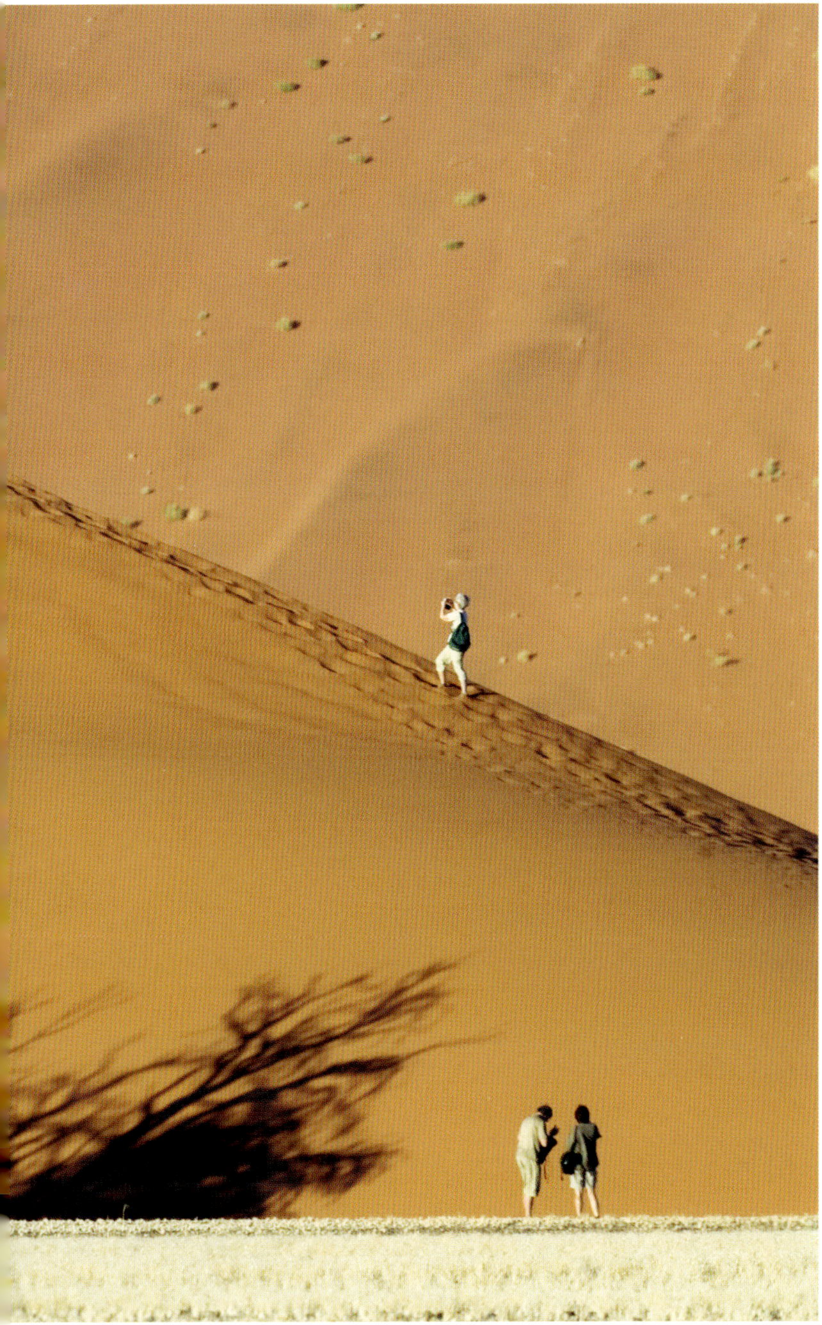

LEFT: With its towering red dunes and scattered camelthorn trees, the endless sea of sand that makes up the Namib-Naukluft has become symbolic of the entire Namib Desert. Despite the heat, aridity and challenging terrain, tourists gather, cameras in hand, to experience the dunes underfoot.

OVERLEAF: The Namib-Naukluft's dry pans of dessicated white clay are surrounded by some of the highest desert dunes in the world, said to reach an impressive 350 metres in places. Set on a foundation of sandstone, the shifting sands have surrounded the pans, which are each peppered with dead camelthorn trees.

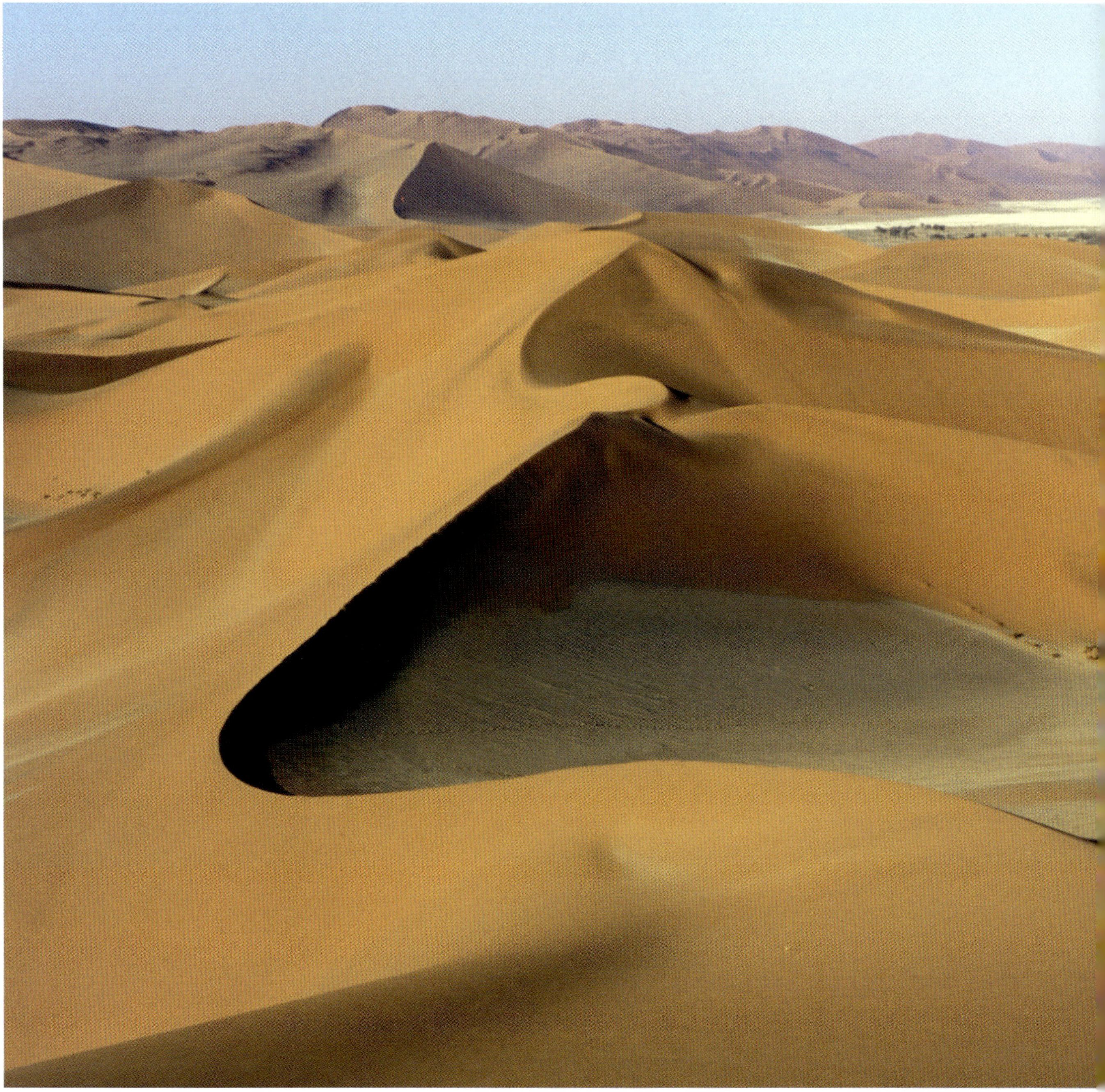

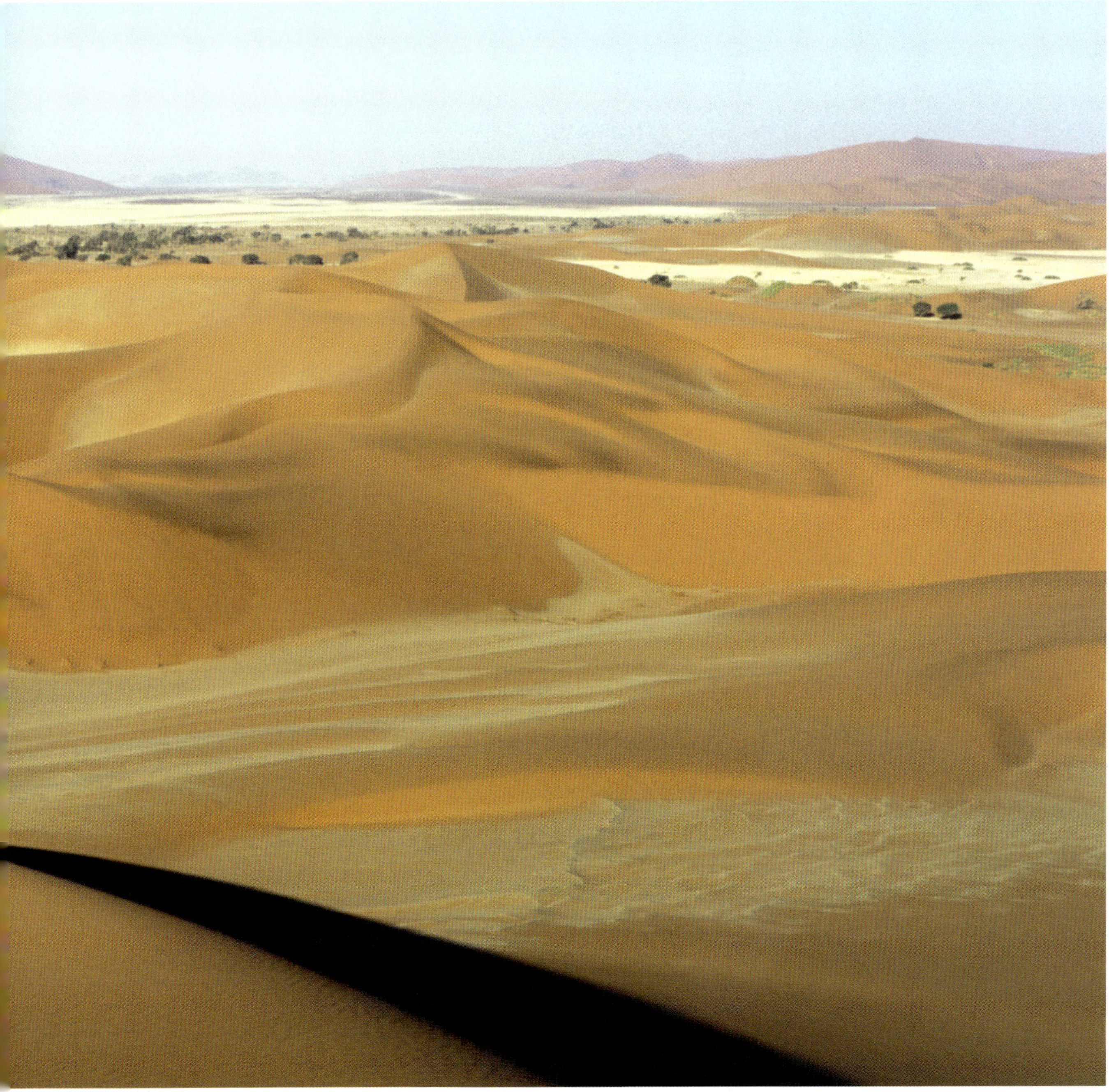

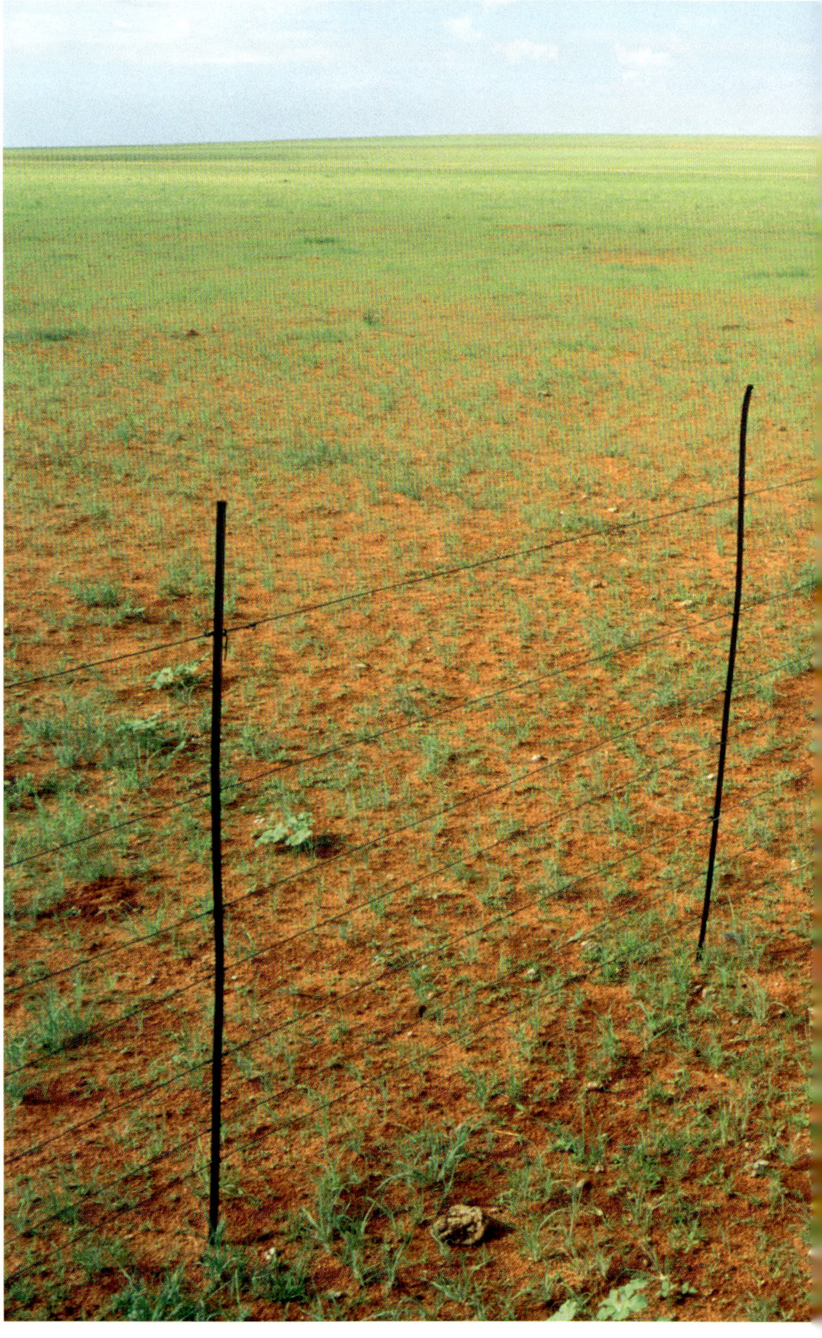

RIGHT: Given the power of the constantly shifting desert sands, delineating farmland is no easy task. A fence separates a farm from the edge of the Namib Desert.

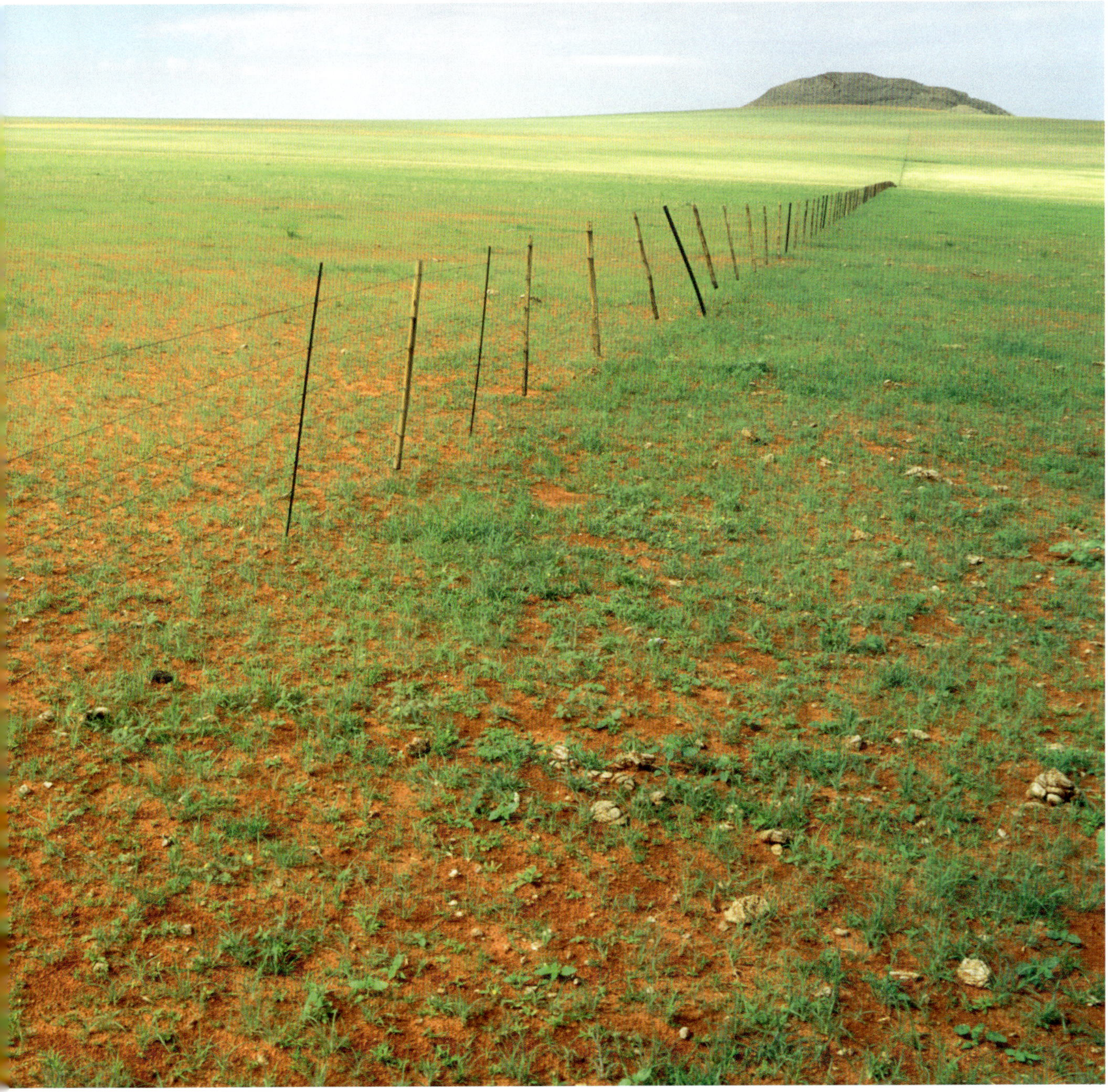

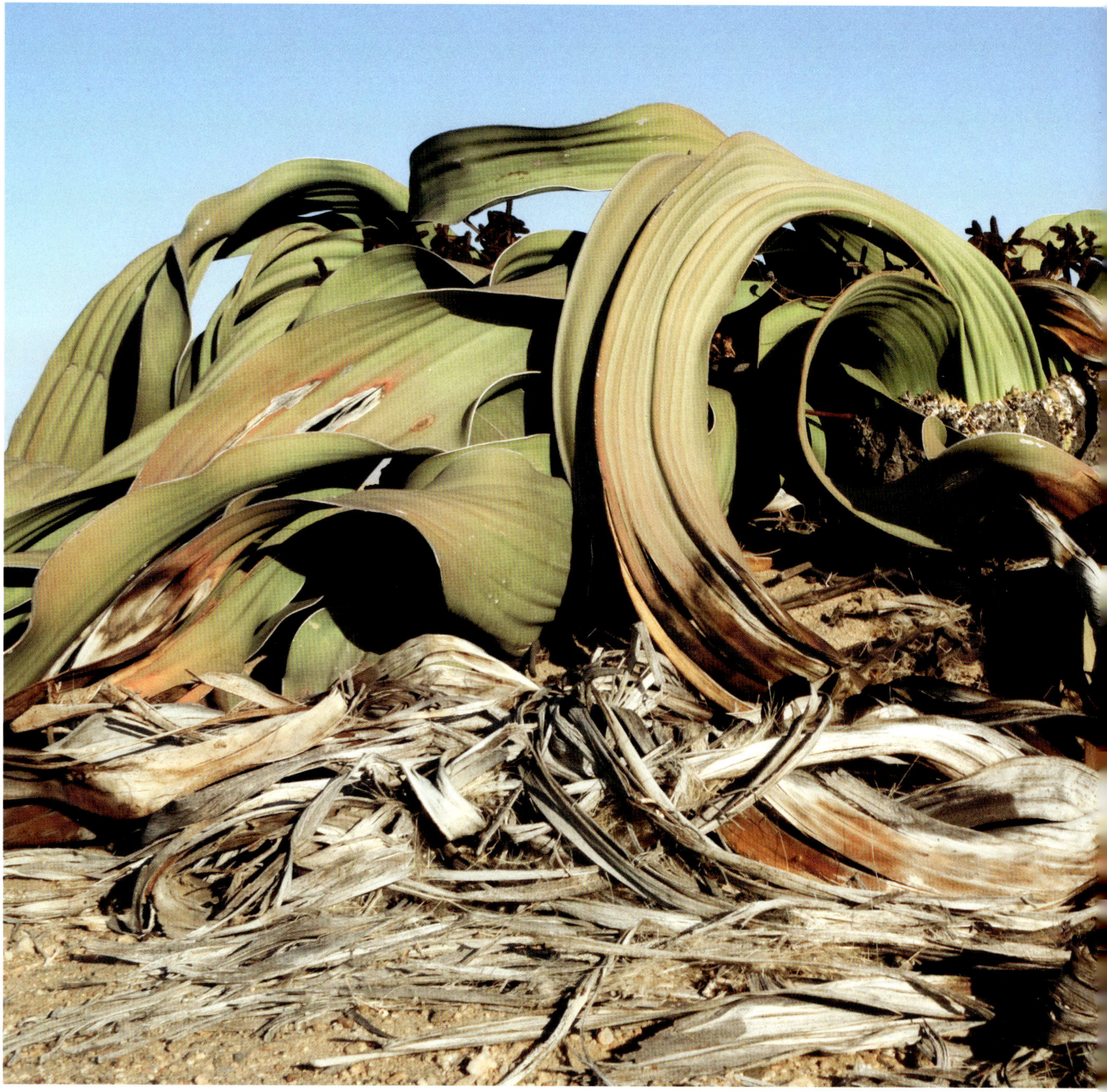

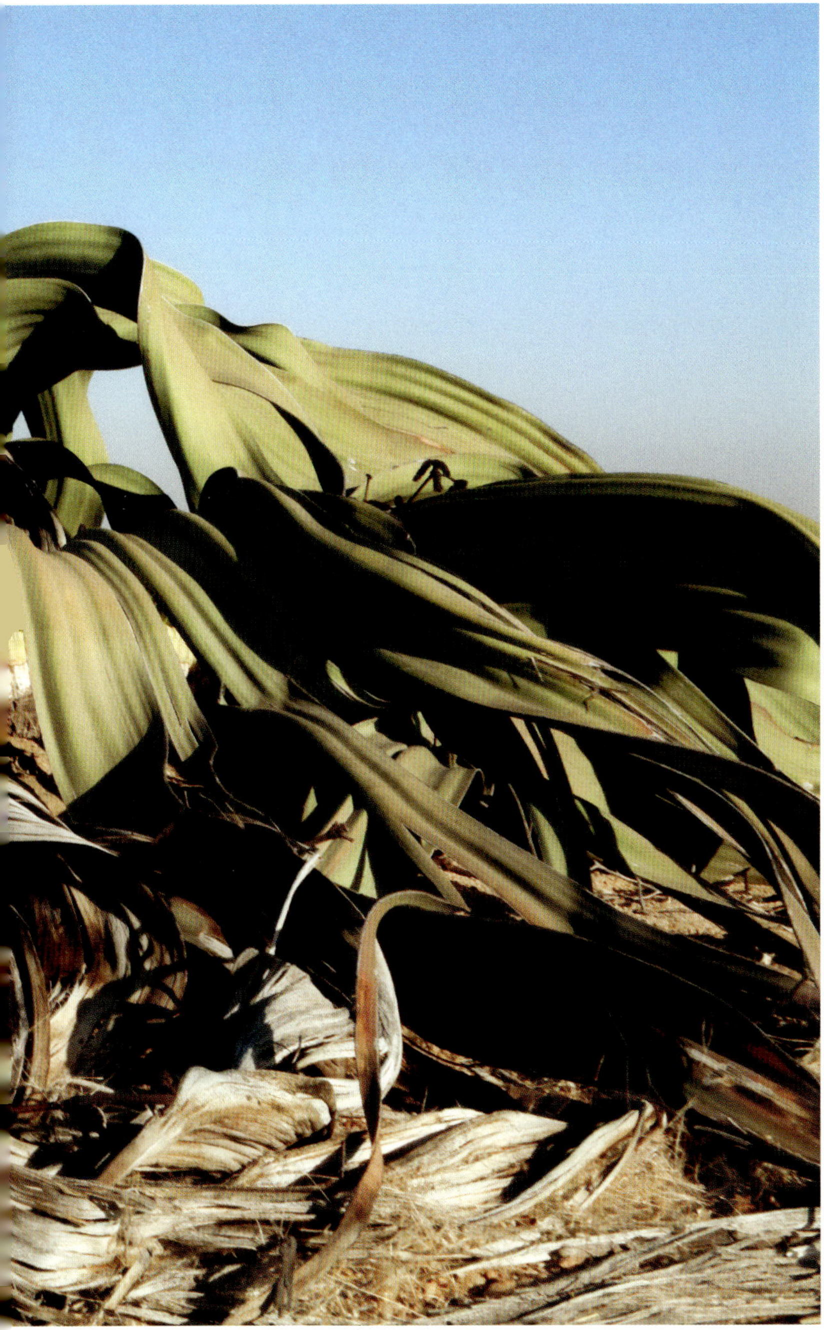

LEFT: Indicative of the unique adaptations of floral life in the Namib, the distinctive welwitschia plant is endemic to this desert landscape. Although the parent plant consists of only two broad leaves, over time these become entangled and ragged so that they appear to be multiple appendages.

OVERLEAF: The Moon Landscape, Namib-Naukluft Park, east of Swakopmund. Given the severity of the landscape and its limited water resources, it is little wonder that both the fauna and flora have had to make any number of critical adaptations in order to survive. Although the Namib-Naukluft and its surrounds seem to harbour few life forms, the Namib is indeed a living desert, with an extraordinary diversity of wildlife and floral species.

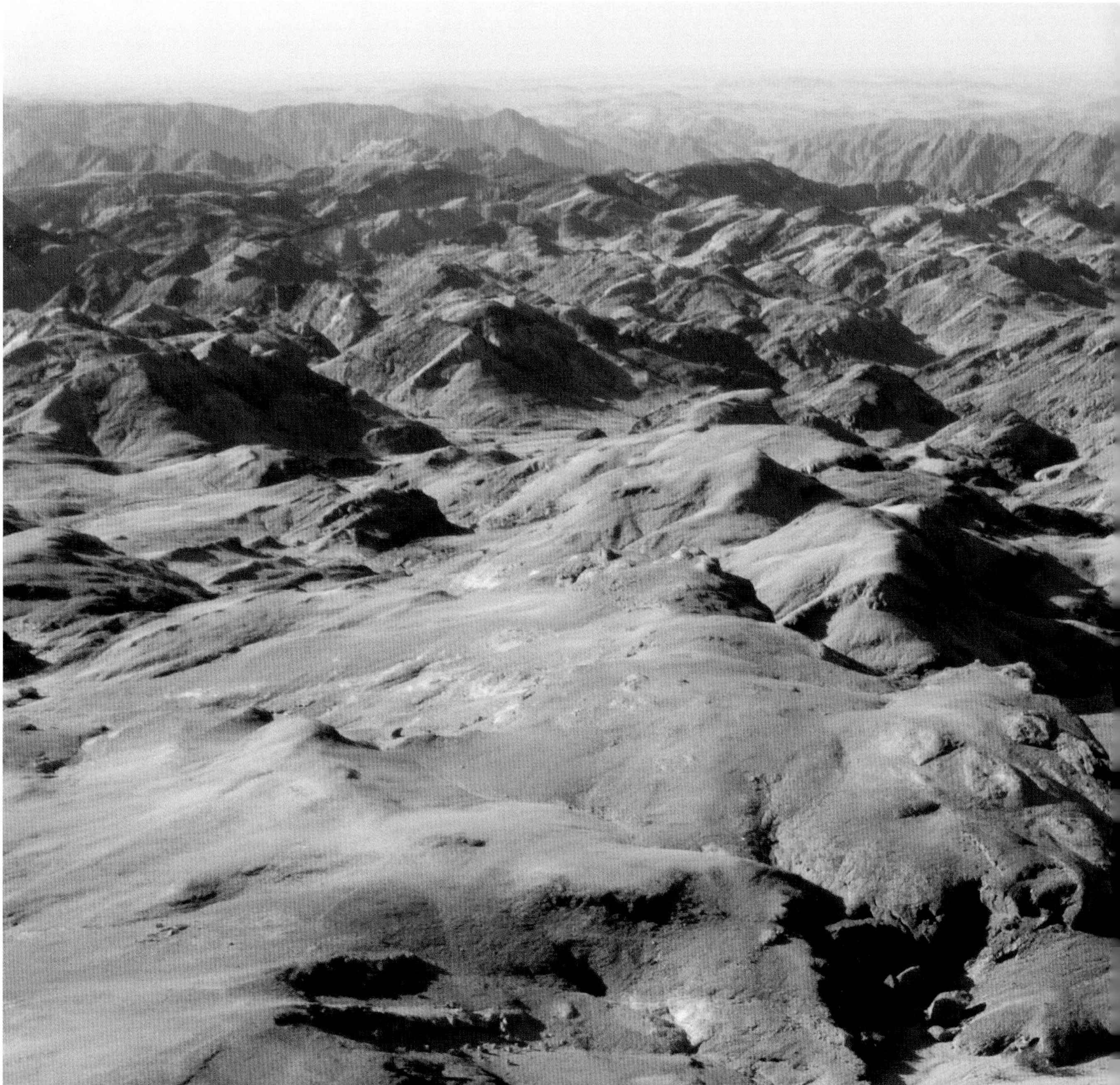

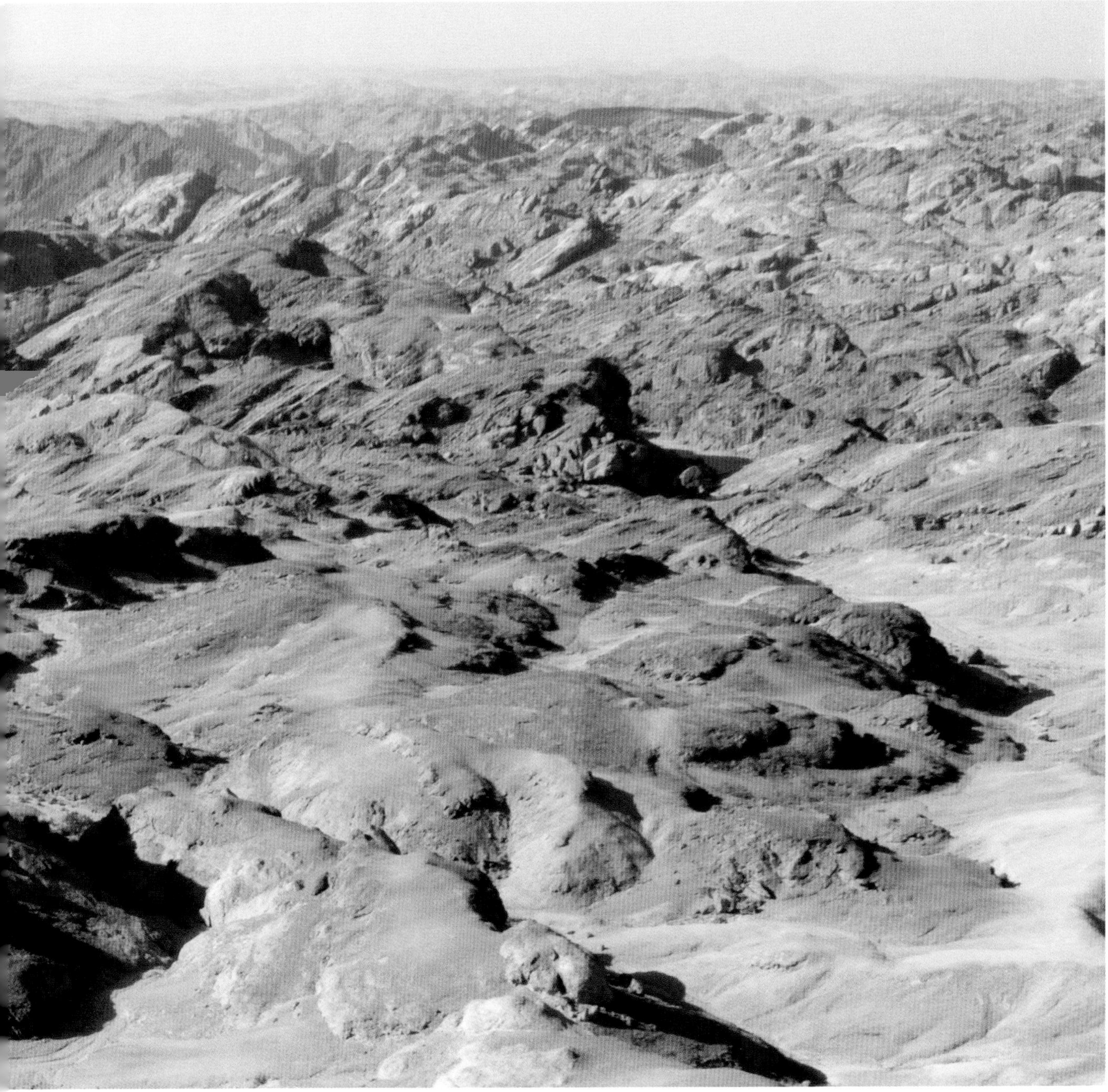

RIGHT: While true deserts are generally considered devoid of water – and this is at least partially true of most deserts – the sands of the Namib encroach so far that they reach right up to the Atlantic shoreline, with only a barely discernible line between desert and beach sand.

OVERLEAF: Because all-important water sources are so few and far between, birds such as these wading flamingos tend to gather in their numbers at the Salt Pans near Walvis Bay.

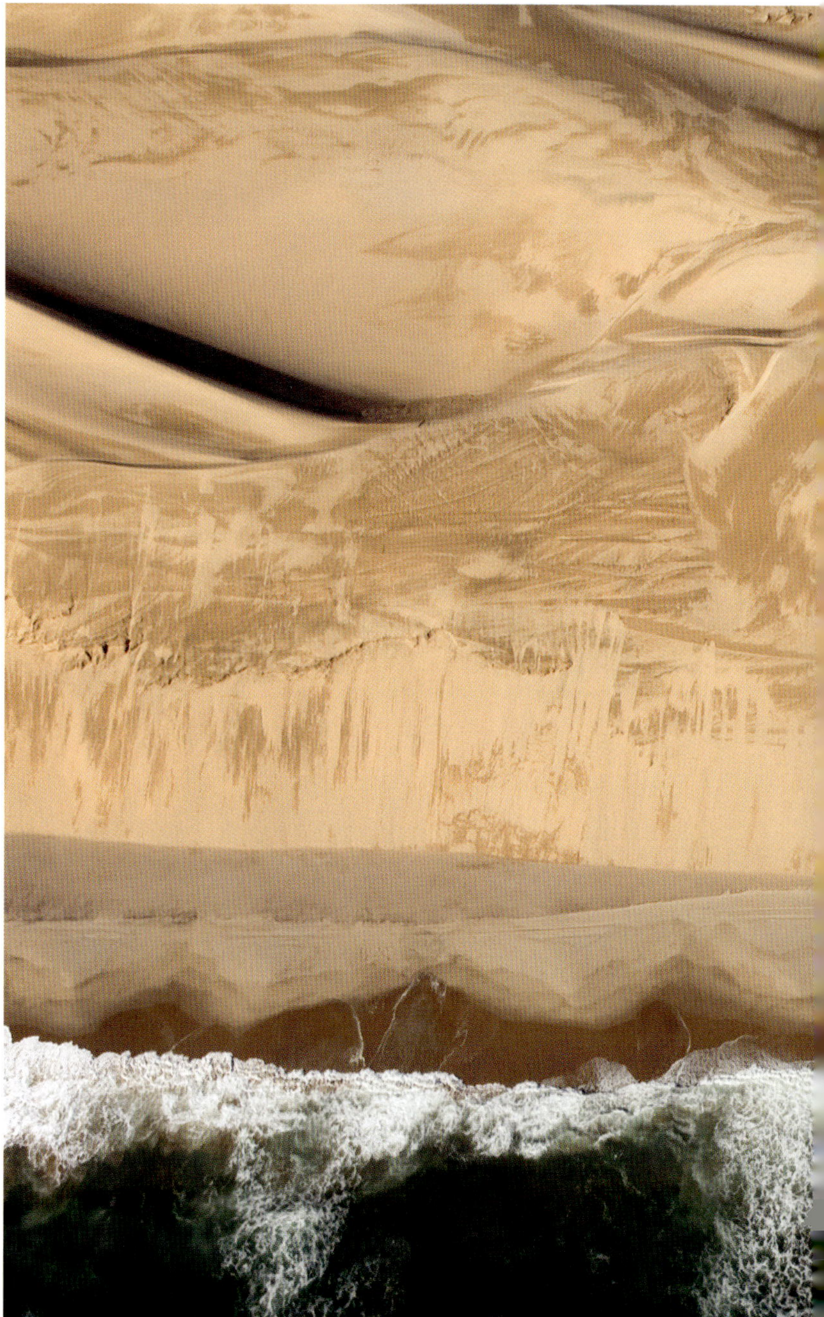

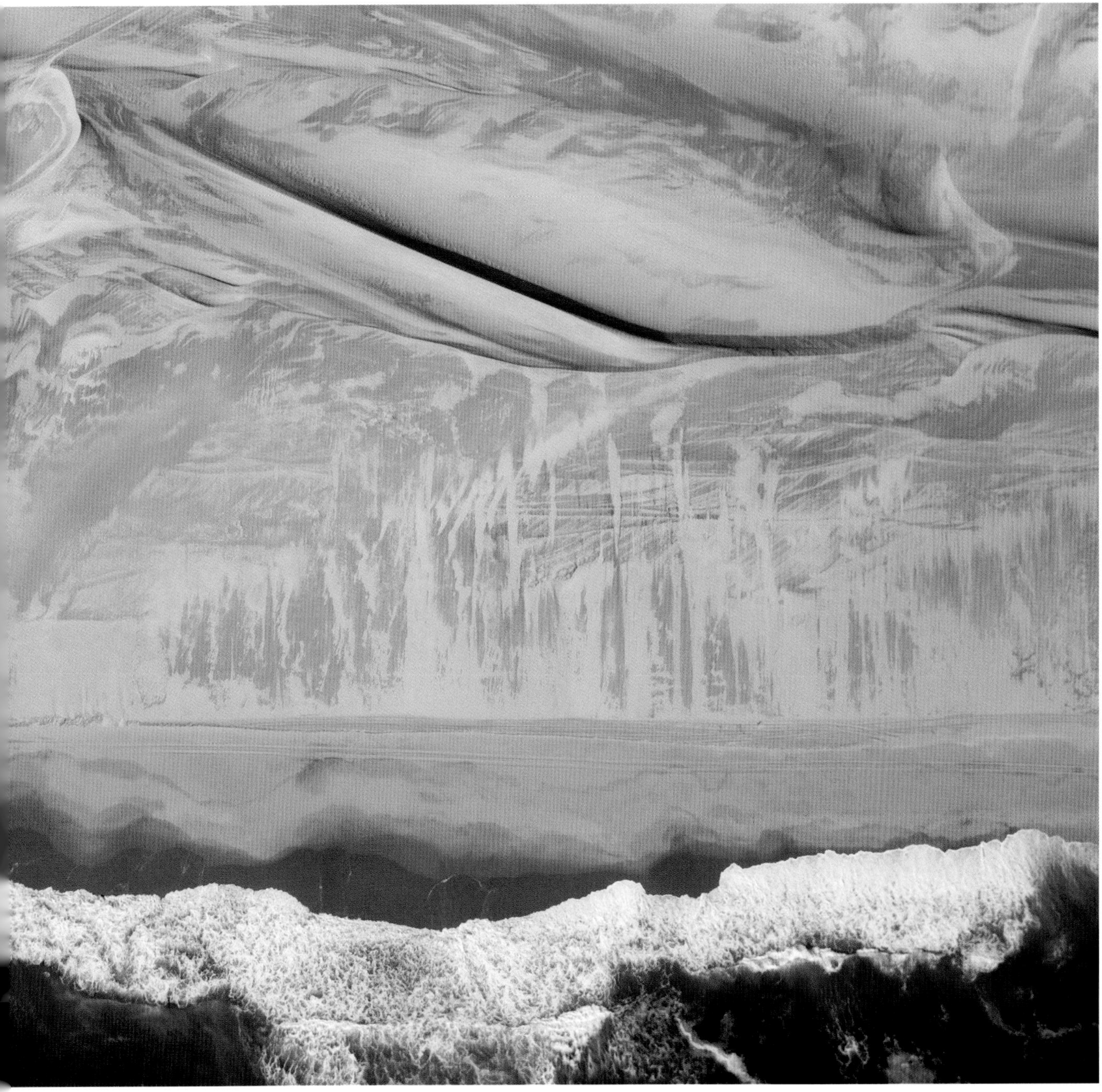

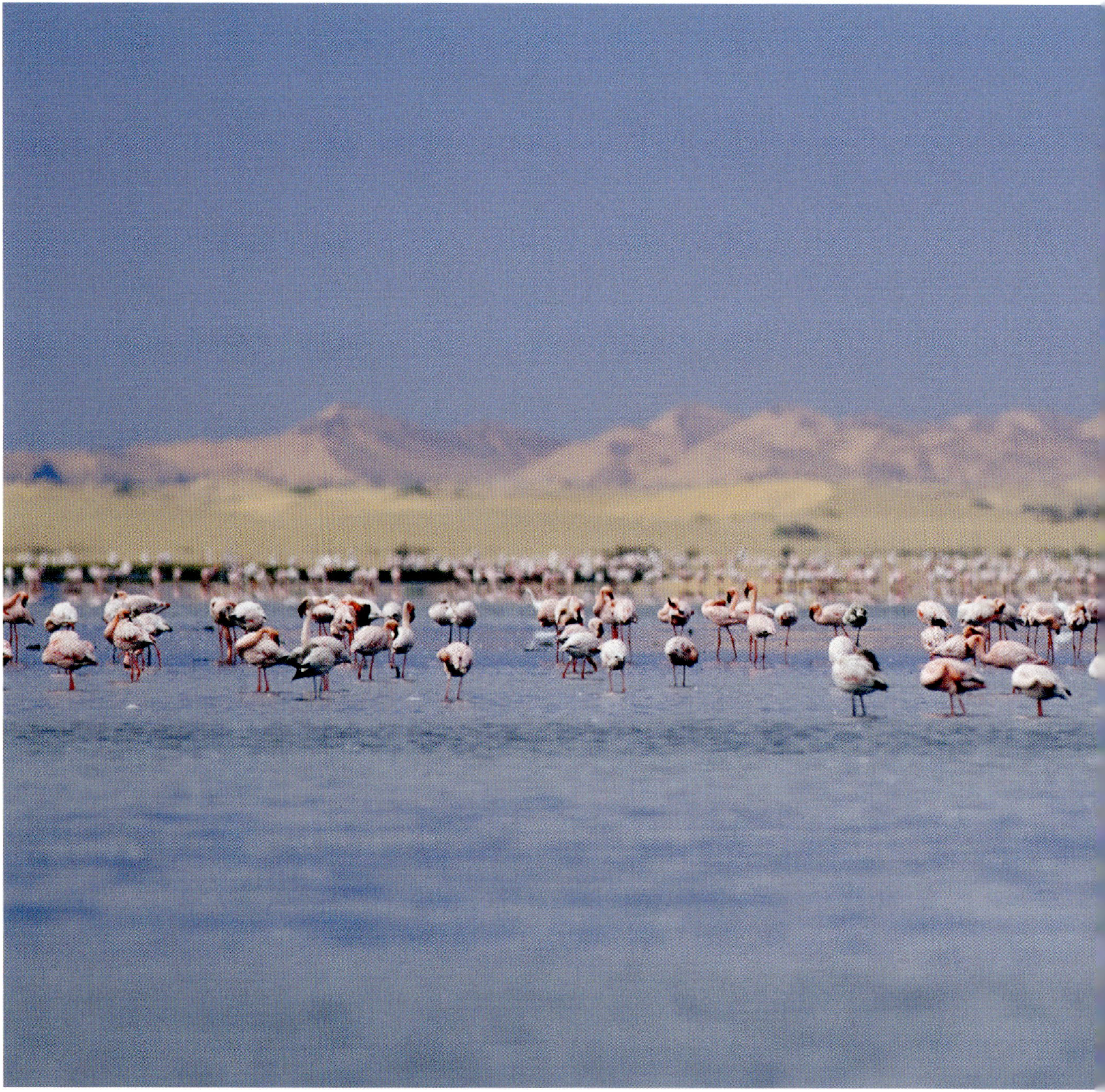

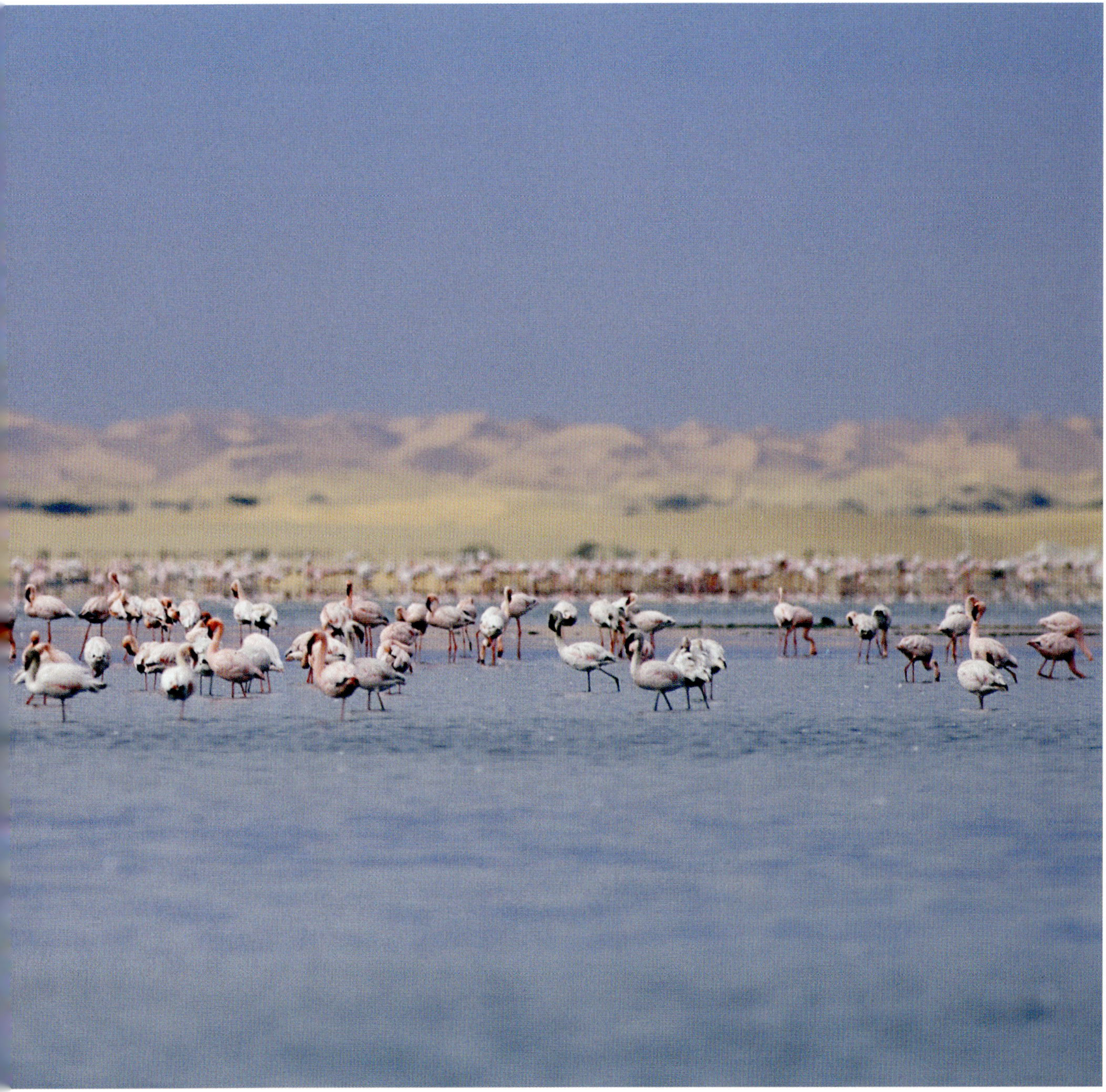

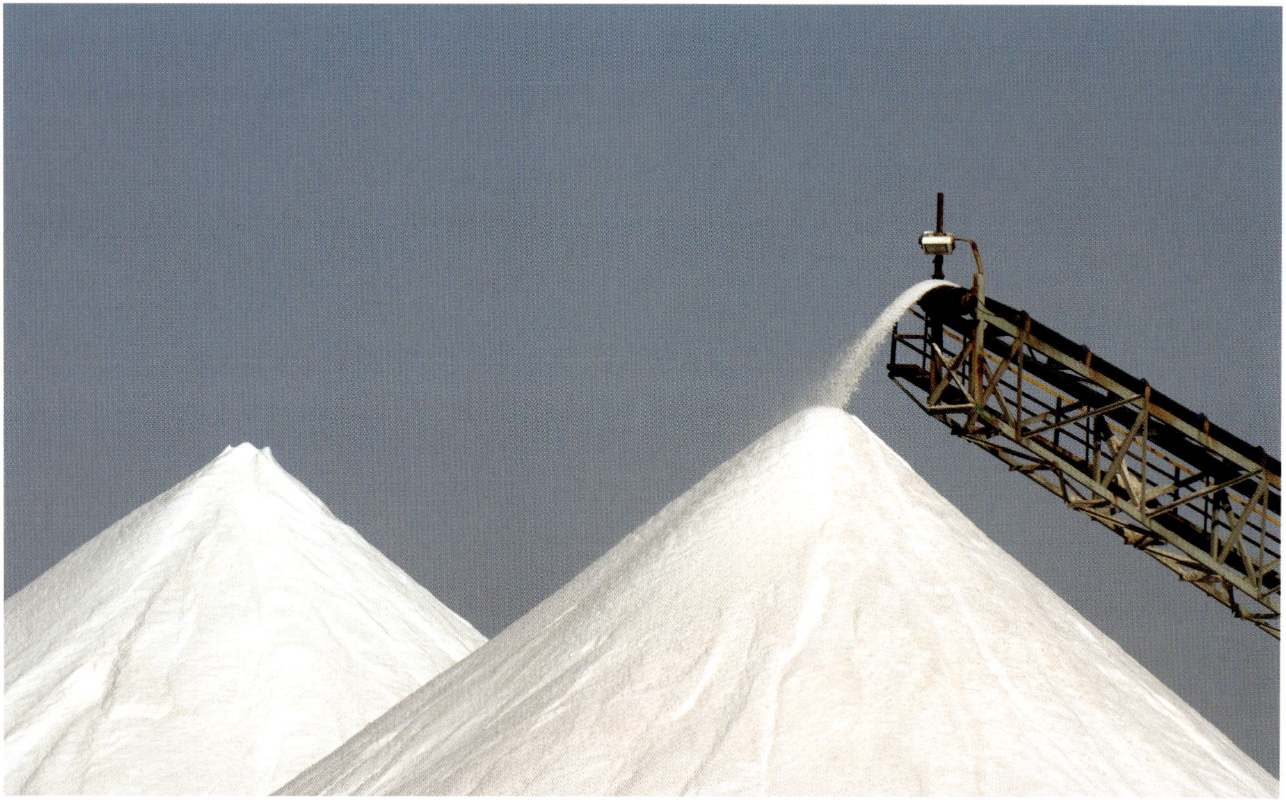

ABOVE: With an apparent abundance of salt pans, salt mining continues to make a significant contribution to the economy of towns such as Walvis Bay, where giant salt works dot the coast.

OPPOSITE: Massive evaporation pans ensure that salt is extracted from saline waters in an operation that has left an indelible mark on the local economy as well as the landscape.

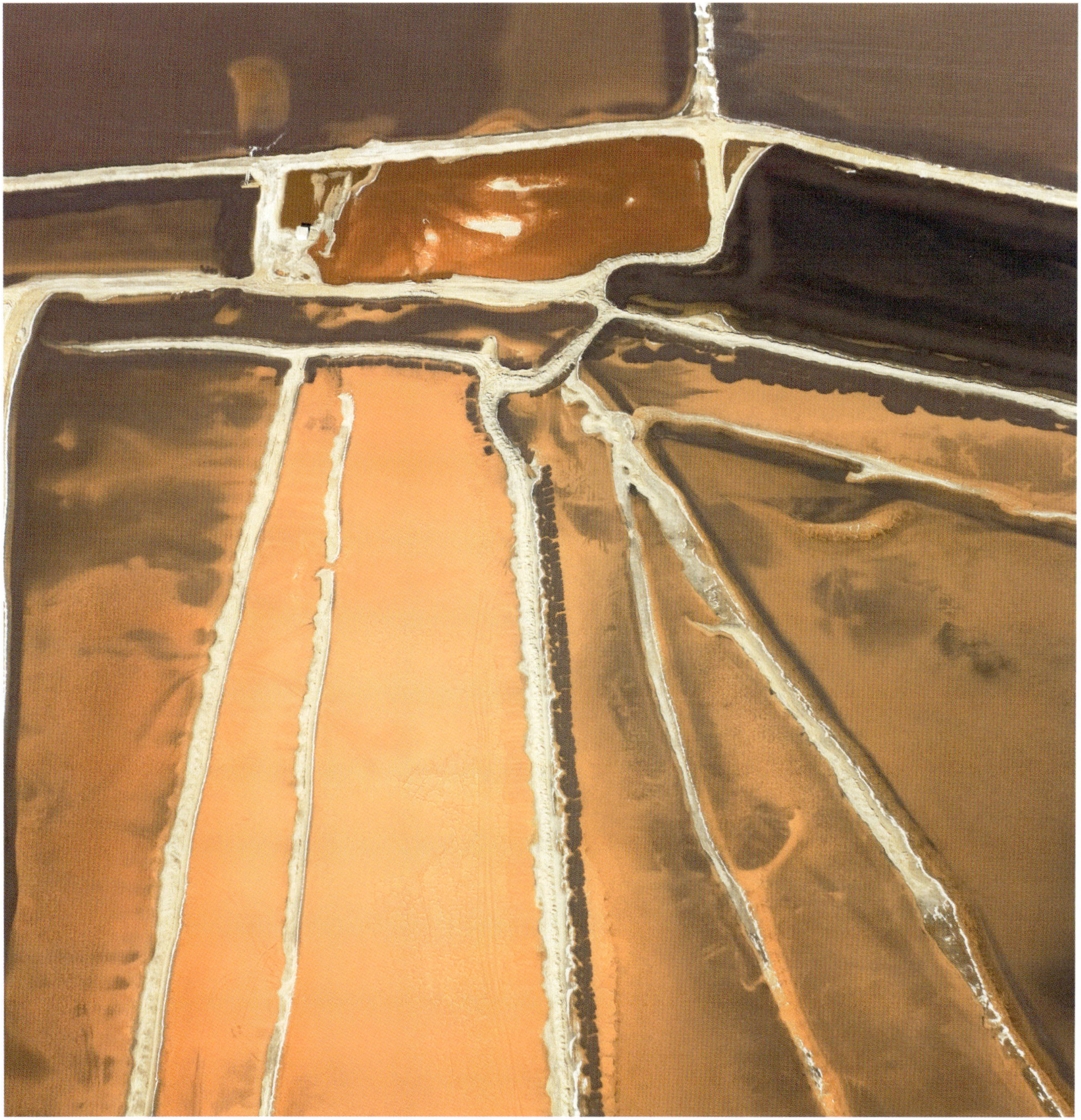

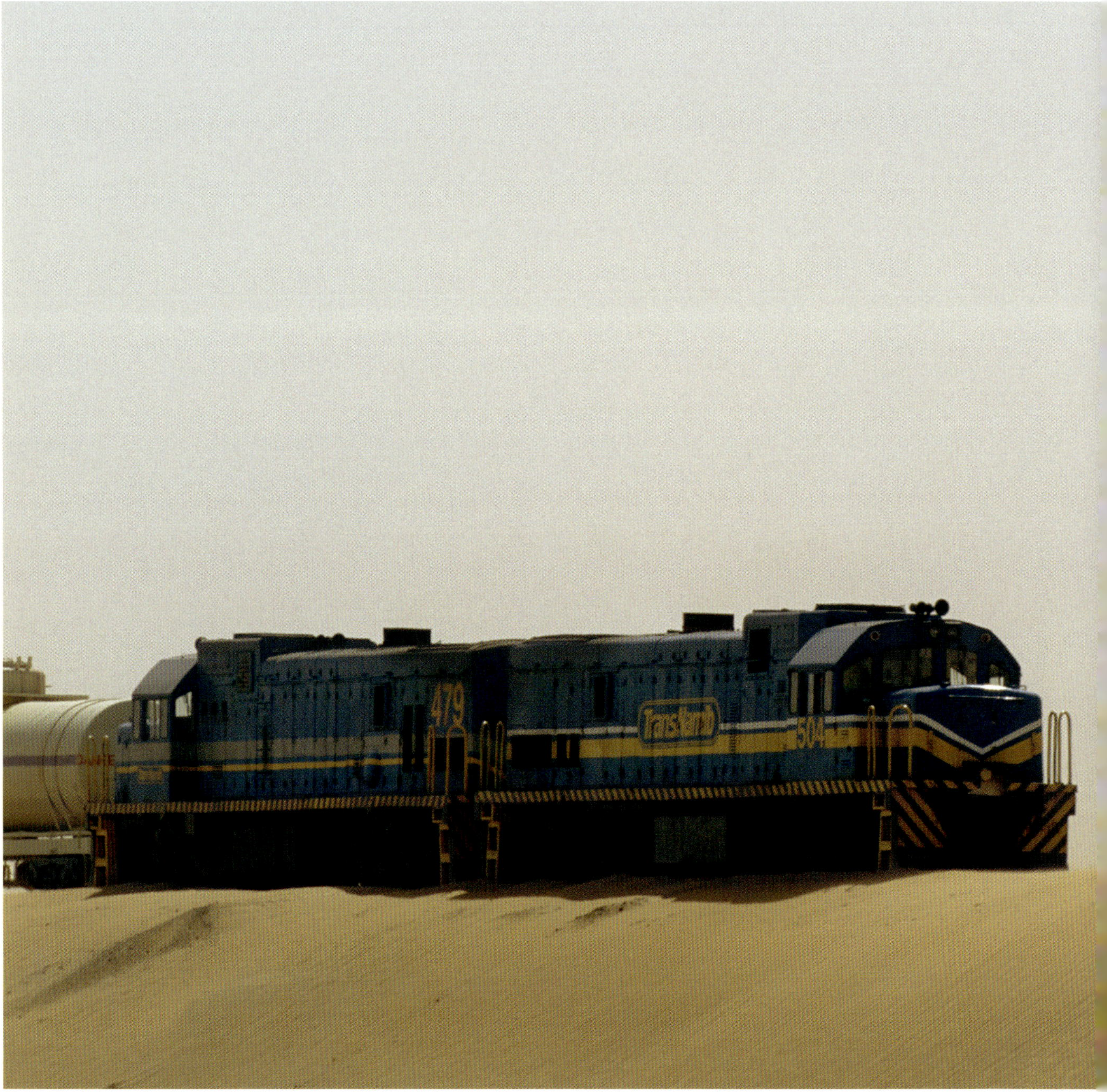
479
TransNamib
504

LEFT: Heavy industry is not easily accomplished in a land where nature plays such a significant role in everyday life. While infrastructure in Namibia is generally regarded as fairly reliable, there can be no certainties. Rail tracks in and around the Namib are often buried under sand and have to be shovelled free.

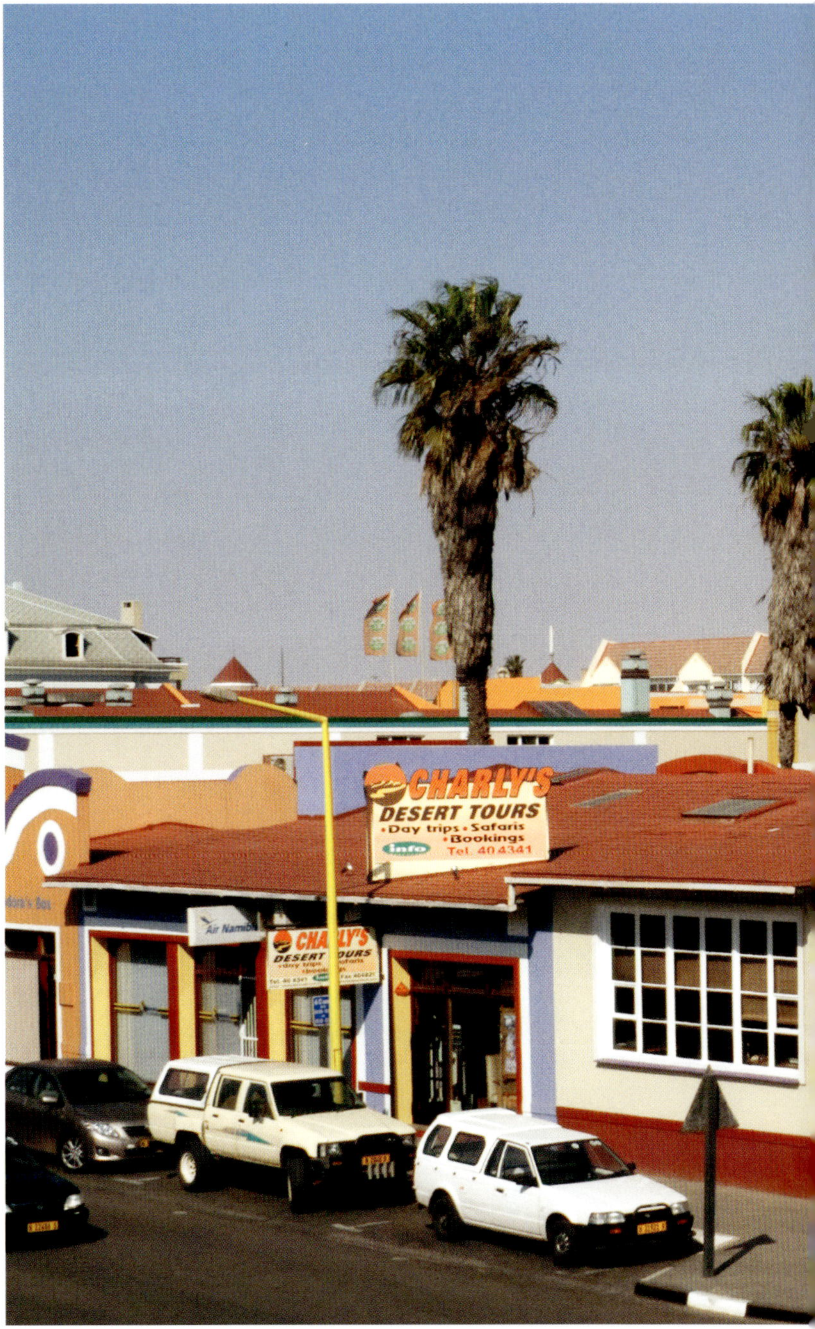

RIGHT: Swakopmund is a simple, laid-back town that is steeped in colonial history and yet retains an engaging local flavour. Here distinctly European structures now house bustling retail outlets and offices – all watched over by the Damara Tower, a nod to its African locality.

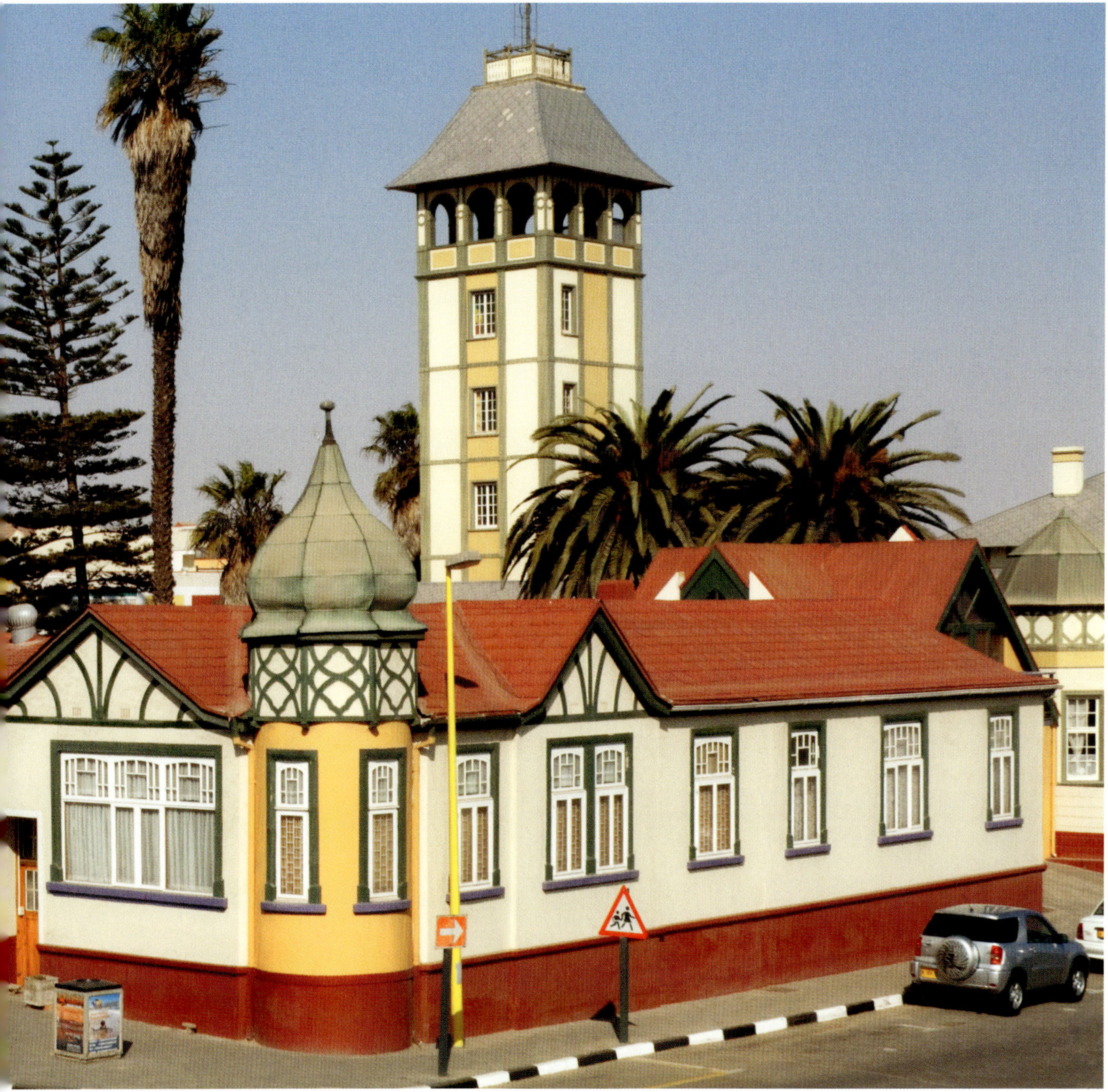

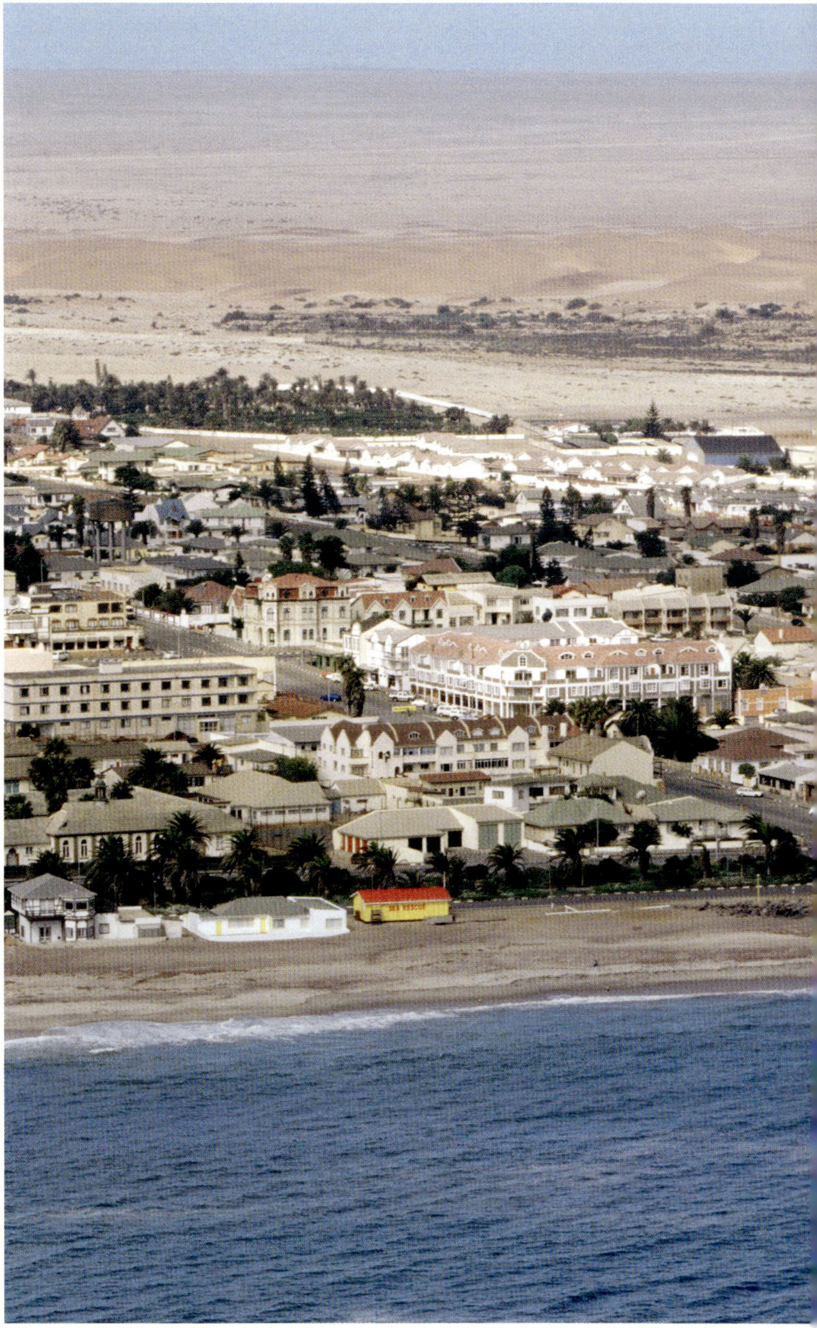

RIGHT: Situated as it is on Namibia's coastline and at the mouth of Swakop River, Swakopmund – with a permanent population of little more than 30 000 – is an attractive little resort town, the administrative centre for the entire Erongo district. Its museums, galleries, colonial architecture and scenic hinterland make it a popular drawcard virtually year round.

OVERLEAF: A pair of squabbling white pelicans perch atop a street lamp in the heart of the urban settlement that is Swakopmund.

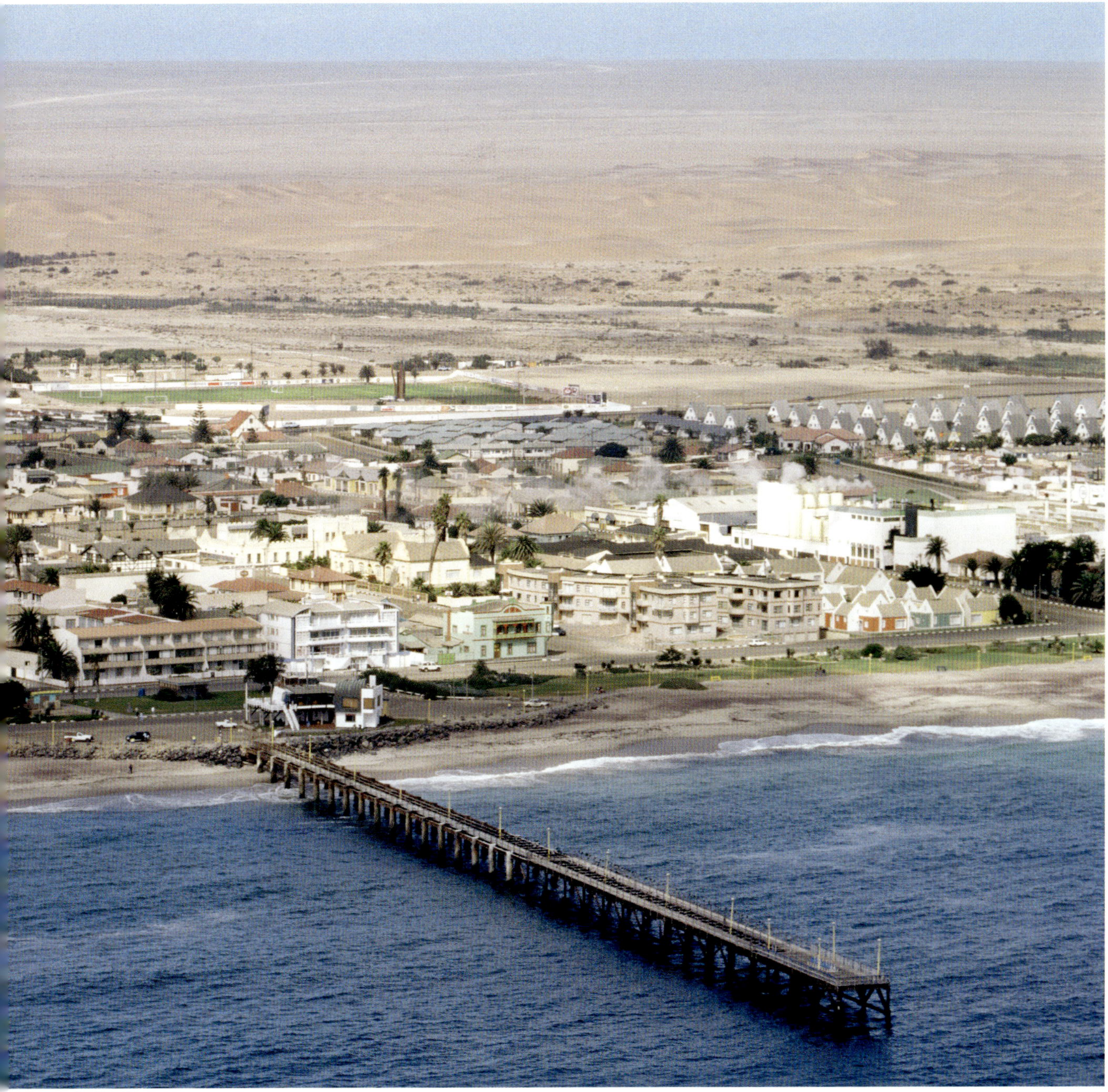

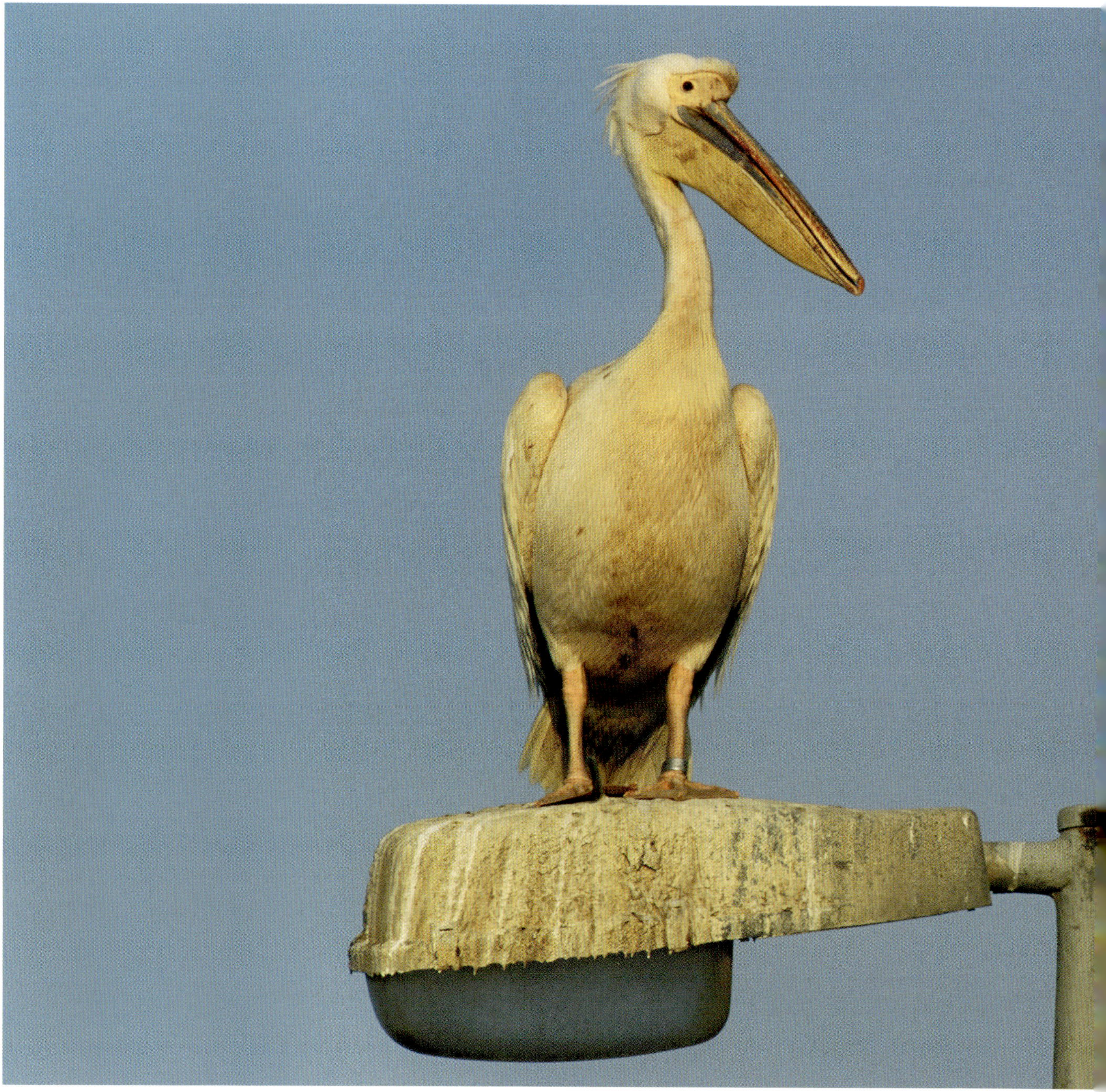

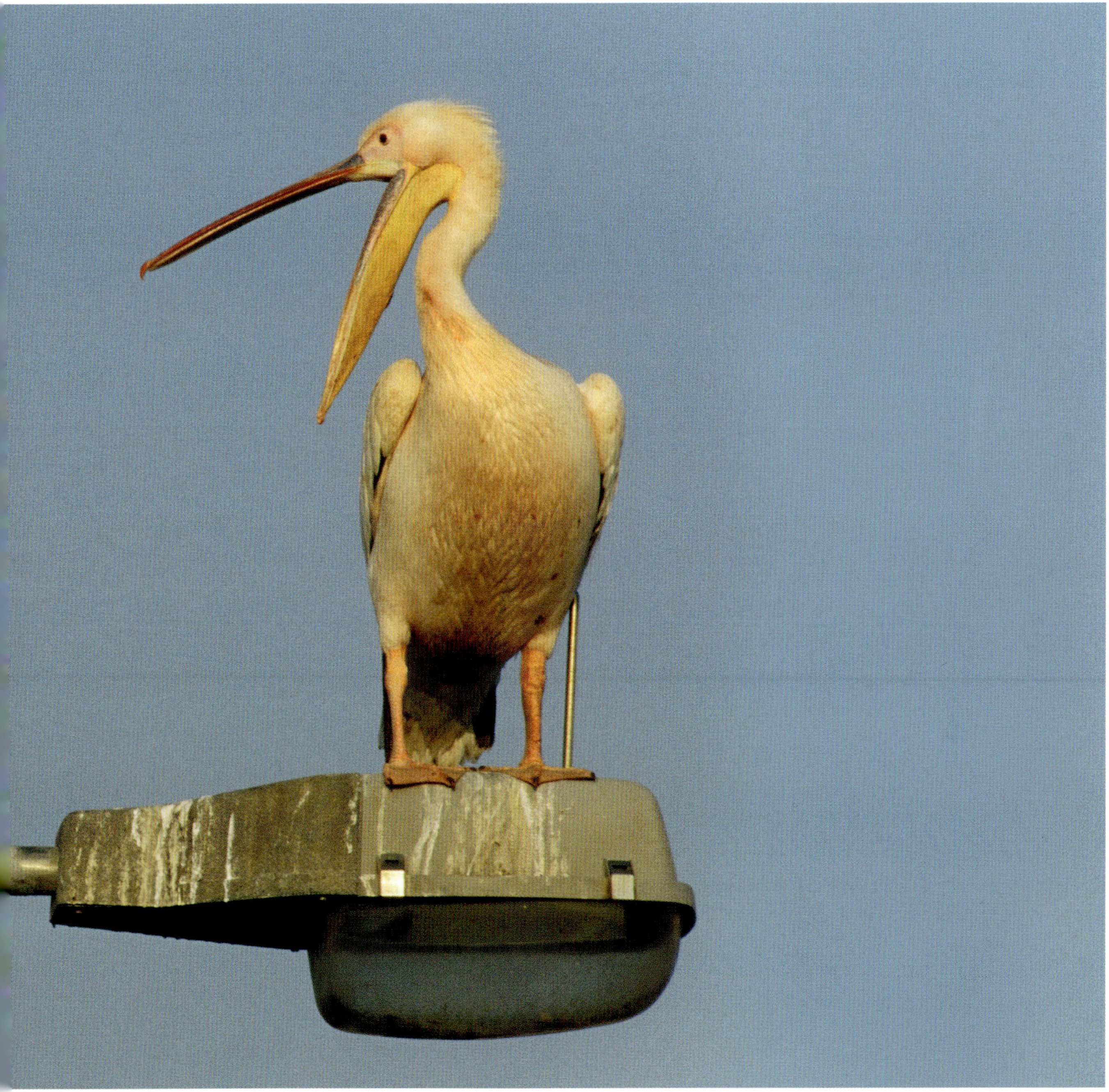

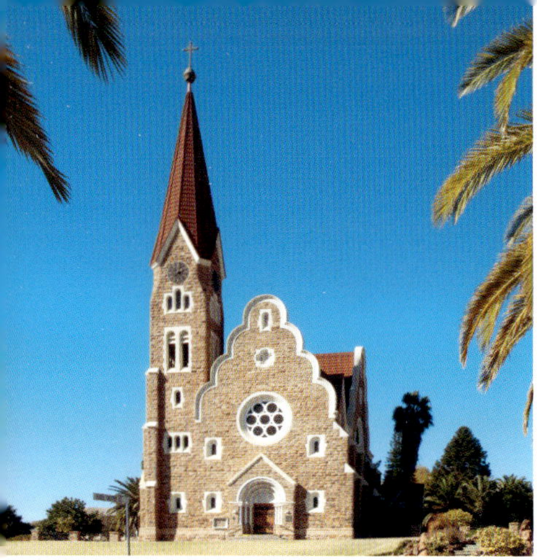
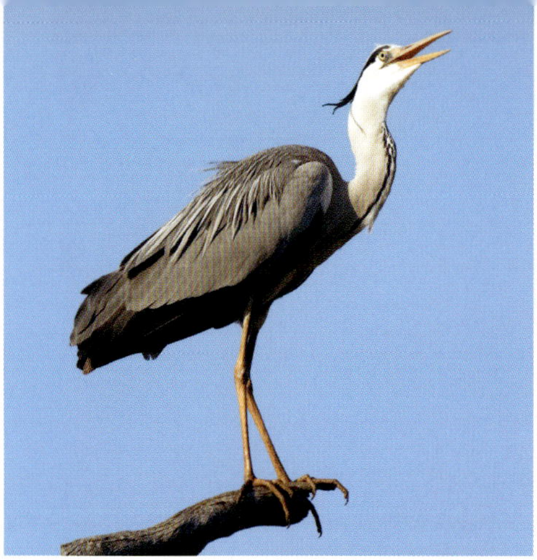
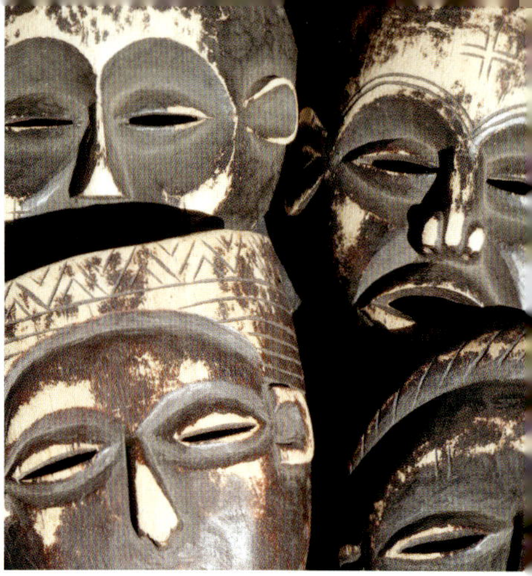
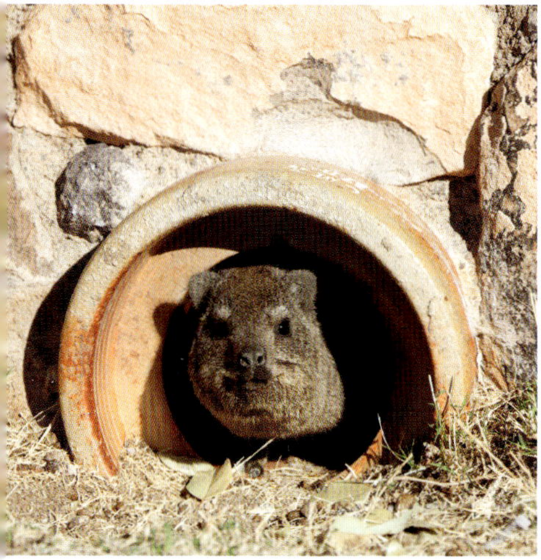
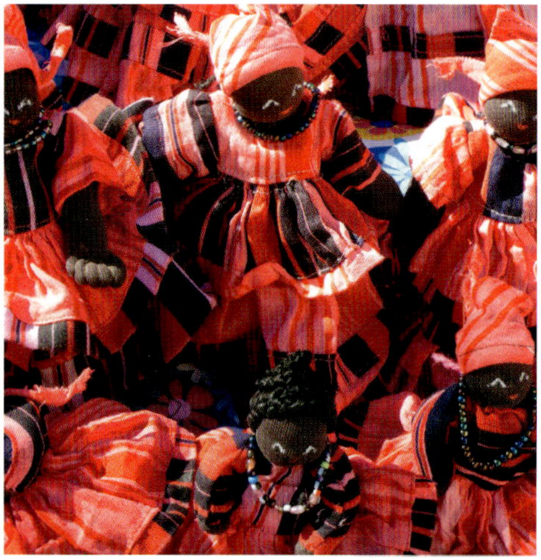
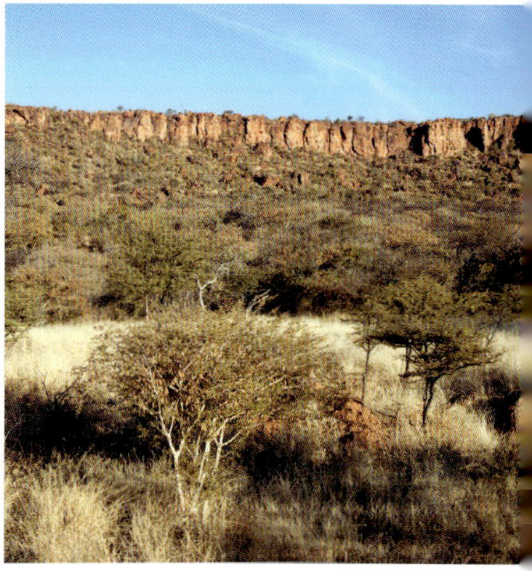
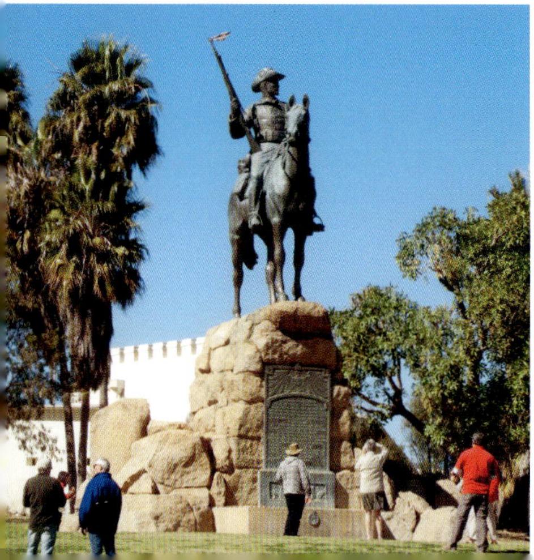
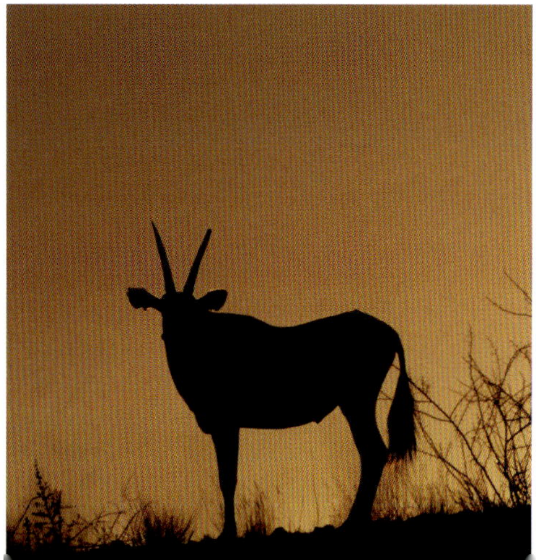
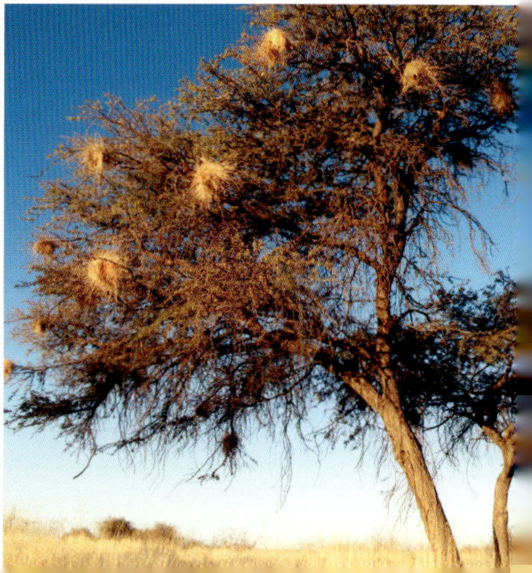

Central Region

Virtually surrounded by desert sand – the Namib-Naukluft Park and the Namib in the west and the Kgalagadi Transfrontier Park in the east – it is not surprising that Namibia's central region is a harsh and arid land. Rainfall around Windhoek is seldom more than 300 millimetres a year, dropping to about 200 millimetres around Mariental to the south. Human settlements are few and very far between – distances seem endless wherever you go in this vast landscape – with most towns and villages scattered along the main artery of the B1 highway, which cuts right through the central region north to south. Dotted along this route are the towns of Mariental, Rehoboth, Okahandja and the capital city of Windhoek.

The broad central region, vast and insulated as it is, is not without its natural wonders. On the western periphery is a series of spectacular mountains, their ragged peaks towering above the surrounding sands: the Tiras, Zaris, Gamsberg and Erongo ranges, each with its own natural splendour. The canyons of the Zaris mountains, for example, boast fascinating limestone strata and rock terraces peppered with the ghost-like silhouettes of corkwood and phantom trees. The Erongo range is equally imposing, its circle of cliff faces comprising granite and volcanic rock weathered and hammered by wind, water and a ruthless sun. Further north, between the cityscape of Windhoek and Etosha National Park, lie the plains of the Waterberg Plateau, a protected conservation area. Unsurprisingly, considering its name, natural hollows that fill with life-giving water during the rainy season are scattered along its perimeter.

OPPOSITE FROM LEFT TO RIGHT:

- The famed Christuskirche, cherished landmark in the nation's capital, Windhoek.
- A grey heron perches high above the waters of Hardap Dam in Namibia's dry central region.
- Local masks, carefully handcrafted, for sale at one of the open-air markets in Windhoek's city centre.
- Rock hyrax (dassie) peeps out of a drainpipe at the Hardap Recreation Resort.
- Handmade Herero dolls add colour to a market stall in the tourism hub that is Windhoek.
- The sandstone rockface of the Waterberg Plateau watches over the savanna plains of the surrounding conservation area.
- An equestrian statue commemorates German losses during the campaigns against local Nama and Herero in the early 1900s.
- Gemsbok gather at dusk along the waters of the Hardap Dam in Central Namibia.
- Chattering weavers congregate at their communal nest in the Hardap Recreation Resort on the banks of the dam.

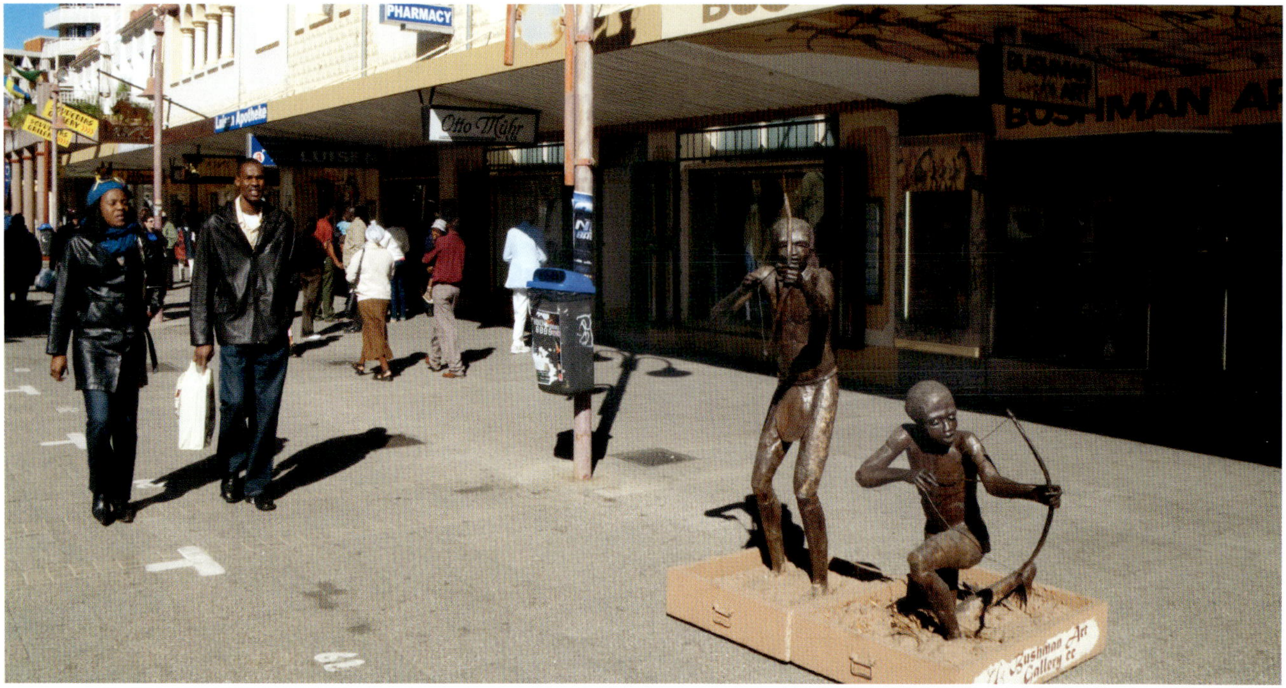

ABOVE: Once known as Kaiserstrasse, Independence Avenue remains Windhoek's main thoroughfare. It is the heart and soul of the modern city, neatly bisecting the capital.

OPPOSITE: Today the face of the inner city reflects the more diverse cultural elements of Windhoek, the grand architectural styles of Europe interspersed with local markets selling traditional crafts and souvenirs.

Windhoek, Namibia's capital, is small and relatively undeveloped even by Africa's standards, but it is precisely that which makes it so alluring. While it has its fair share of contemporary office blocks and shopping centres, and a network of well-maintained roads, its charm lies in its intimacy.

Its abundance of historic buildings bear testimony to its German occupation, but it also enjoys a unique local flavour, making it a vibrant and modern city increasingly popular among travellers in an ever-growing tourism industry. Informal street markets – colourful and lively – are interspersed among old colonial structures that today serve as administrative centres, offices and even retail outlets. Windhoek is the gateway to the adventures promised by the coast, the desert and the wilderness beyond.

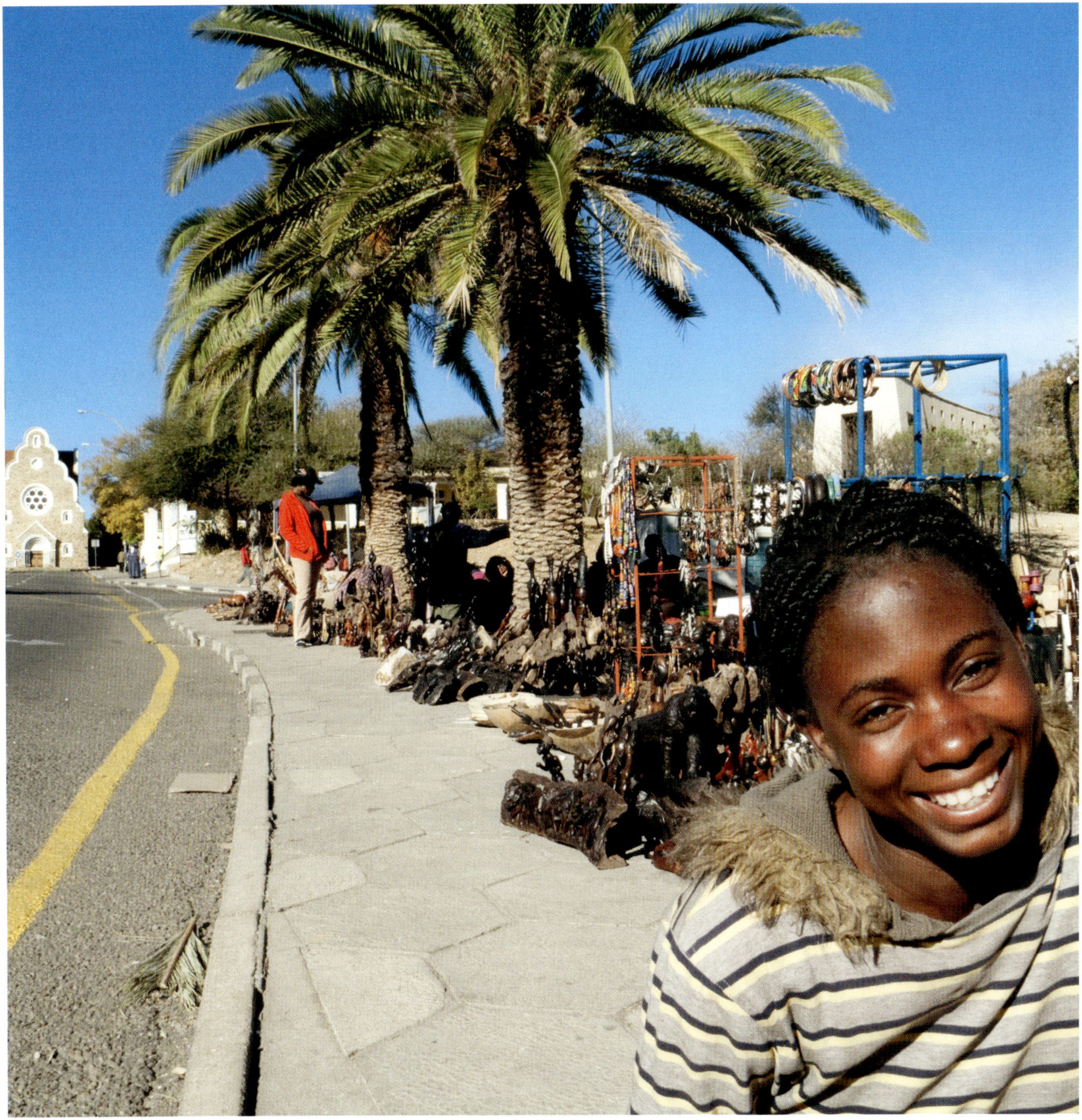

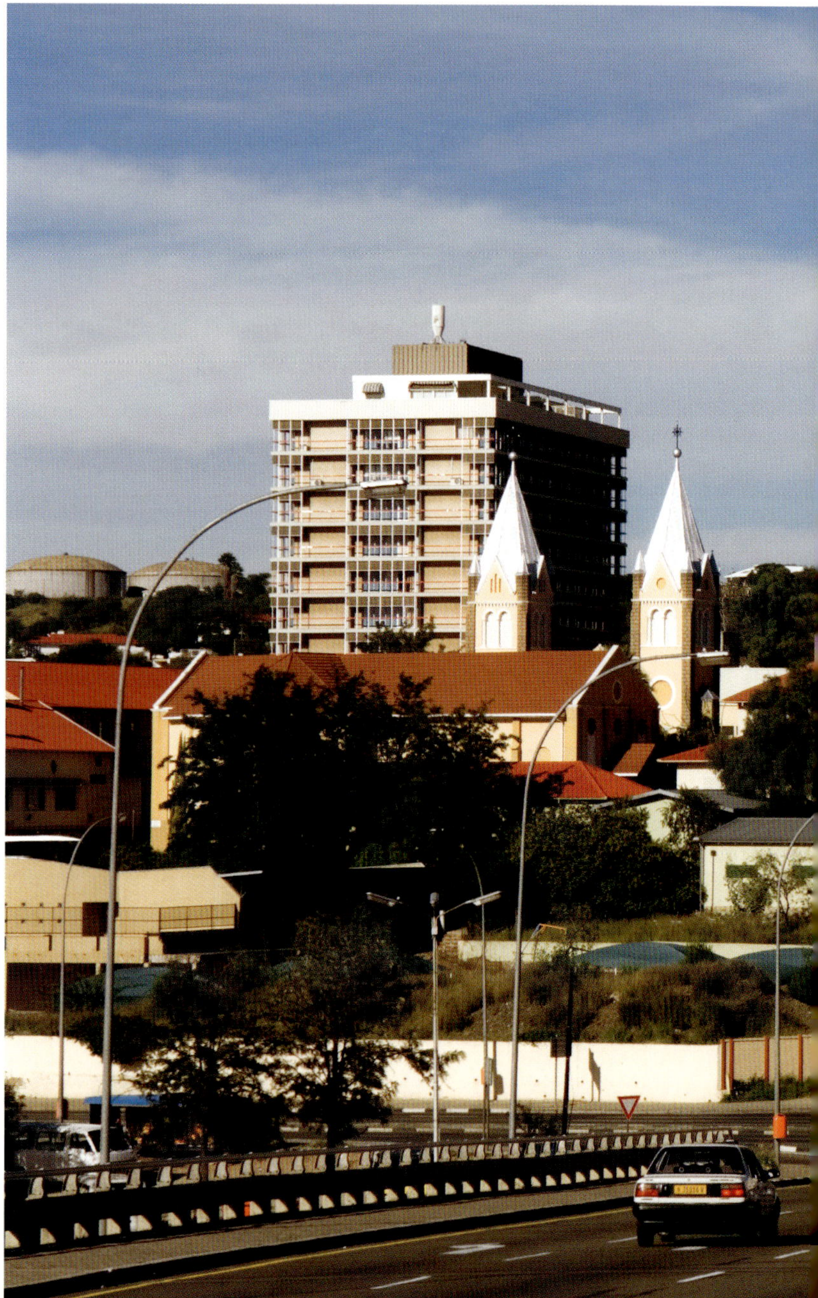

RIGHT: With no more than about 300 000 citizens and presiding over a country with a total population of less than two million, Windhoek is a capital city in every sense of the term. It is the undisputed heart of the country, home to virtually all its industry, economy and socio-political activity.

OVERLEAF: National coffers have come to rely more and more on an expanding tourism market, and the country's recreational facilities range from basic tents to luxuriously appointed chalets, such as these at the Waterberg Plateau Lodge.

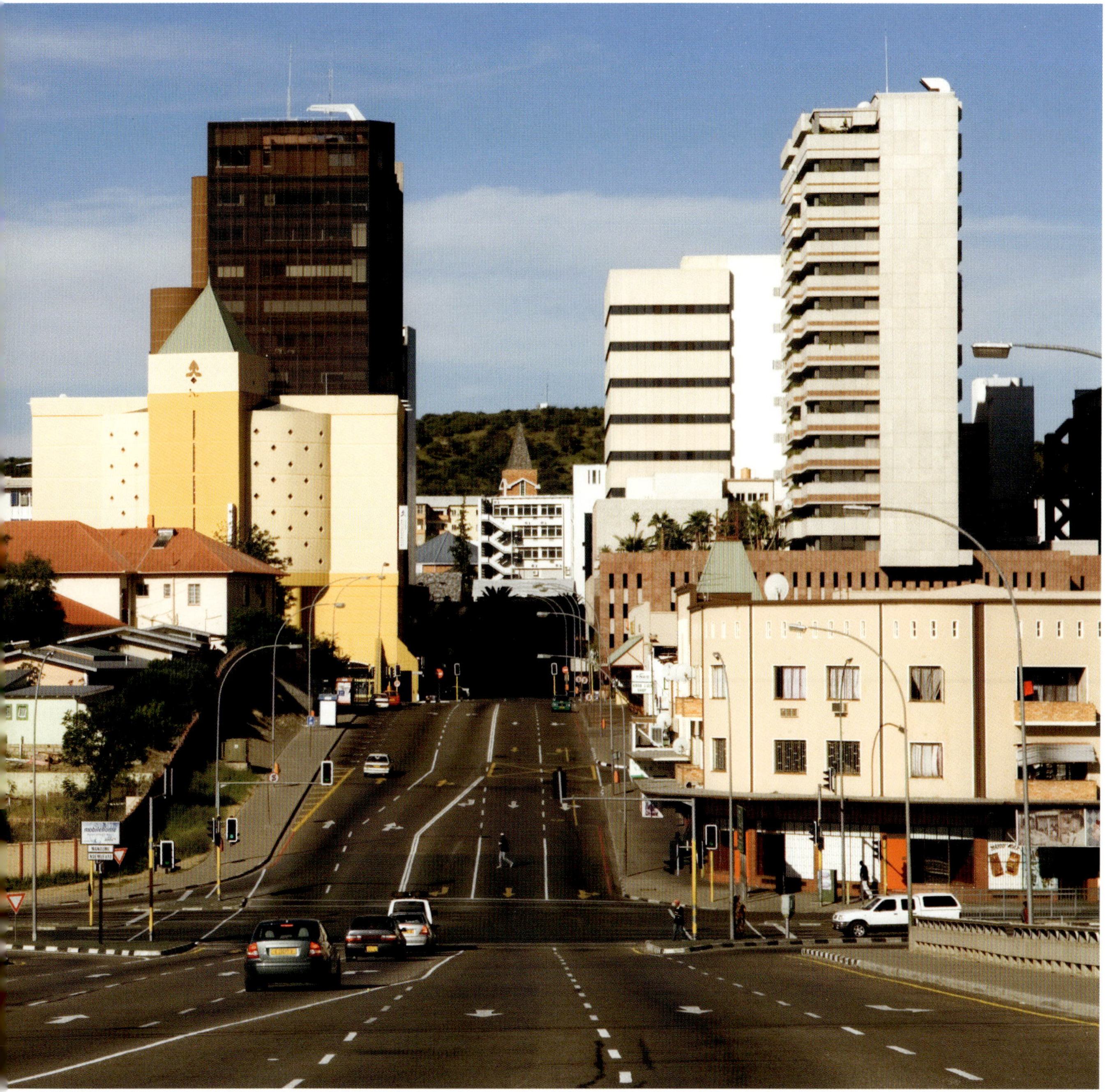

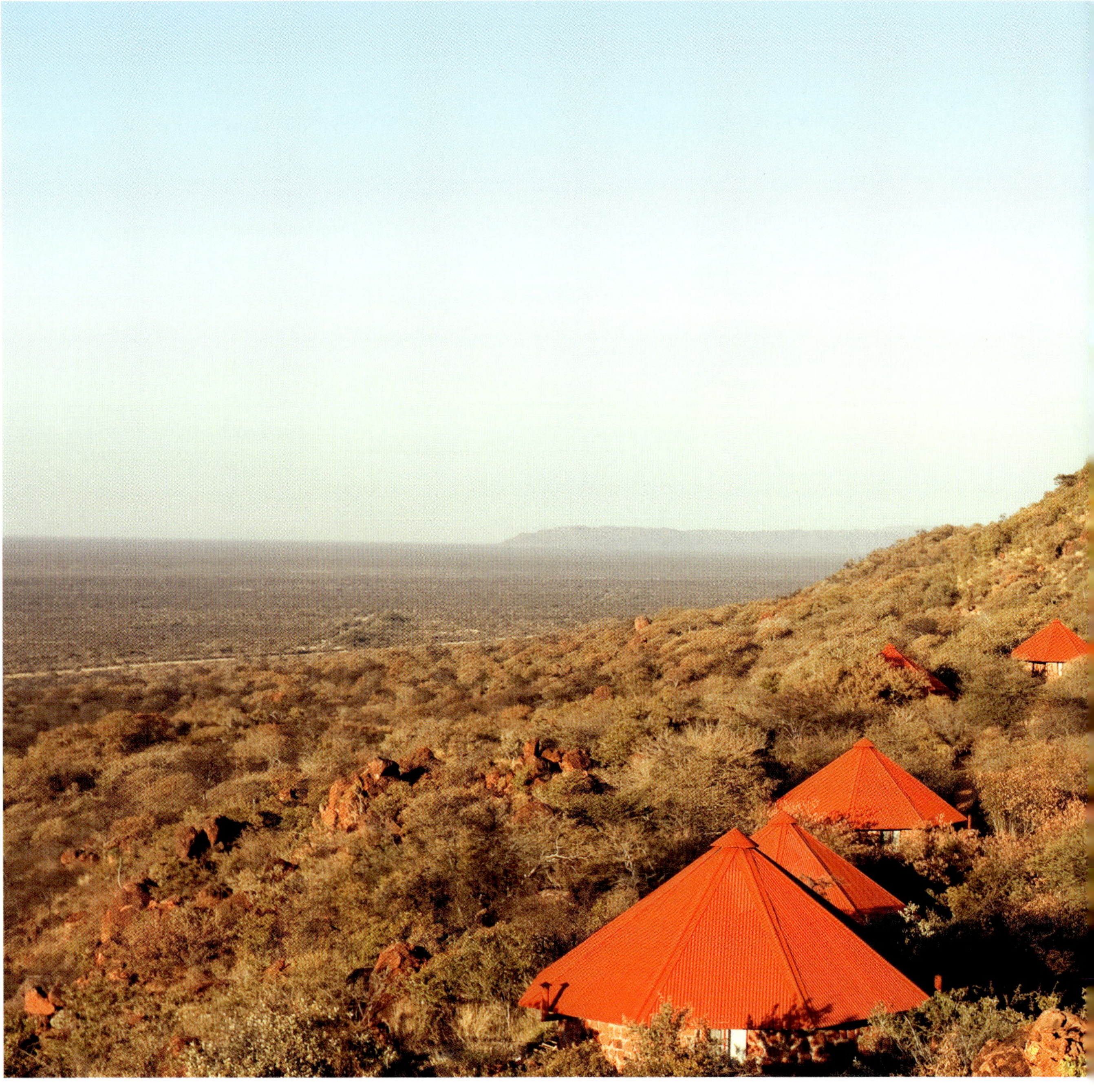

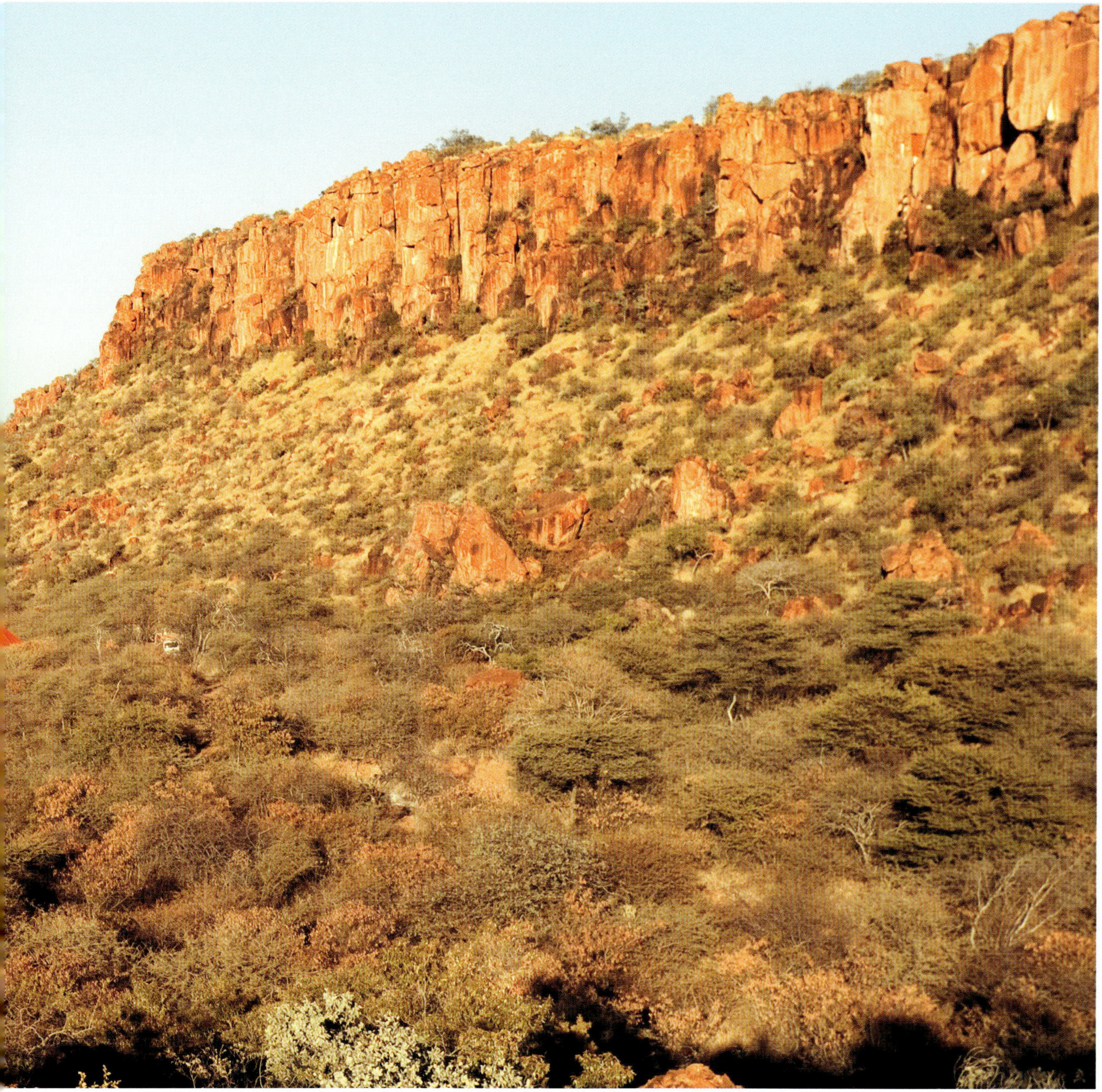

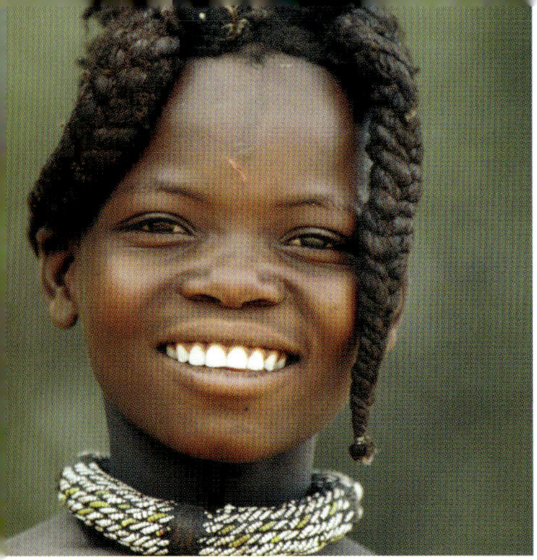
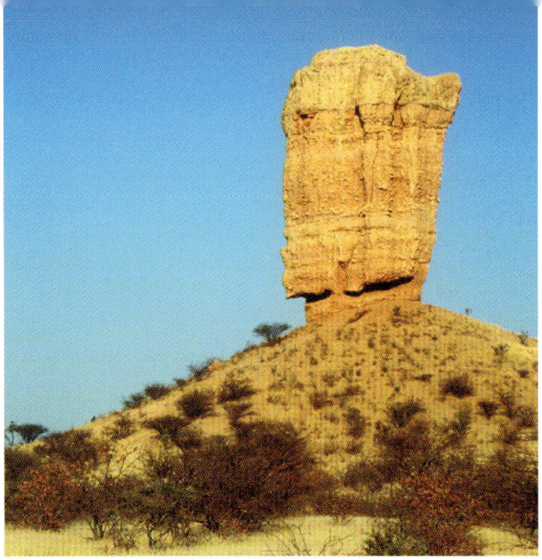
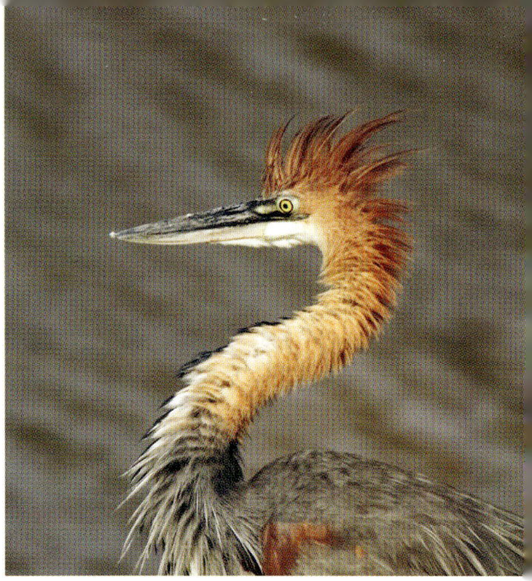
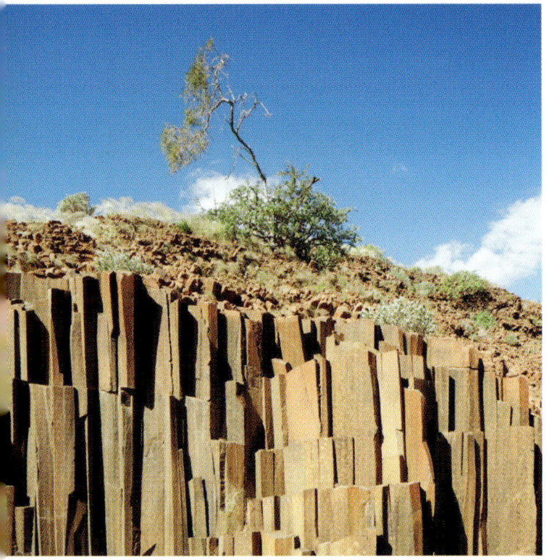
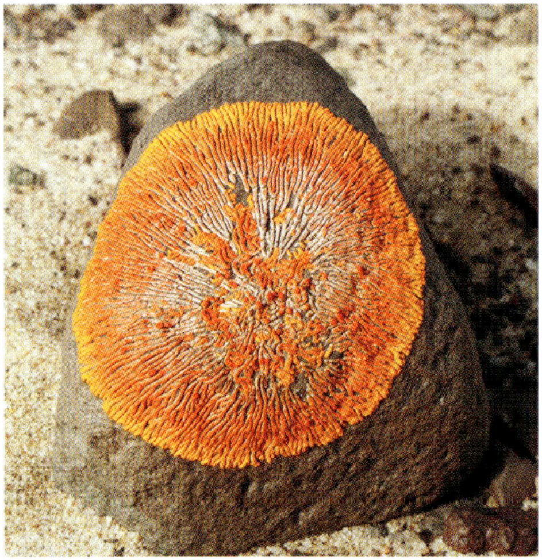
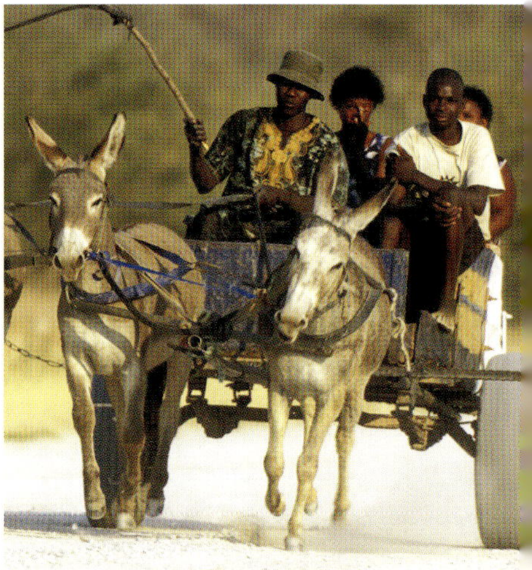
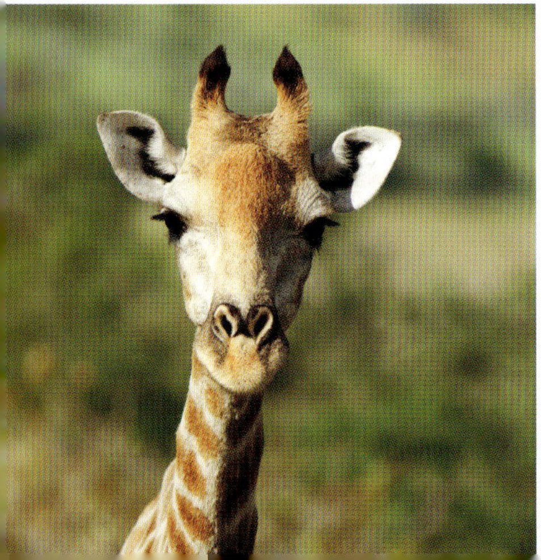
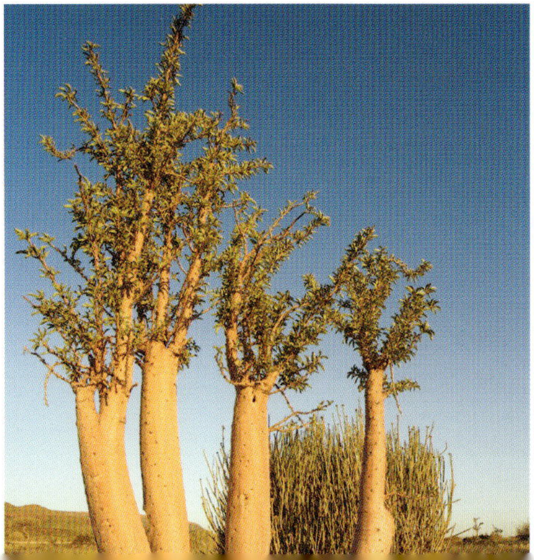
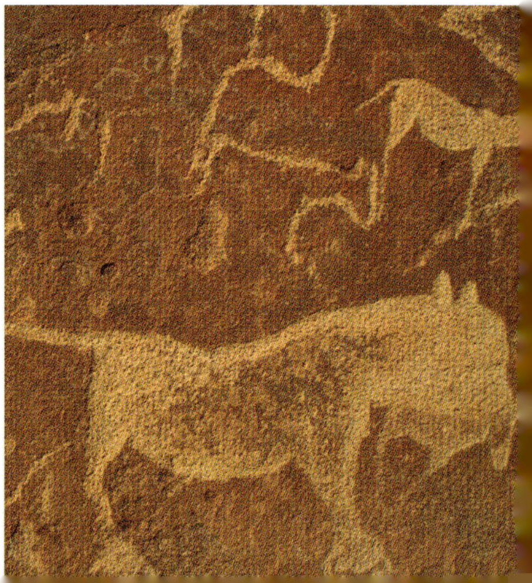

Northwest

The northwest of Namibia includes the Skeleton Coast, Damaraland, Kaokoland and the hinterland south of Etosha National Park and west of the B1 highway, which runs more or less down the centre of the country. It is characterised by basaltic and sandstone rock formations – for example the natural formations of the Brandberg, Vingerklip and the Organ Pipes near Twyfelfontein – and savanna vegetation, which includes bushman grass, succulents and trees, such as mopane, ana, thornbush and bottle trees. While its dry and dusty plains give the appearance of a terrain that is apparently inhospitable and relatively lifeless, the region – home to hardy welwitschia plants and petrified forests – transforms after the rains have fallen. Its yellow, red and ochre face changes into a green panorama alive with the renewed activity of birds and other wildlife species. The river waters, most notably those of the Kunene and Uniab, speed up on their course towards the ocean before tumbling into the Atlantic on the west coast. Life here is slow and relaxed, even for the animals. Wildlife is diverse and thriving, ranging from the desert elephant and the brown hyena of the Skeleton Coast to the fur seals at the Cape Cross Seal Reserve. The region's human origins date at least to early settlements of San, whose rock engravings at places such as Twyfelfontein provide a fascinating record of the presence of humankind. More recently, it is the Himba, Herero and other indigenous groups who have made their homes here, and many traditional Namibians are still claiming ancestral lands across the northwest.

OPPOSITE FROM LEFT TO RIGHT:

- Young Himba girl of Kaokoland, with hair braiding typical of pre-adolescence.
- Striking finger-like rock formation of Vingerklip, Damaraland.
- Goliath heron, with shaken plumage, hunting on the banks of the Kunene River in the northwest of Namibia.
- The vertical and almost perfectly symmetrical columns of the Organ Pipes near Twyfelfontien, Damaraland.
- Caloplaca lichen grows on rocks and stones along the Skeleton Coast in the northern reaches of the Namib.
- Damara villagers continue to use traditional donkey carts as the principal means of transport in Damaraland.
- Southern giraffe are fairly common among the wildlife in the northwest.
- The bottle tree, best known for its irregular bottle shape, is endemic to the pre-Namib areas in the northern regions.
- Acclaimed Lion Panel, part of the world-famous San rock engravings found at Twyfelfontein.

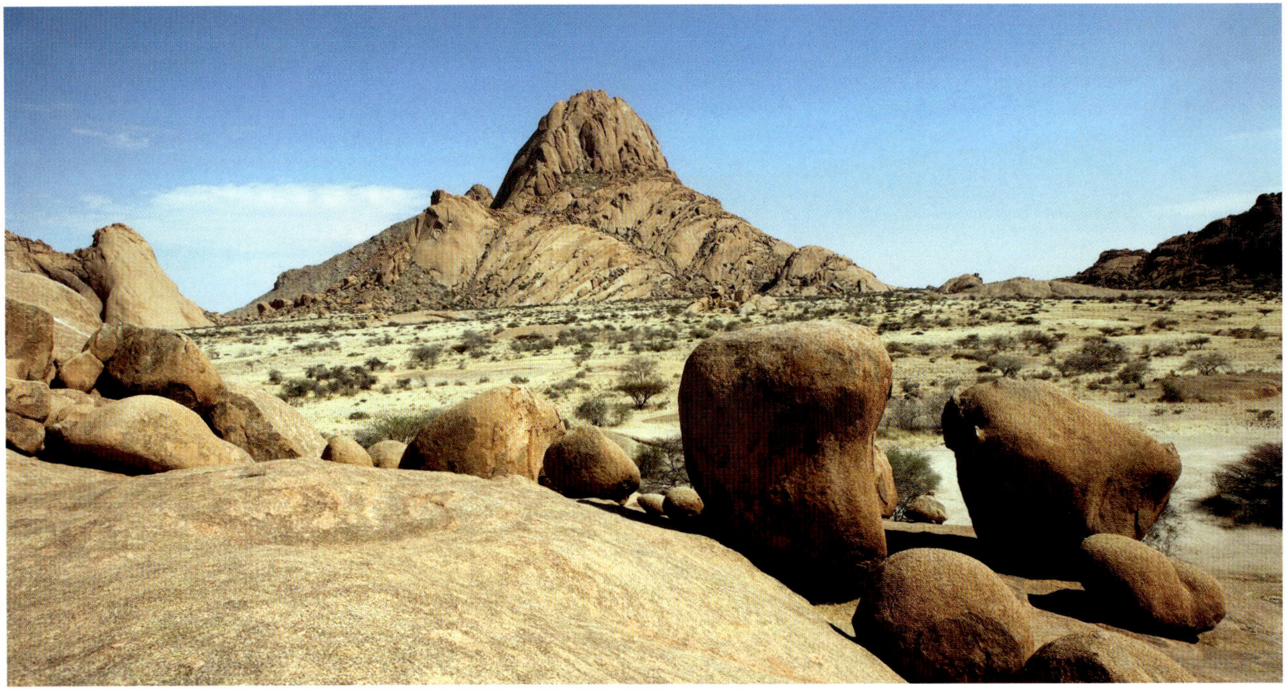

ABOVE: The granitic mountains of the towering Spitzkoppe in the Erongo region loom some 1 800 metres above the boulder-strewn plains that surround the series of rugged peaks. The colours are bold and the contours produce a wave-like line in the rock strata.

OPPOSITE: The arid terrain that surrounds the Spitzkoppe is dotted with rocks and boulders, their polished surfaces either perfectly rounded or sculpted into unusual shapes, many of which balance precariously on the rocky landscape.

Of all the images portraying Namibia as a wild and ancient land, those that most define the character of its northwestern region are of its rock and stone landscapes, such as the isolated Spitzkoppe in Damaraland and the giant granite rock formations to be found on the land of the Ameib Ranch in the Erongo mountains. Sand particles, carried by hammering winds, combined with extreme temperatures have capitalised on even the slightest imperfection in the rock strata – a simple crack, groove or hole – and have been significant in the creation of striking shapes in the rocky outcrops. The resulting abstract and surreal formations of sculpted boulders are the colour of rust, with some sandblasted to near-perfect spheres.

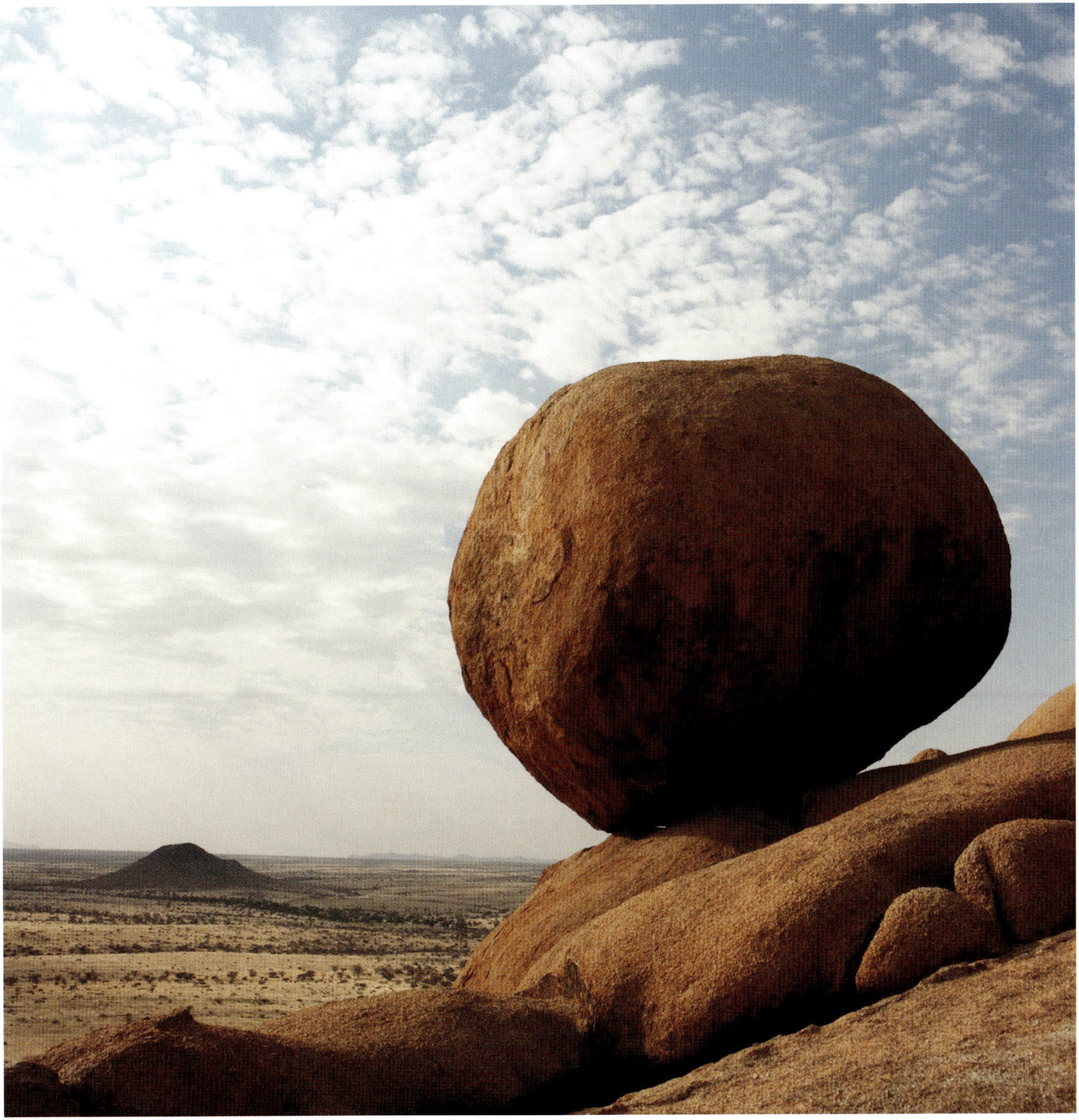

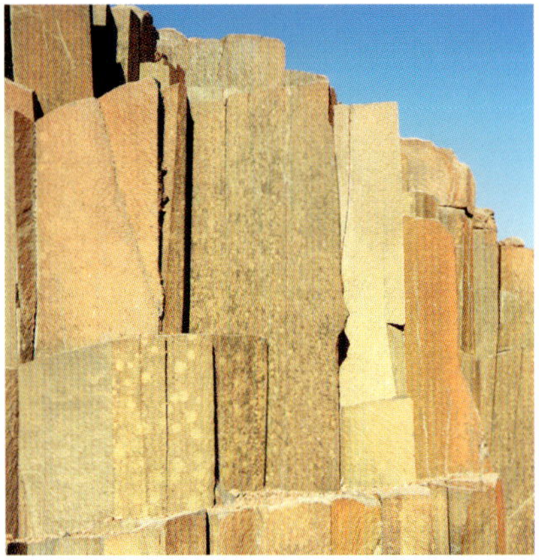

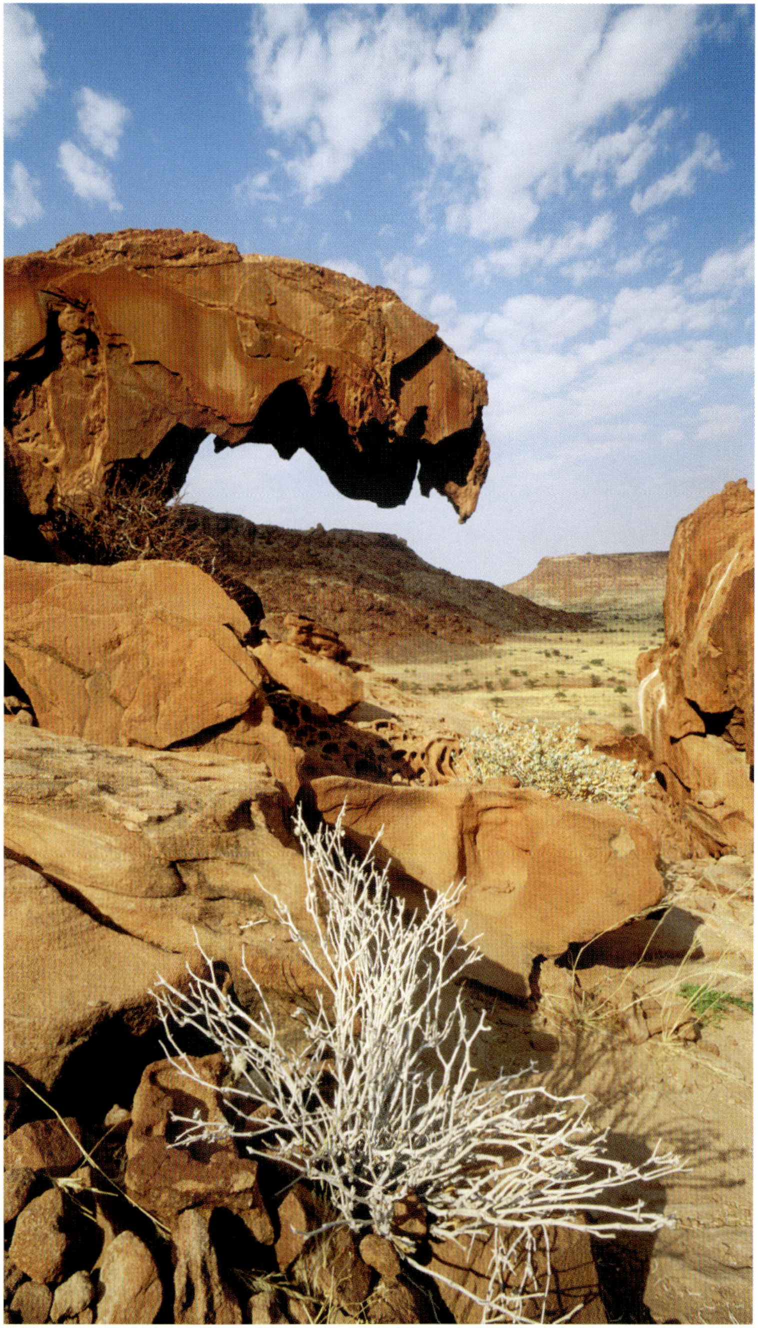

ABOVE: The unusually symmetrical pillars that make up the Organ Pipes near Twyfelfontein consist of basaltic rock exposed after the upthrust of magma 120 million years ago, resulting in these extraordinary geometrical protrusions.

RIGHT: Both Elephant Rock and its equally bizarre neighbour, Eagle Rock, near Twyfelfontein are extreme examples of the erosive action of the wind and sand on protruding granite over thousands of years.

OPPOSITE: The world-renowned rock engravings at Twyfelfontein are said to have been created over a period of 2 000 years and are some 1 000 years old. They were proclaimed Namibia's first World Heritage Site in 2007.

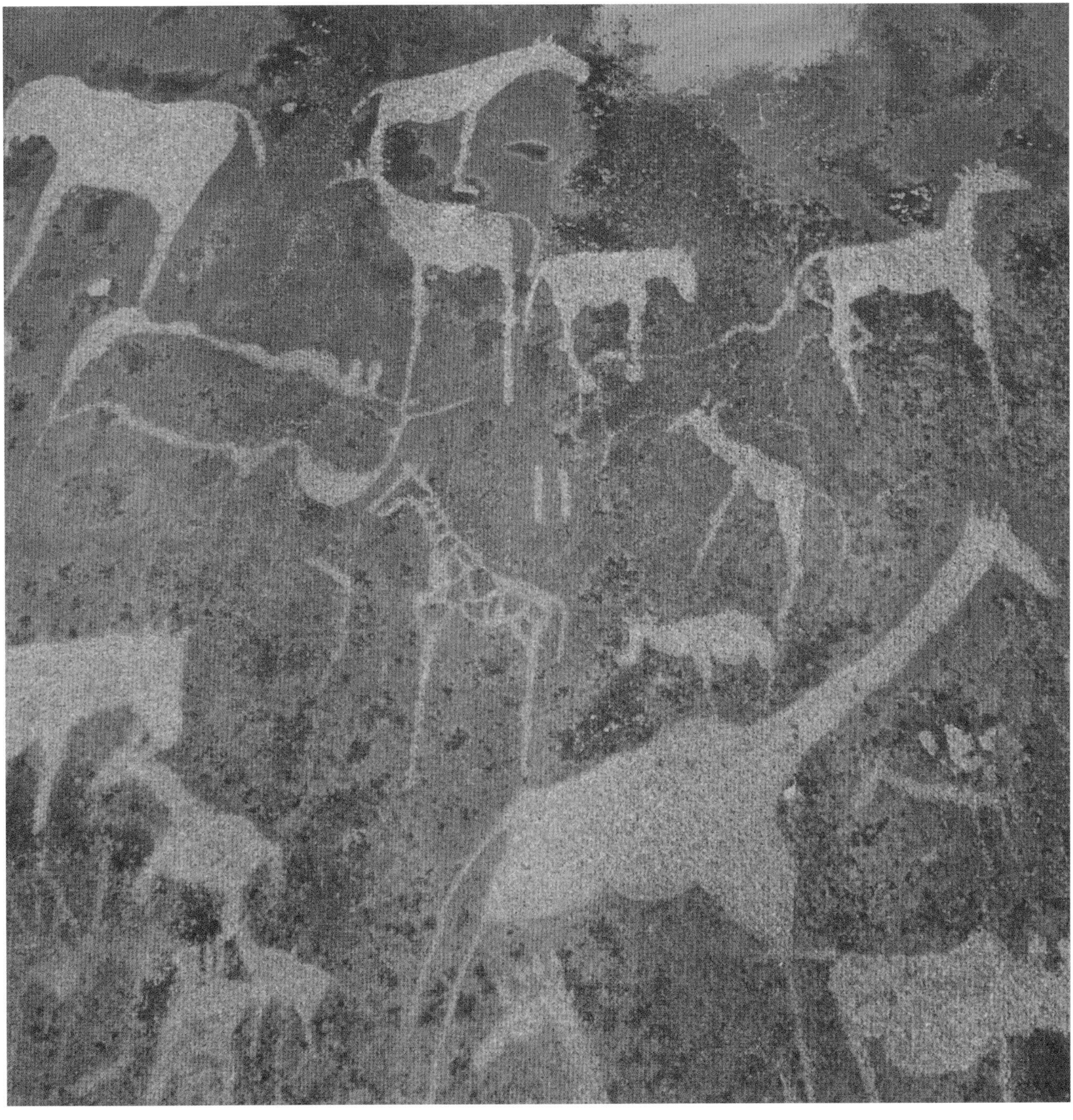

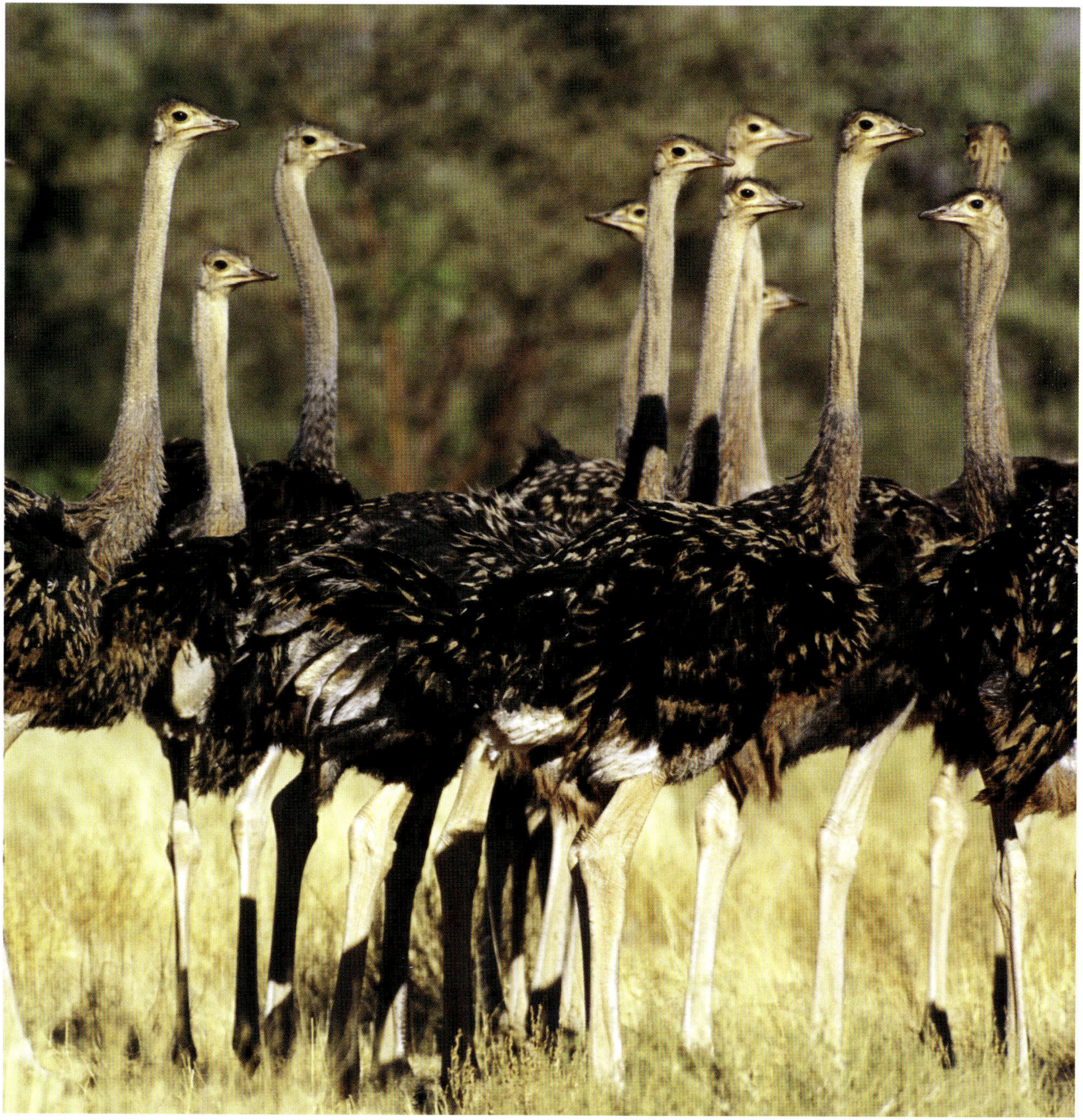

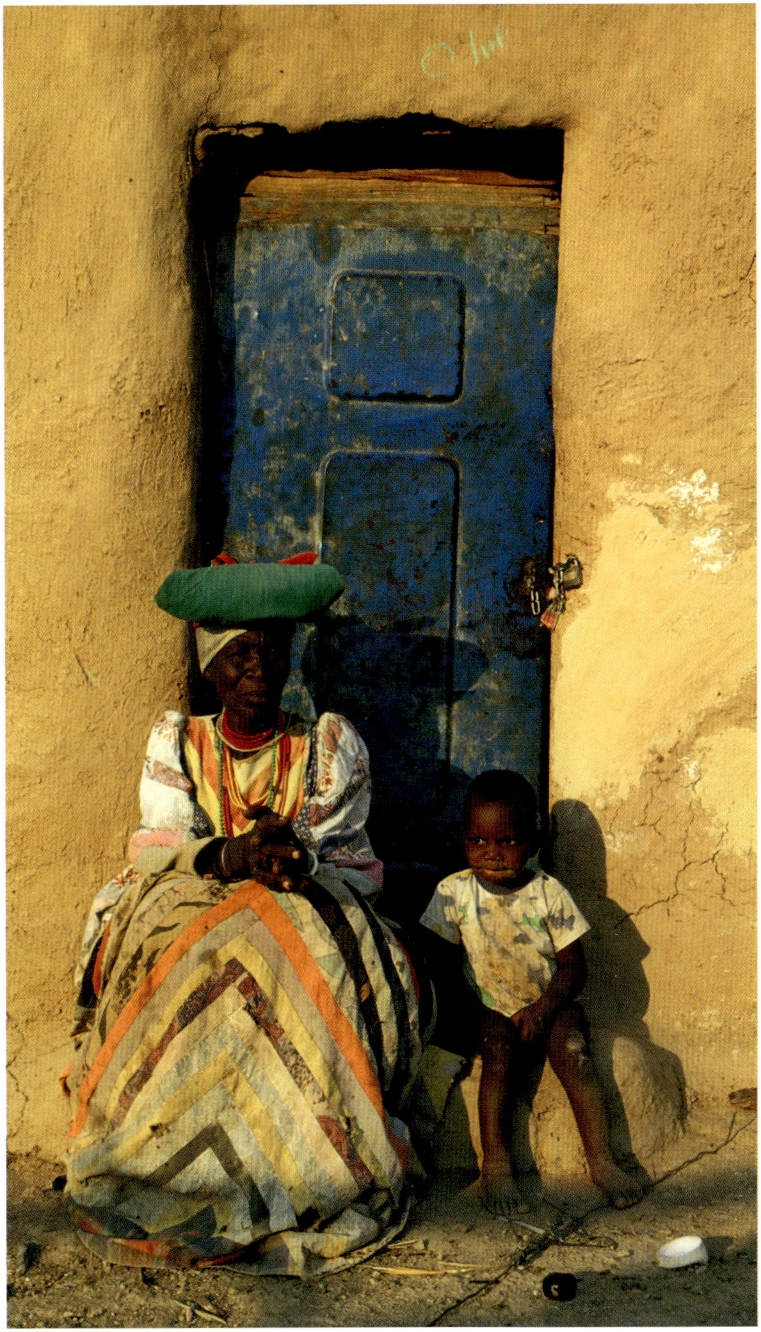

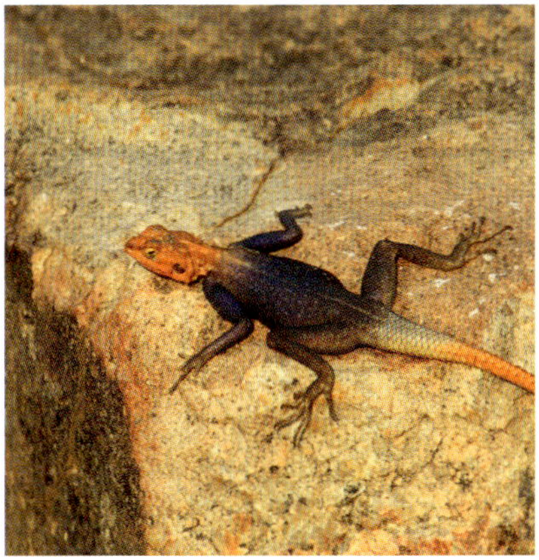

OPPOSITE: The scrubland of Damaraland is home to herds of ostrich that are accustomed to the dry desert and thrive under these harsh conditions.

LEFT: The key to survival in this sometimes desolate land is being able to live in harmony with nature. Indigenous groups such as Herero, who traditionally hail from the northwestern reaches, have adapted well to life in this region.

ABOVE: The plains and rocky terrain of the northwest are home to an astonishing diversity of wildlife, including the Namibian rock agama, seen here on an outcrop in the Spitzkoppe.

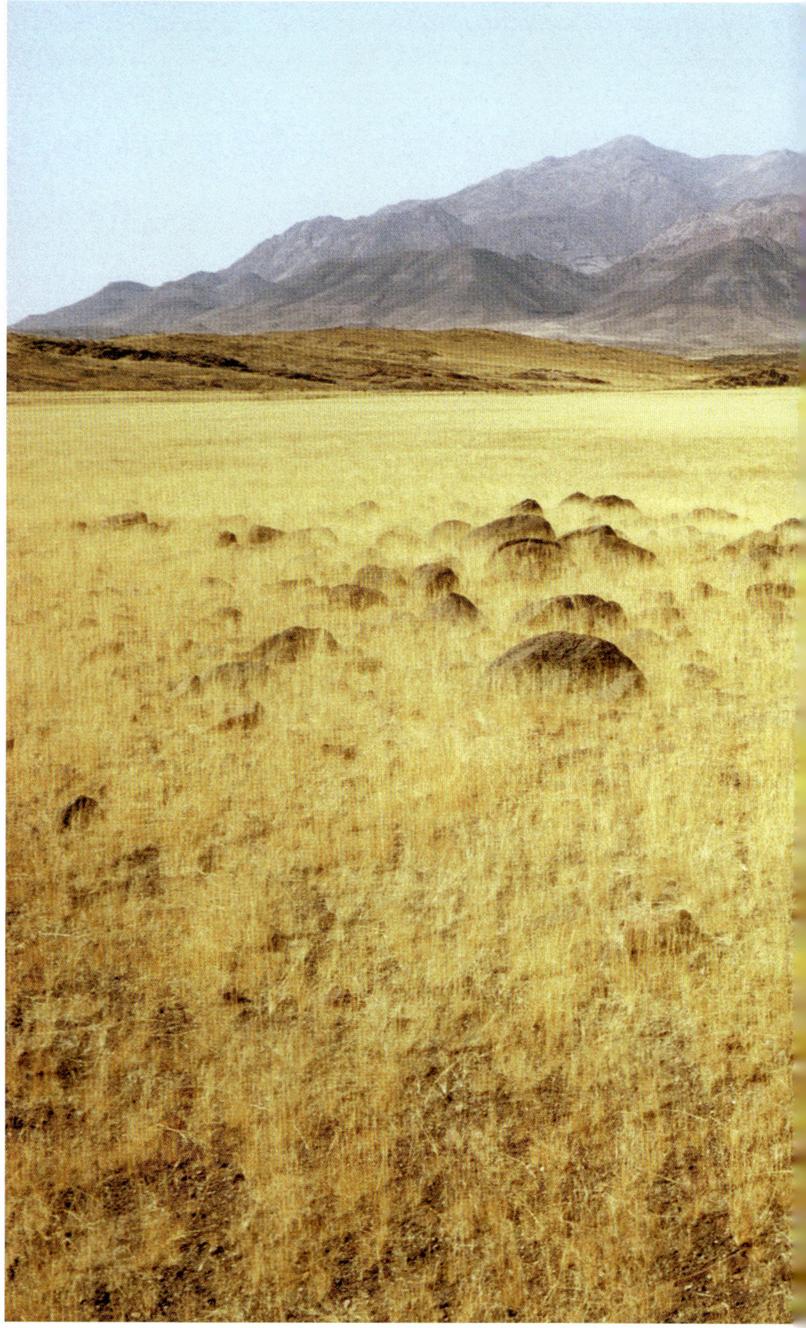

RIGHT: Virtually enclosed by a sea of bushman grass, the Brandberg is a granitic massif covering an area of 650 square kilometres. Rising more than 2 500 metres over the surrounding plains, it is the highest mountain peak in Namibia.

OVERLEAF, LEFT: The rainy season is Namibia's lifeblood, transforming dry and barren landscapes, such as this one at Palmwag in Damaraland, into a sea of green.

OVERLEAF, RIGHT: Many of the indigenous people, such as the Herero, continue to live uncomplicated lives in simple villages, eking a meagre living from the surrounding lands.

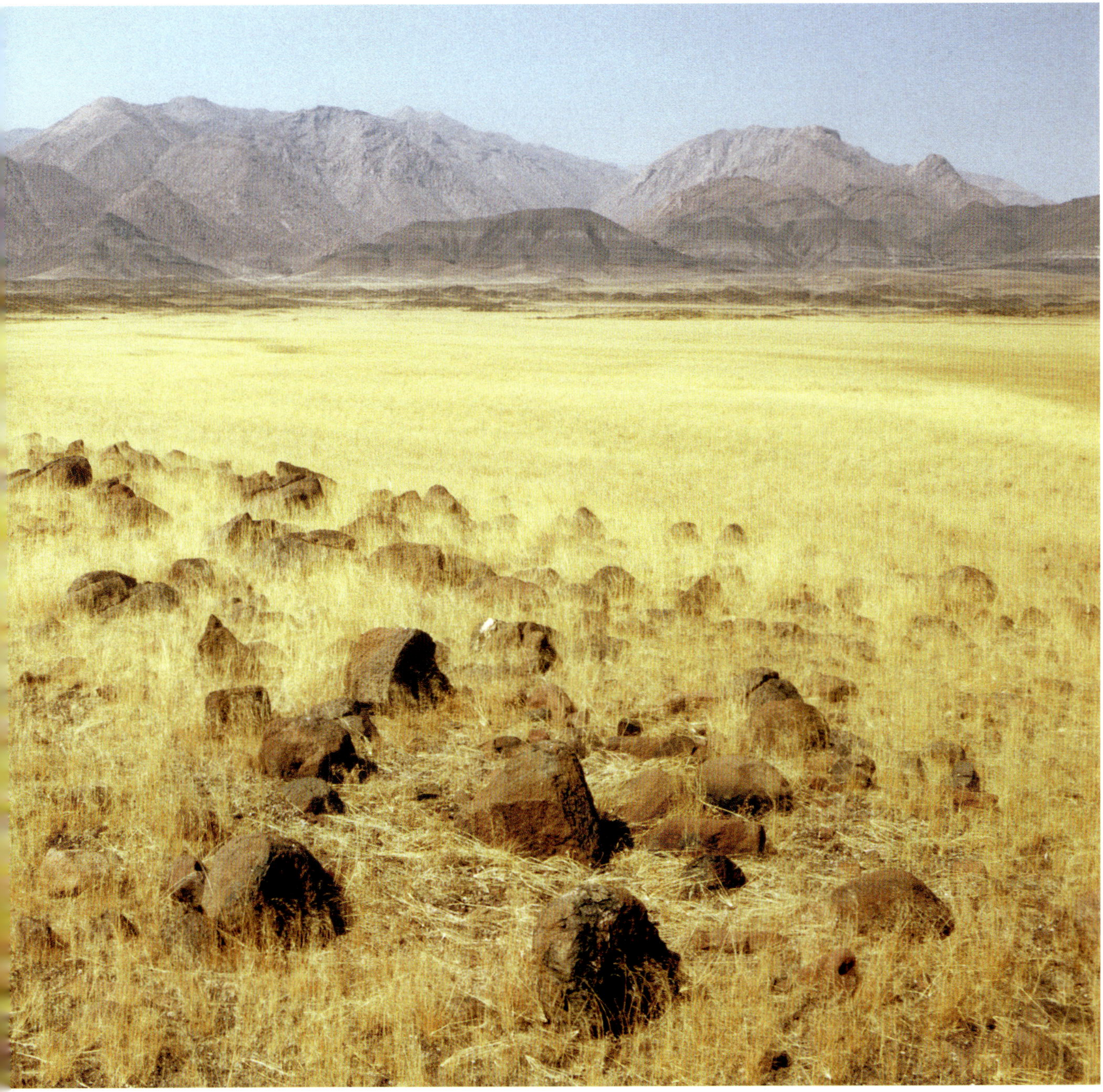

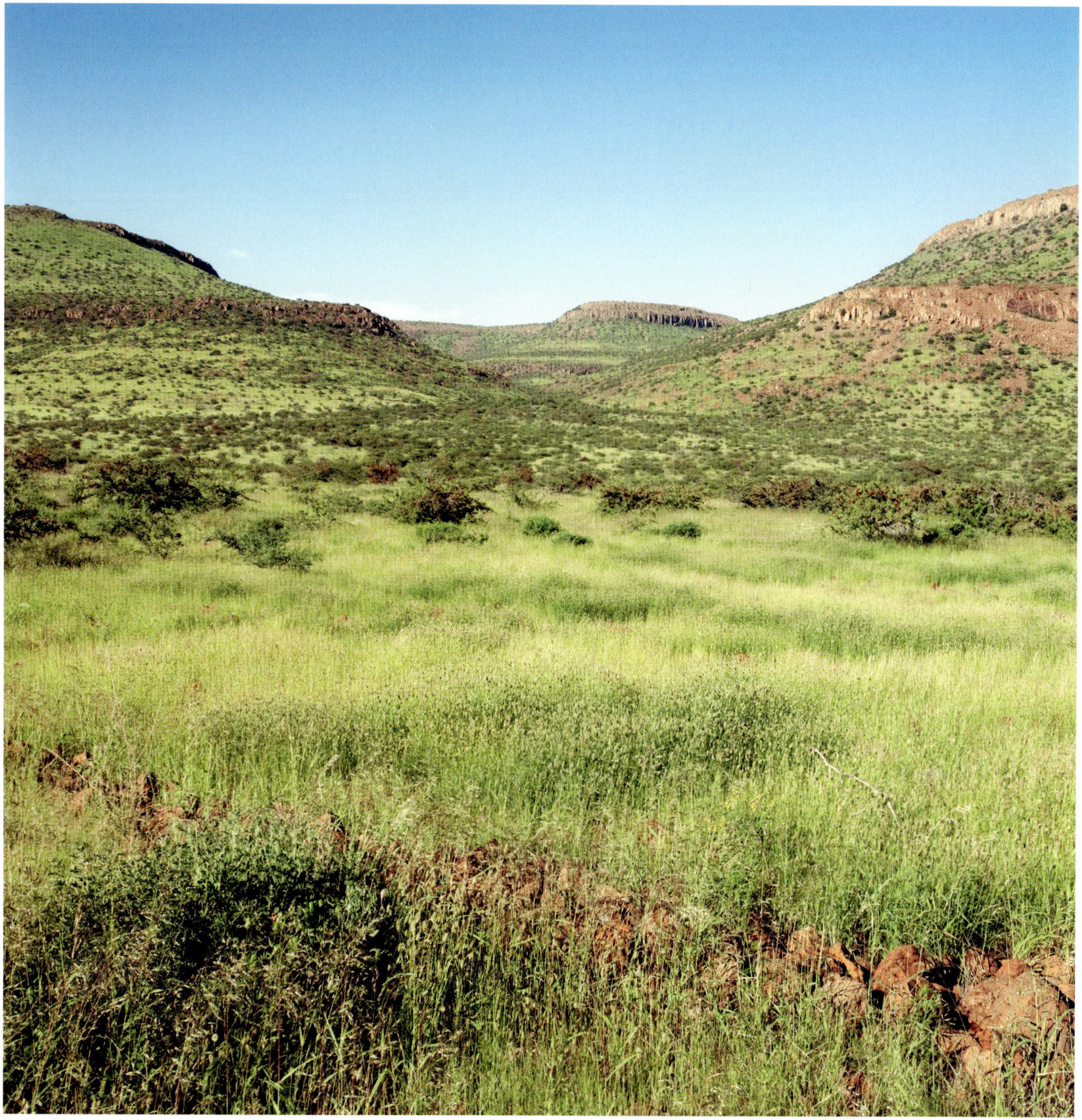

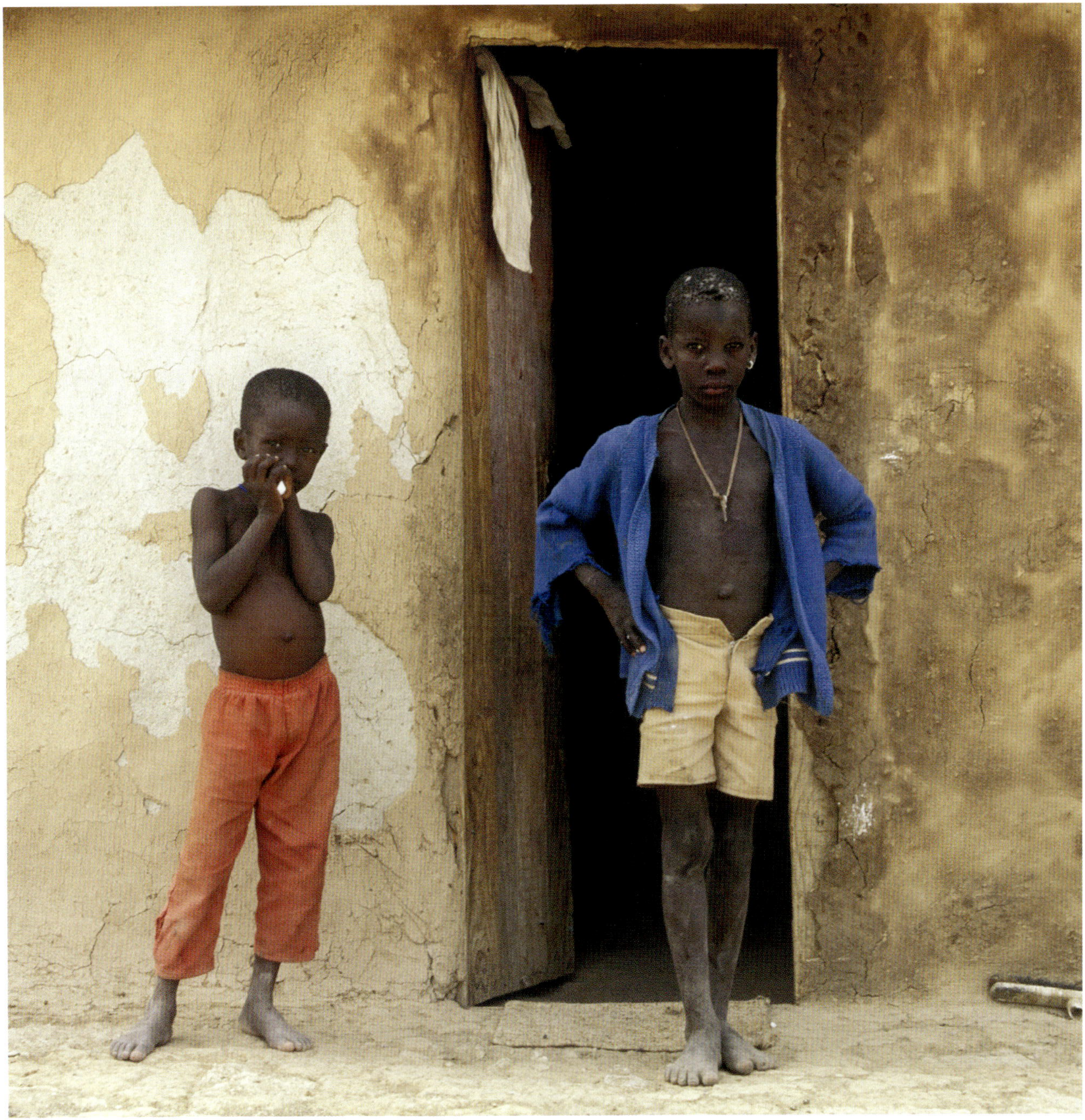

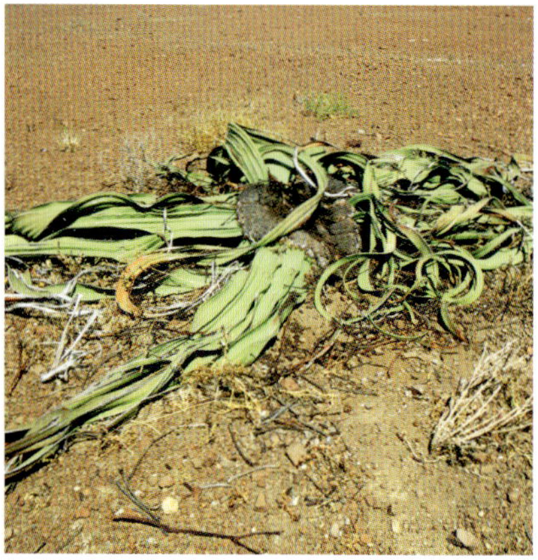

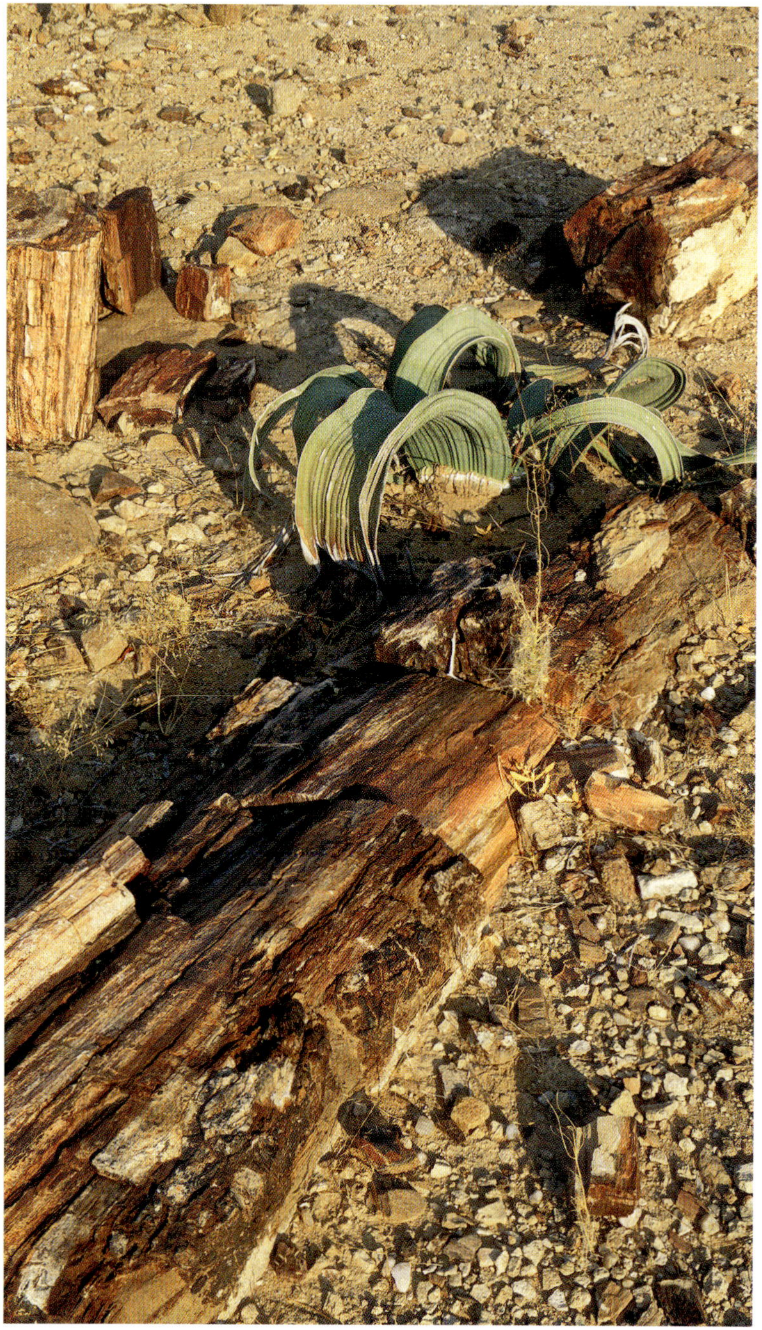

ABOVE: Indigenous to the Namib, the welwitschia is an endemic of ancient origins. These strange-looking plants lie scattered across the desert sands.

RIGHT: A number of fine welwitschia specimens may be found in what is commonly referred to as the Petrified Forest in Damaraland. The 'forest' here is a graveyard of fossilised tree trunks that thrived in the region more than 280 million years ago.

OPPOSITE: Standing tall and proud from the surrounding mopane and thornbush savanna is Vingerklip, a 35-metre finger-like rock tower consisting of limestone layers deposited over a period of 30 million years.

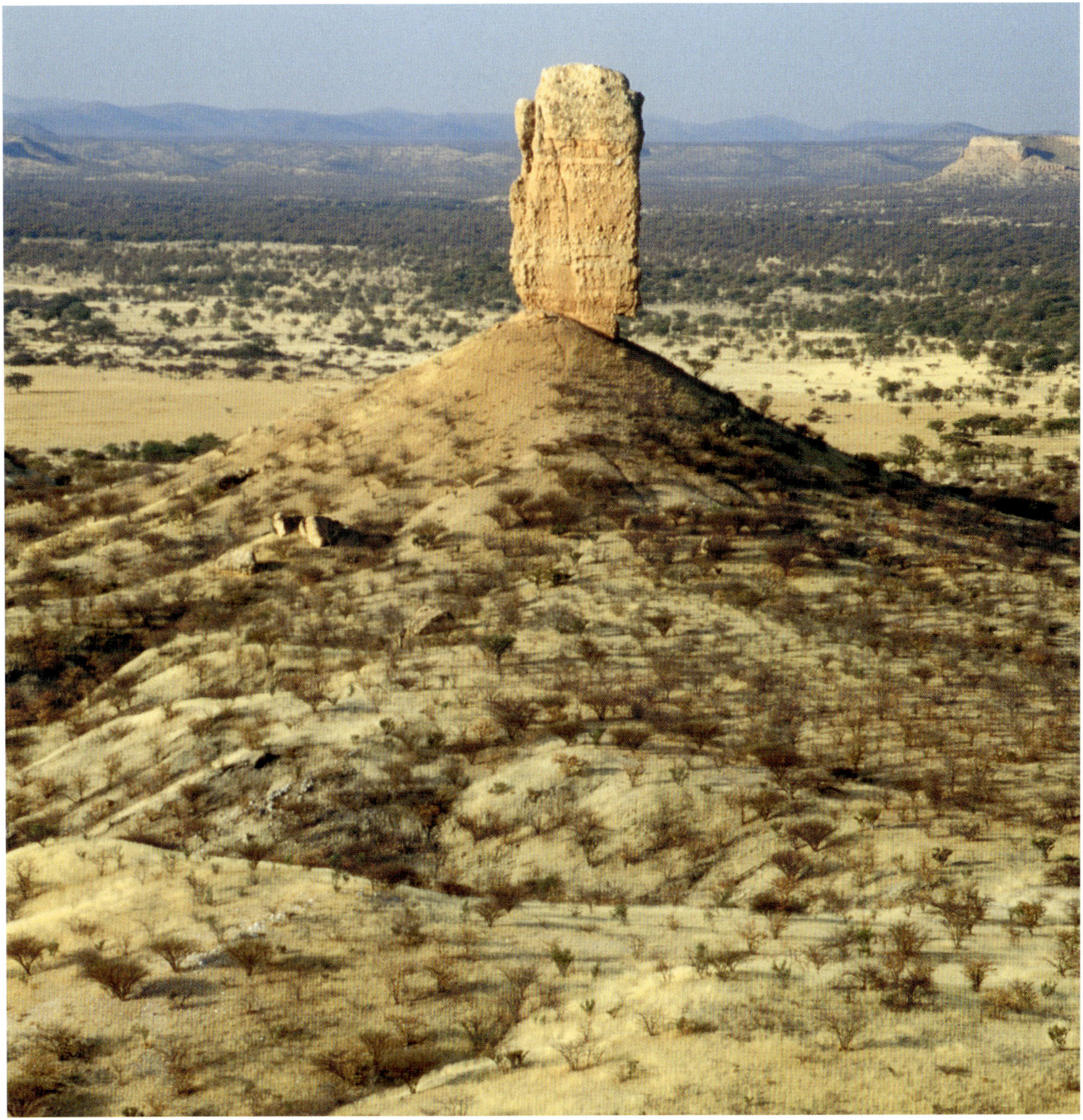

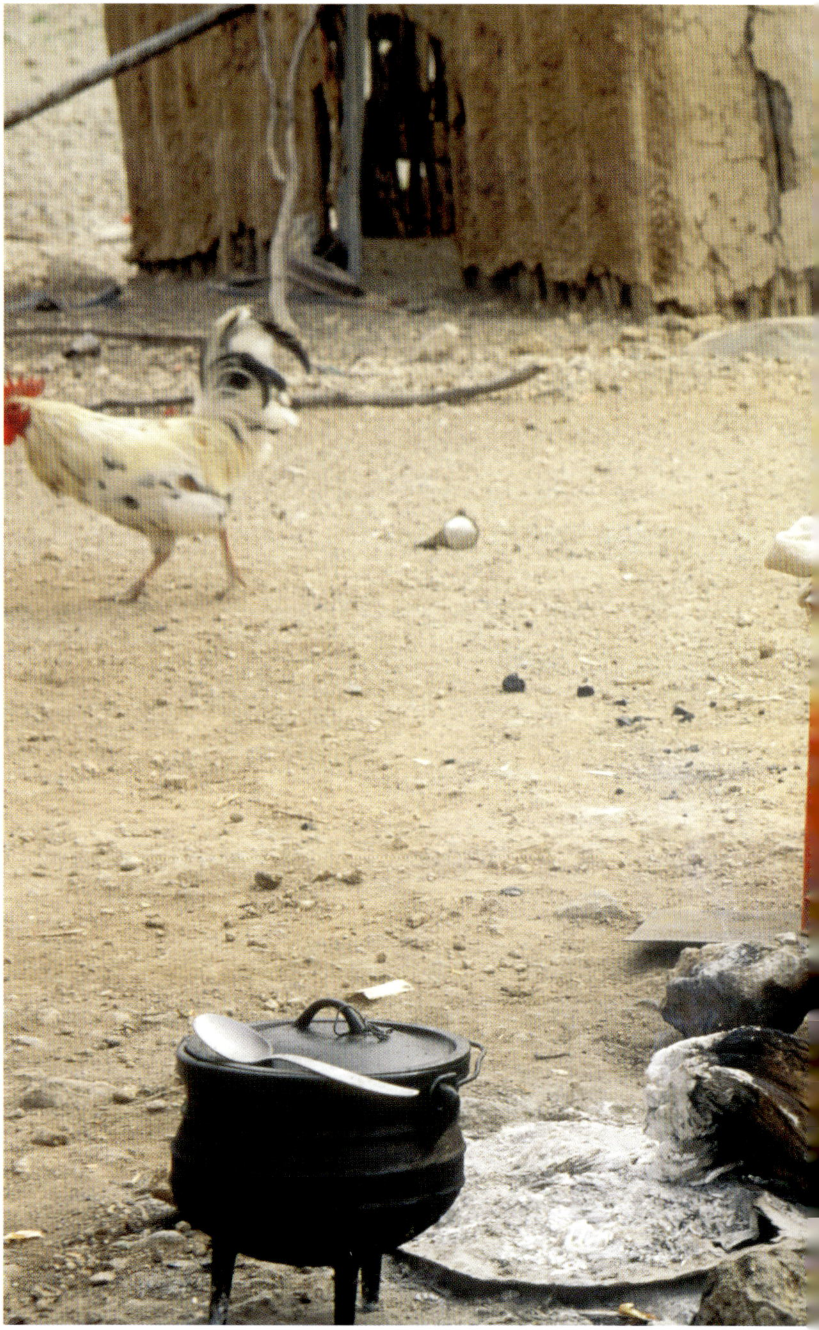

RIGHT: Herero villagers of the Kaokoveld are traditionally pastoralists, maintaining close ties with the land of their ancestors. Today, a large number work on farms in and around Damaraland, whilst others have sought a more Western lifestyle in the larger towns and cities.

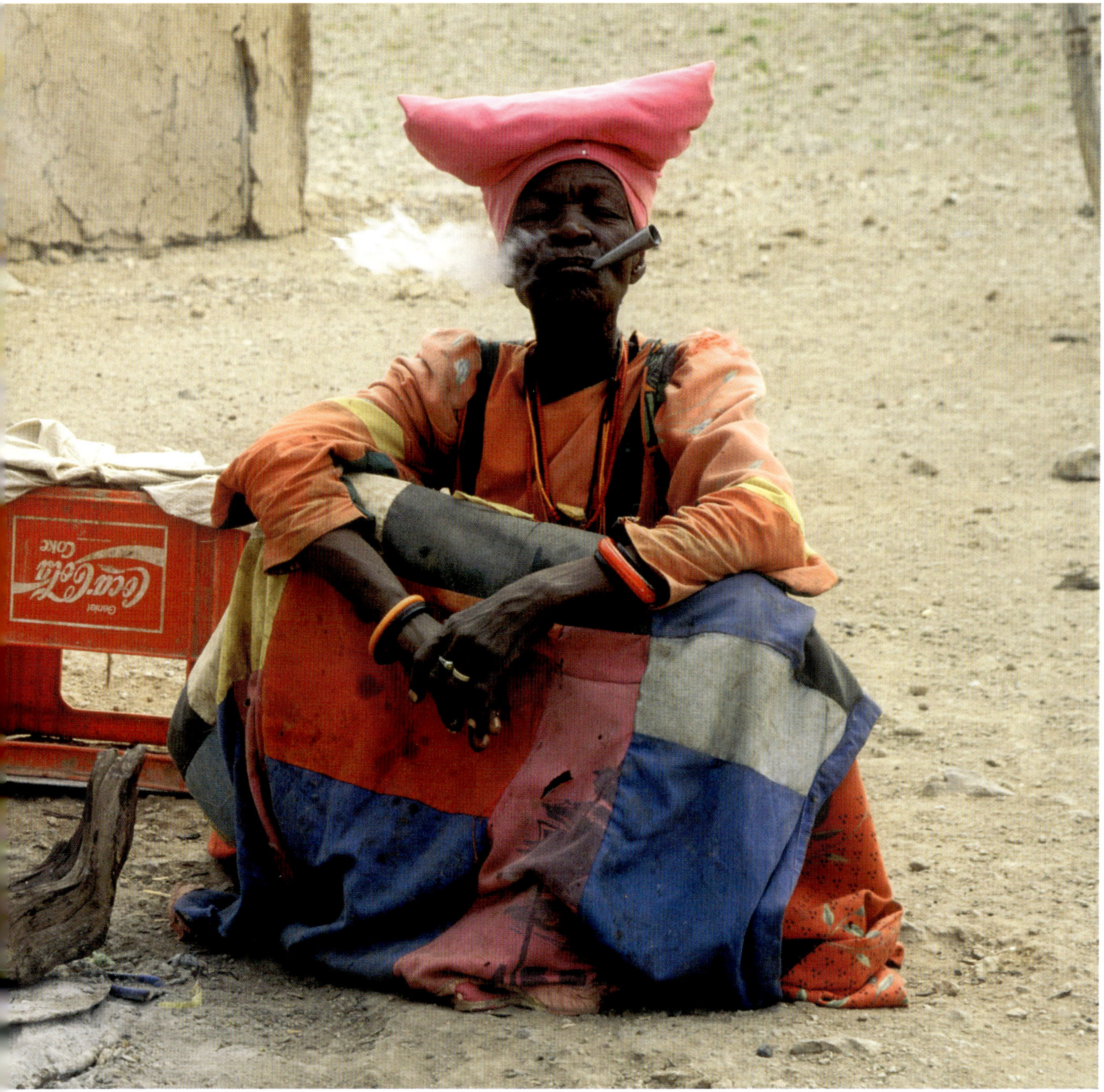

Coca-Cola
Coke

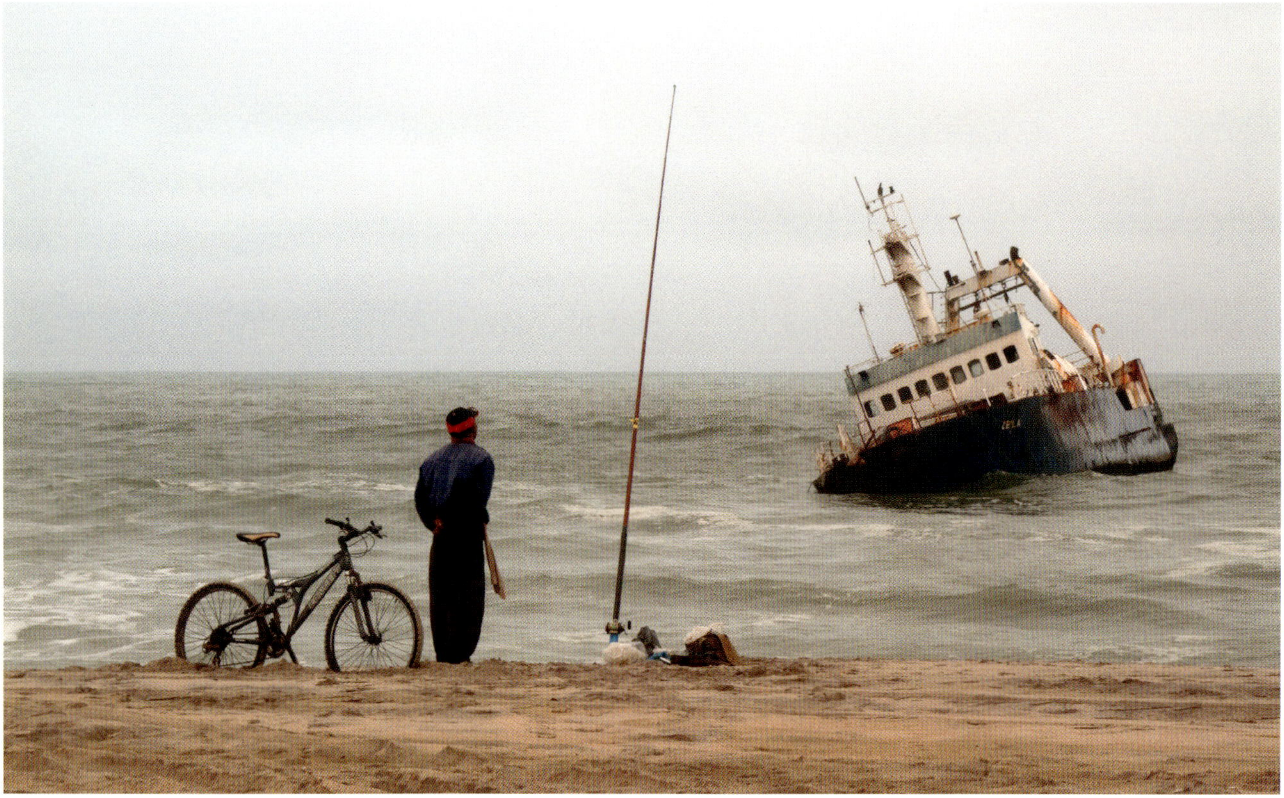

ABOVE: Namibia's Skeleton Coast is one of the country's most intriguing landscapes. It is a remarkable place, where desert sand meets ocean wave in an often volatile environment.

OPPOSITE: One of the curiosities of the Skeleton Coast is its resident population of brown hyena, a mammal species more commonly associated with the dry hinterland.

OVERLEAF: Despite its heavy surf and windblown beaches, the approximately 16 000 square kilometres of the national park are home to a great diversity of plant and animal life, among them succulent mesembryanthemum plants and colonies of Cape fur seals.

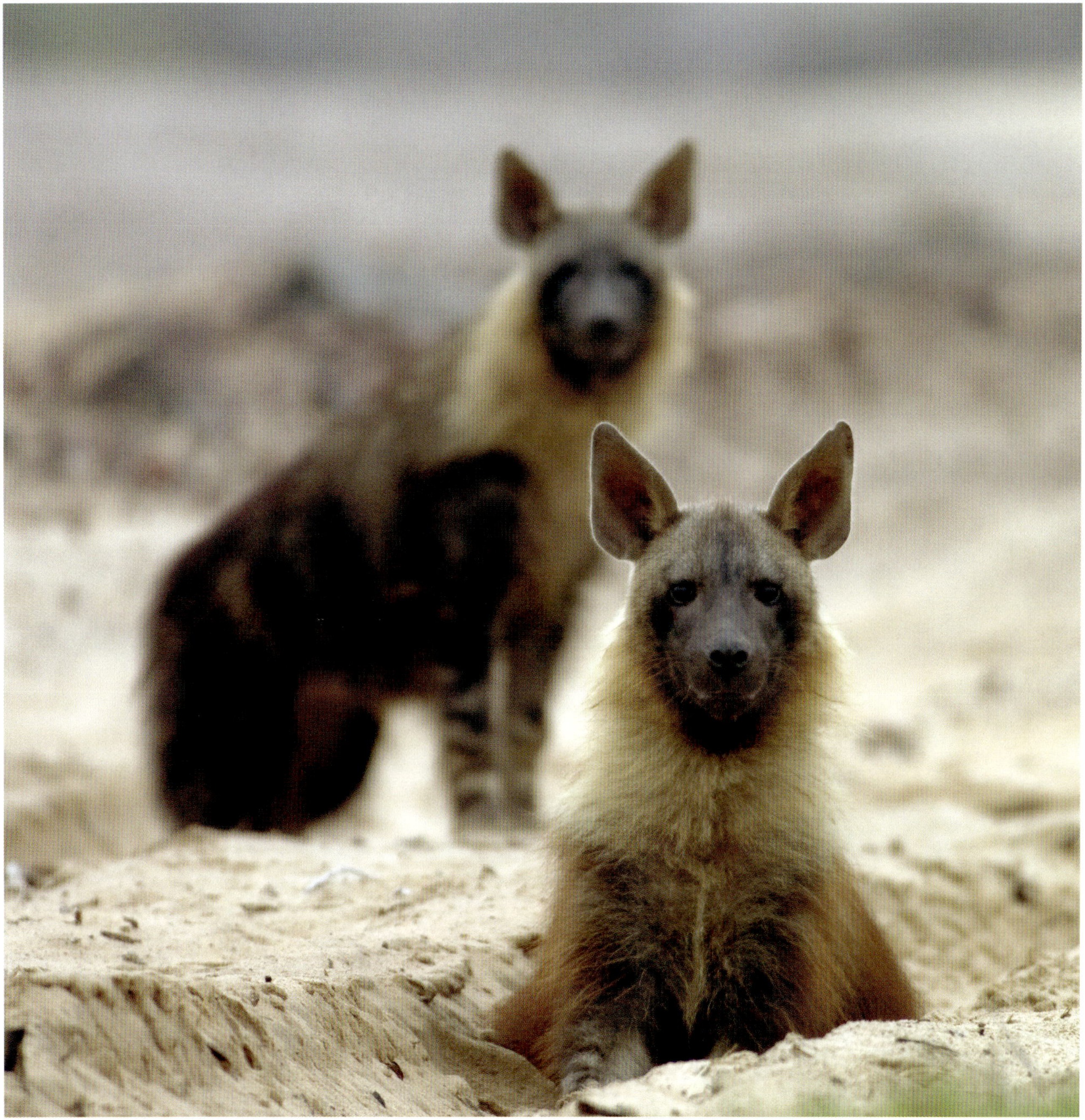

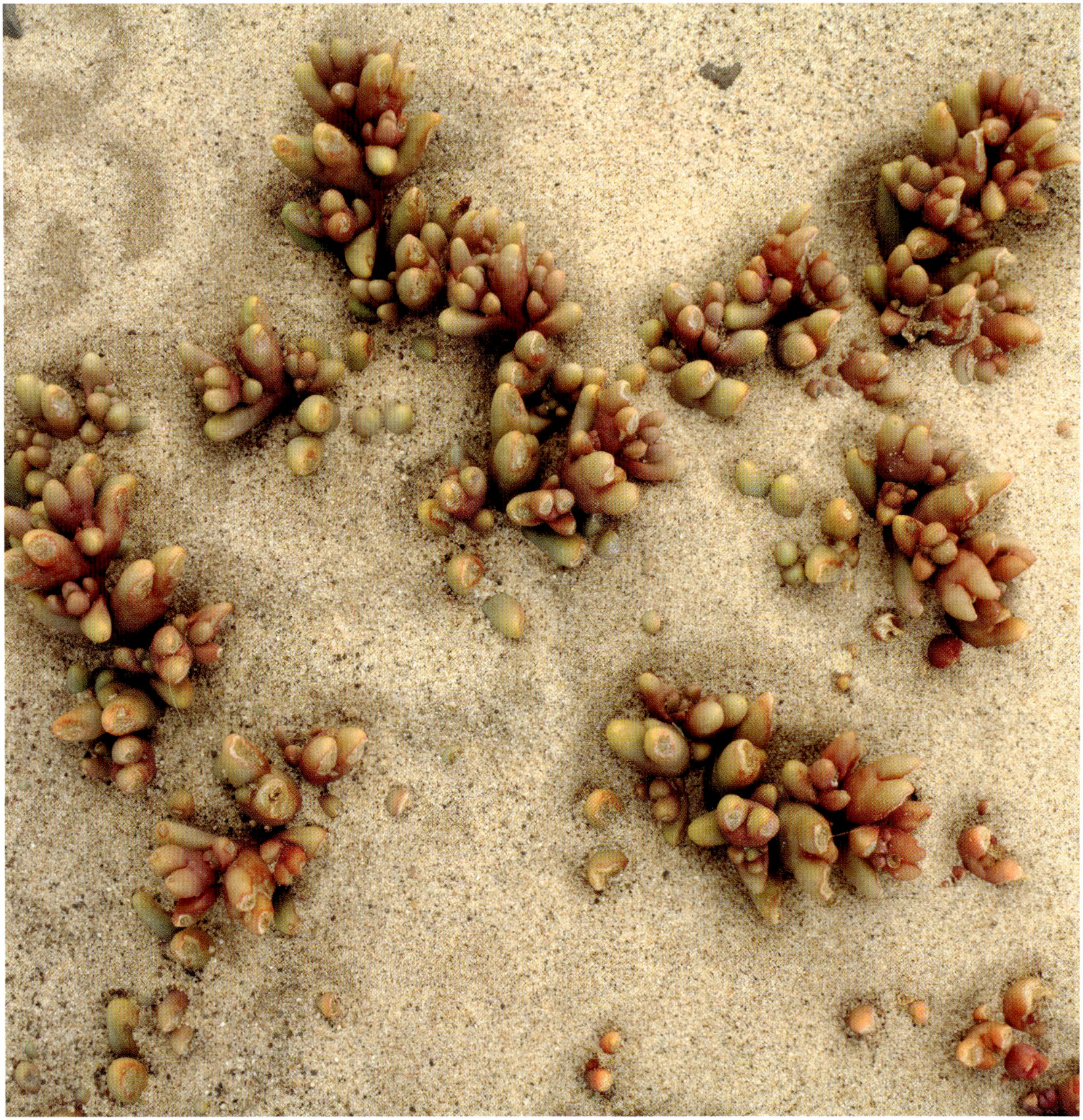

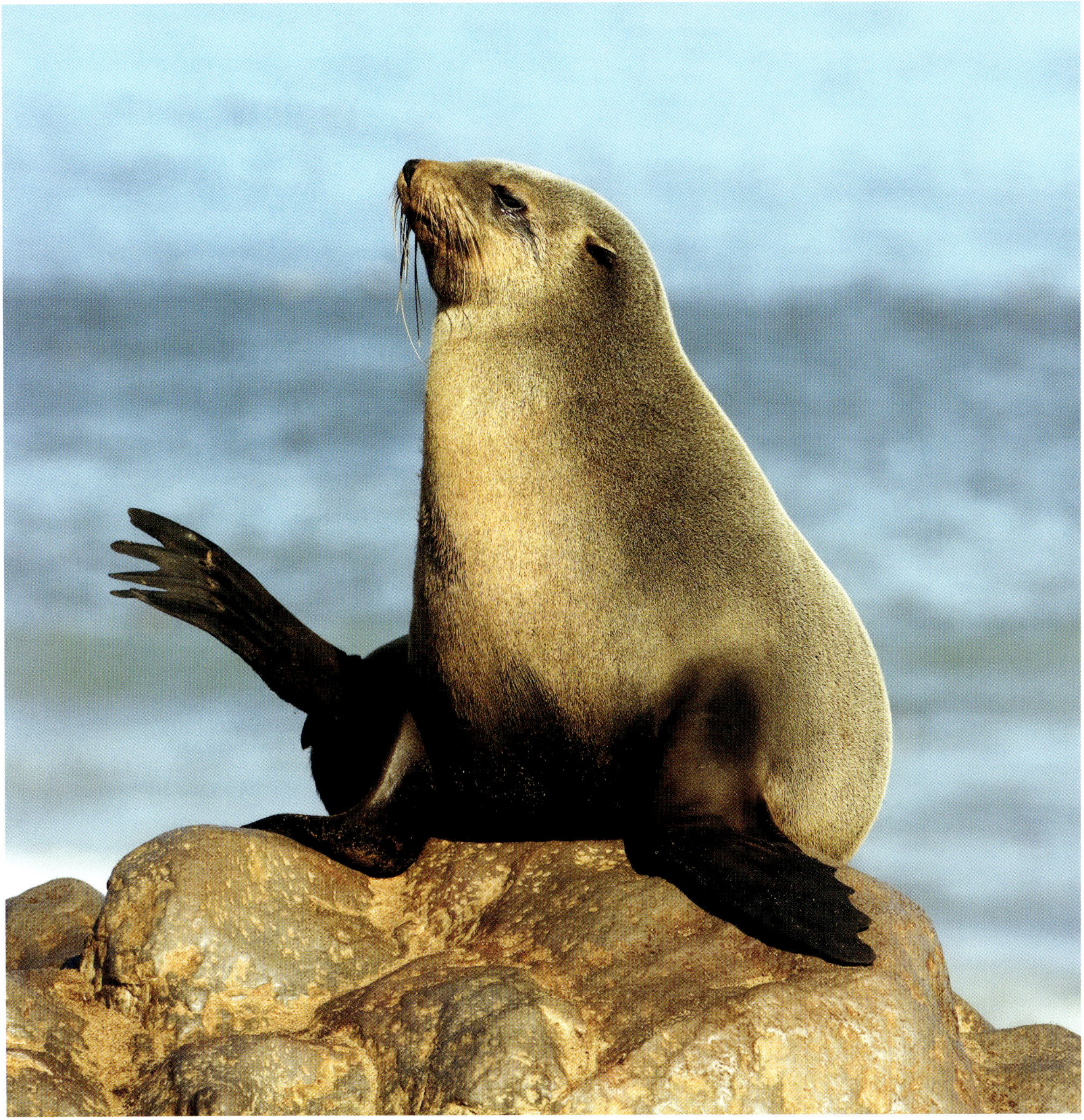

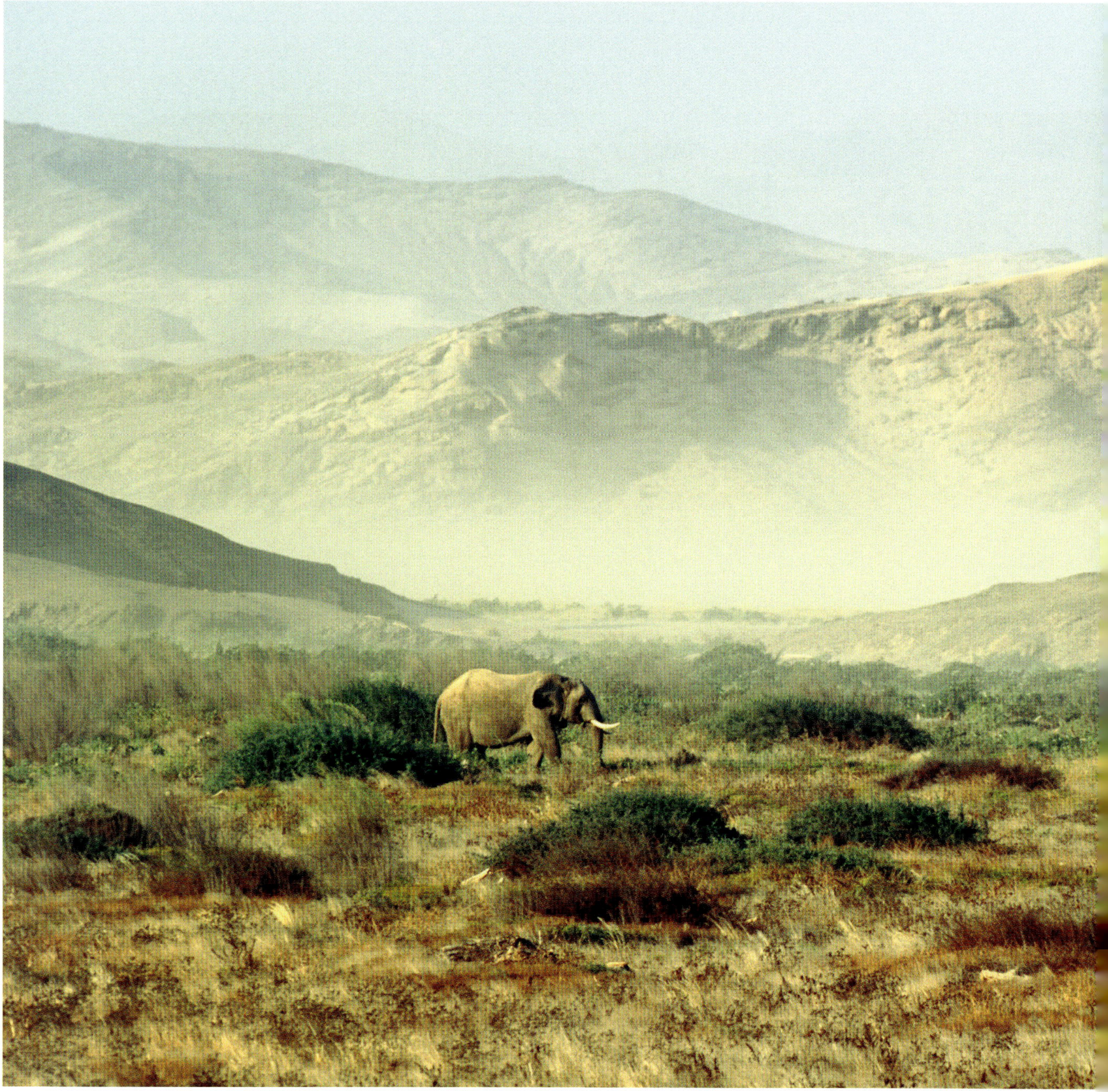

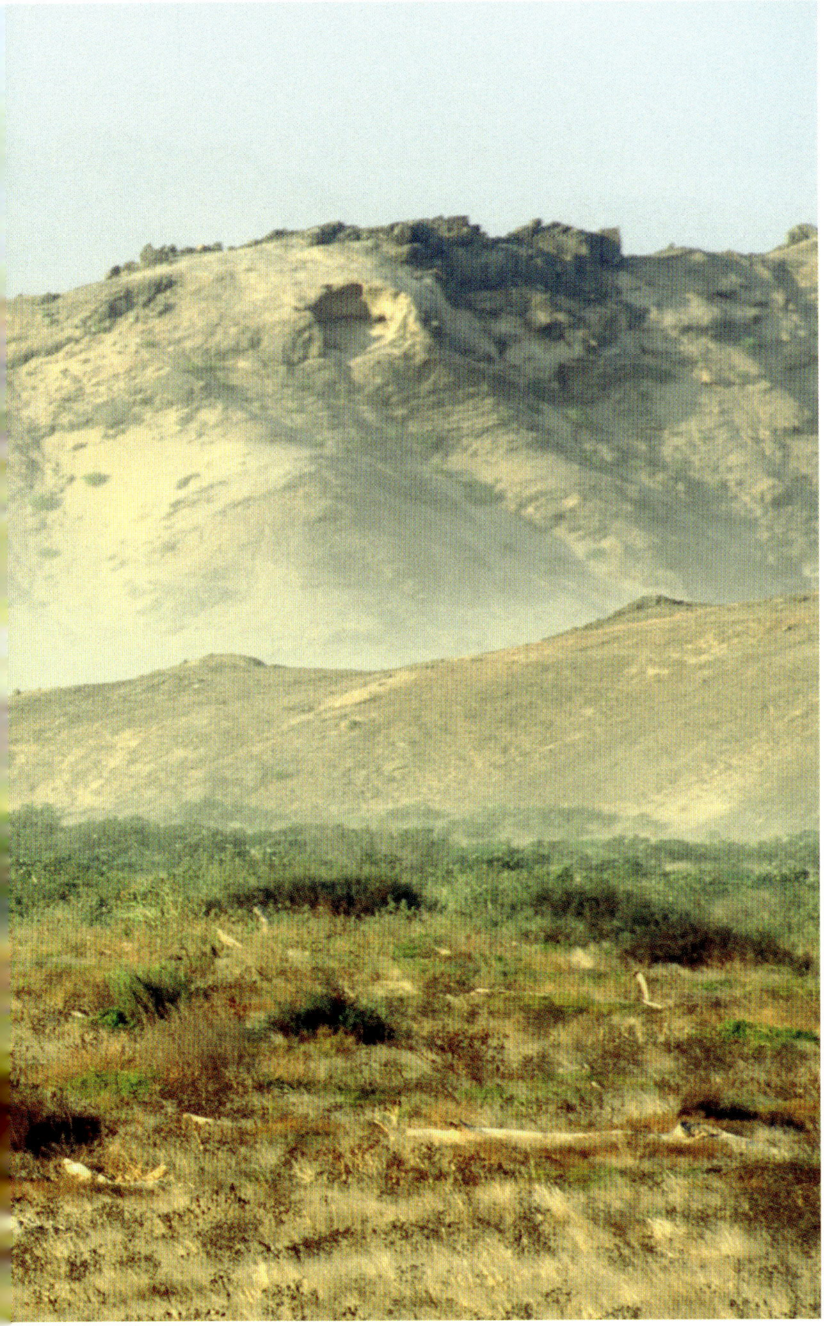

LEFT: Although the so-called desert elephants of the Kunene are no different to other African elephants, they have nevertheless adapted to life here on the dry gravel plains. They are generally smaller than their savannah cousins, and have longer legs and broader feet to help them move across this sandy terrain.

OVERLEAF: Kaokoland in the Kunene region is the ancestral home of the Himba, many of whom remain livestock farmers following traditional lifestyles. Much of the farm labour is done by women, the typical leather headdress shown here indicating that they are married.

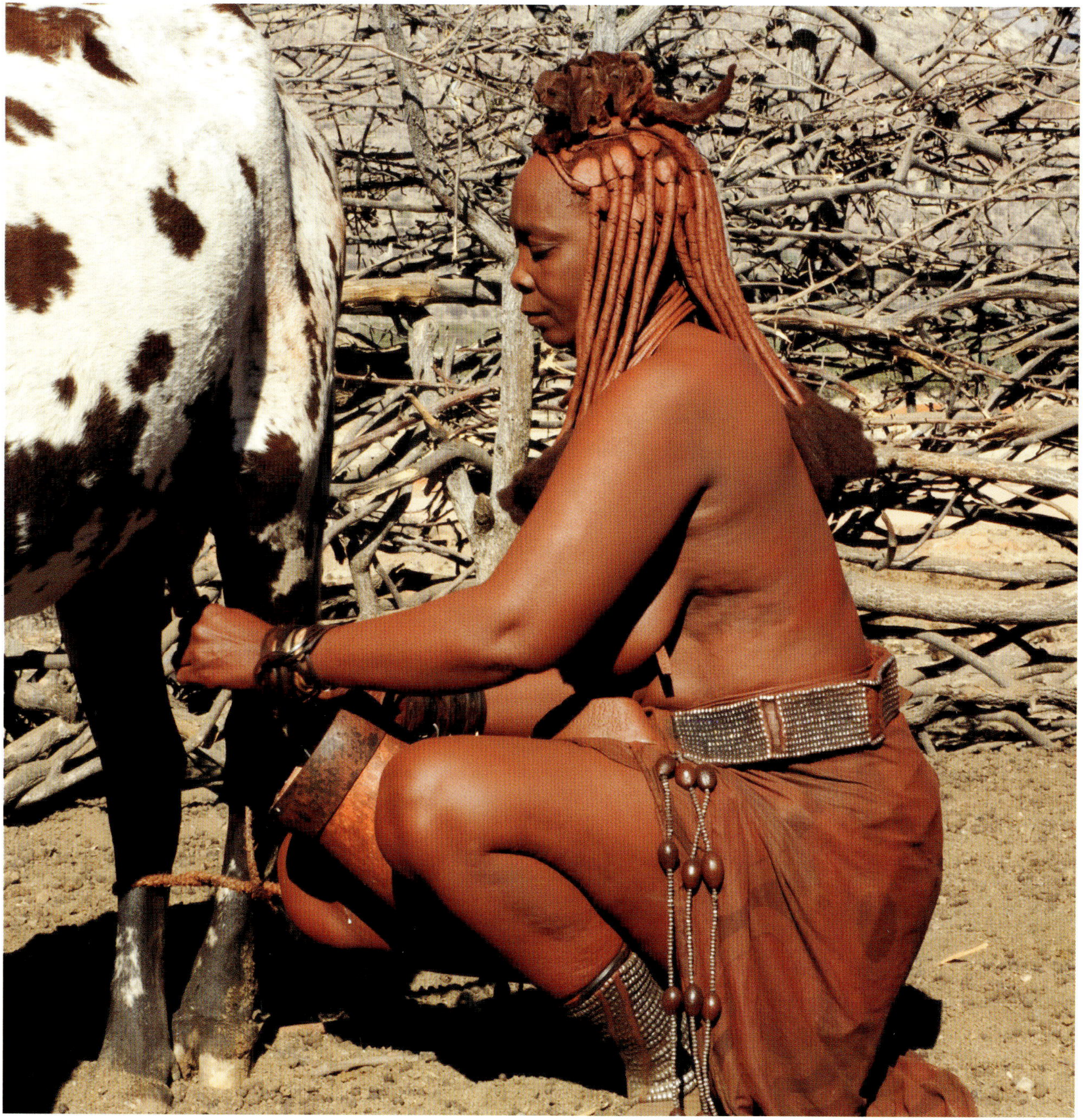

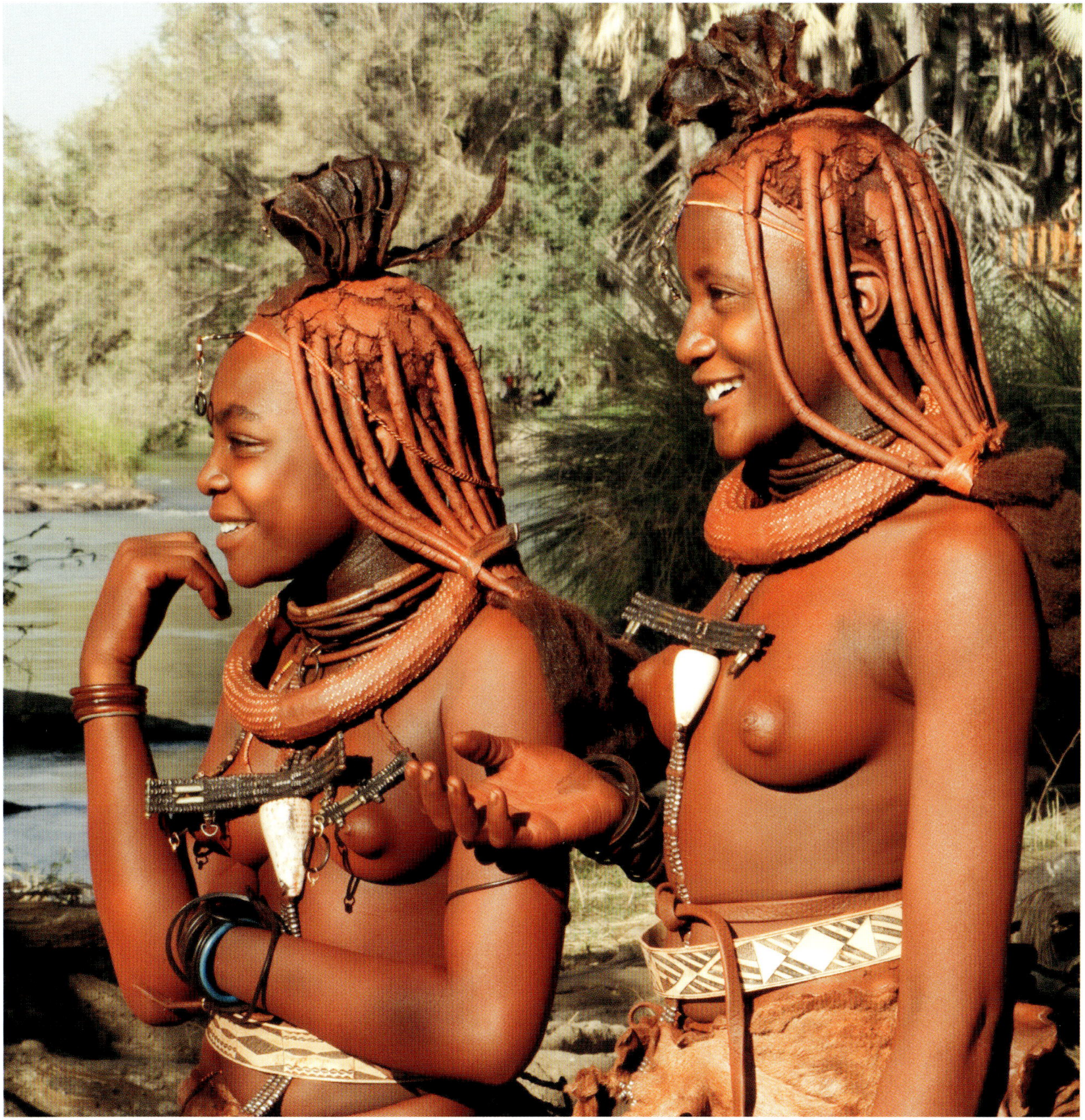

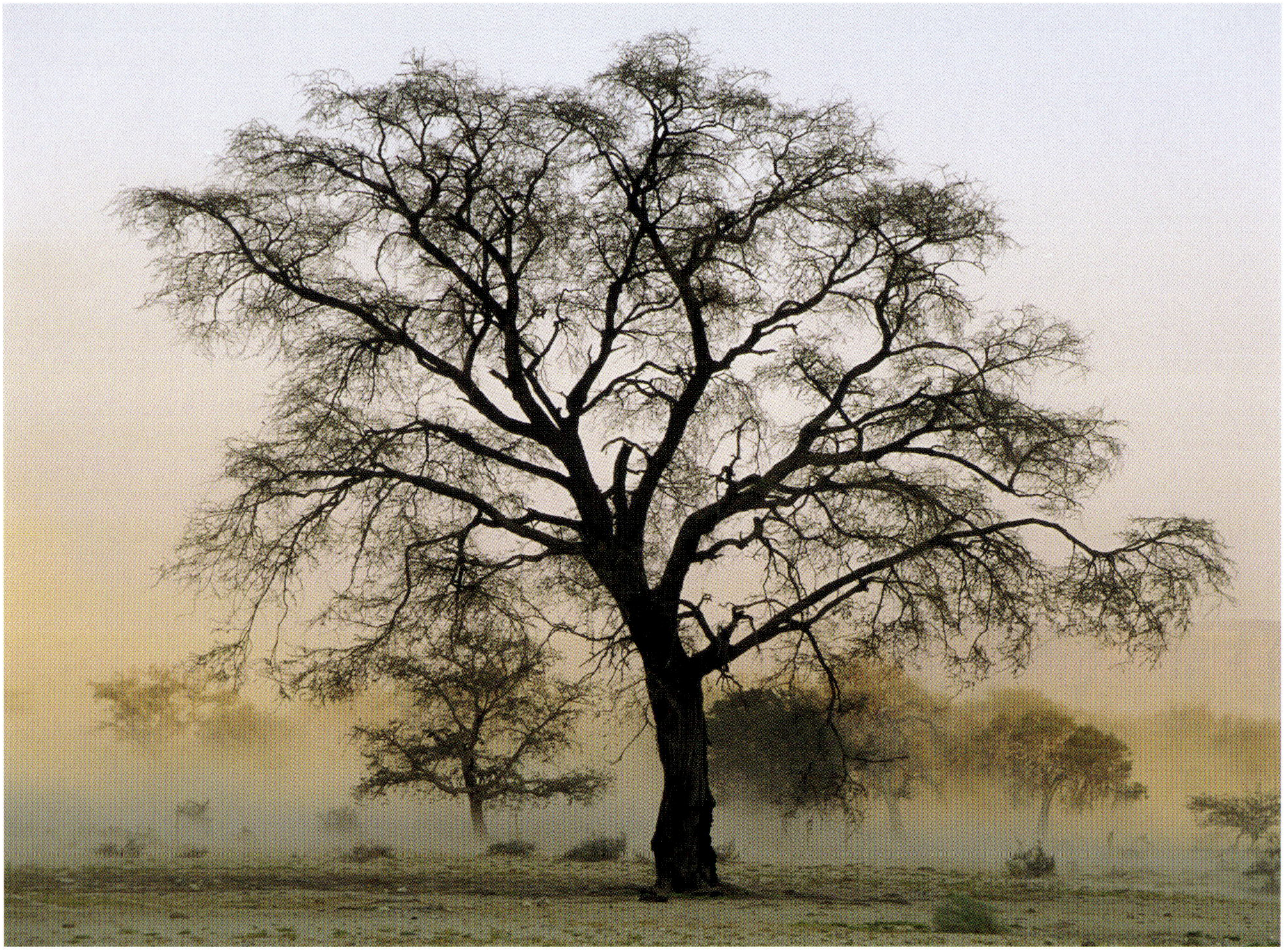

ABOVE: Punctuated with fan-shaped ana trees, Kaokoland and the broader Kunene region is an untamed wilderness, a rare combination of rocky scrub plain and occasionally lush river terrain.

OPPOSITE: In parts, the Kunene River breaks up into a number of cascades, the most impressive of which is Epupa Falls. The falls at Epupa are only 37 metres, but they are one of the most scenic on the subcontinent.

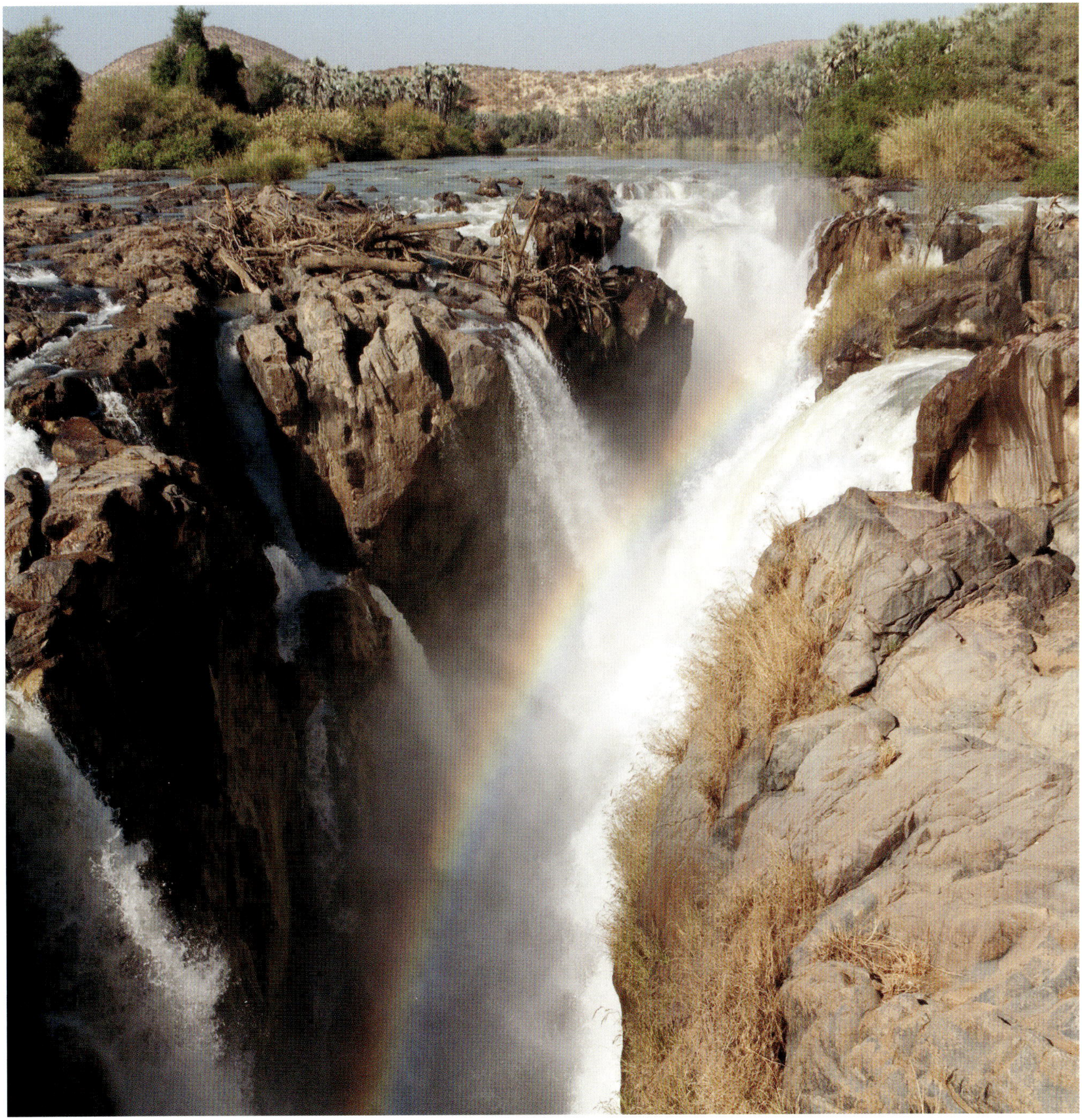

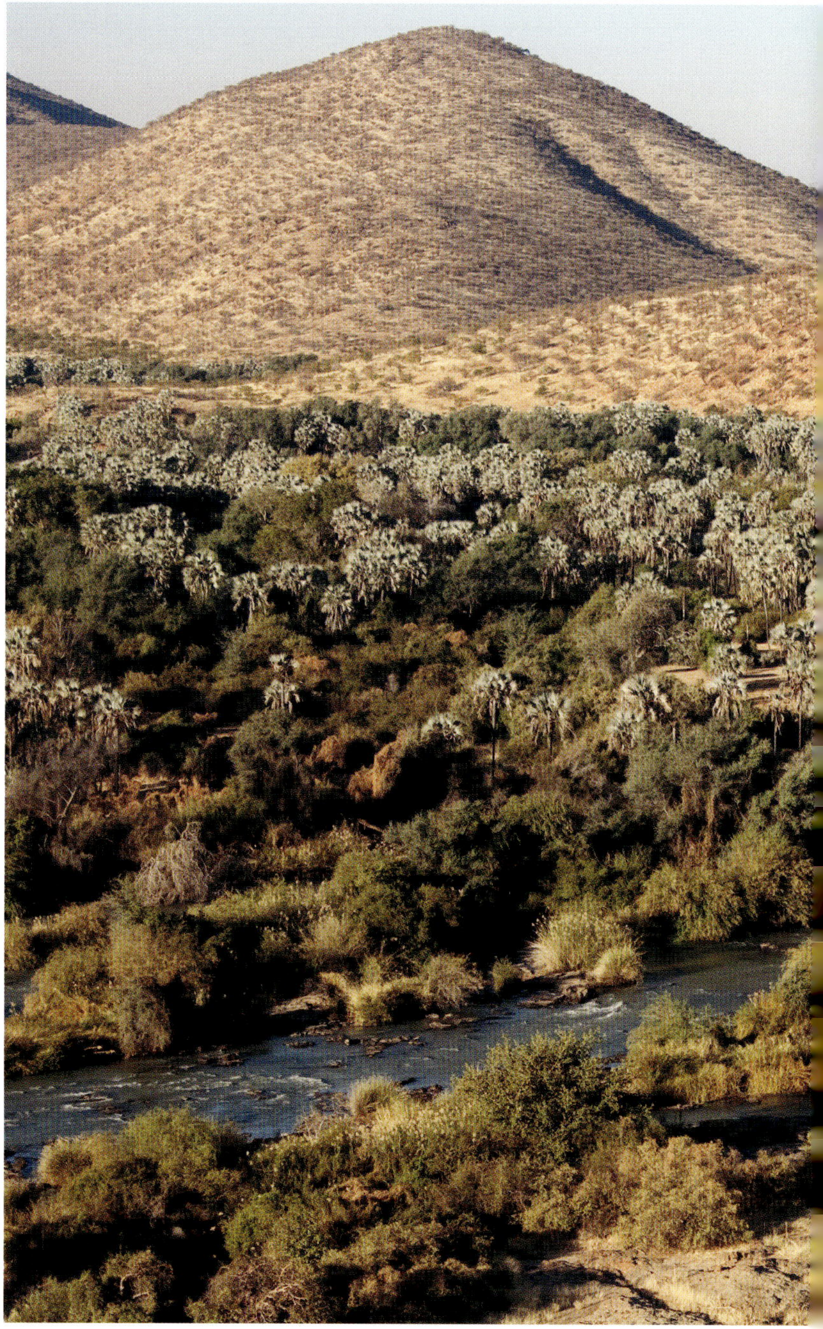

RIGHT: The gorge through which the Kunene winds is 60 metres deep in some sections and the riverbank is lined by makalani palms and intermittent shrubland. The river, which originates in the highlands of Angola, is just over 1 000 kilometres long, its most southern reaches separating Namibia from its northern neighbour, Angola.

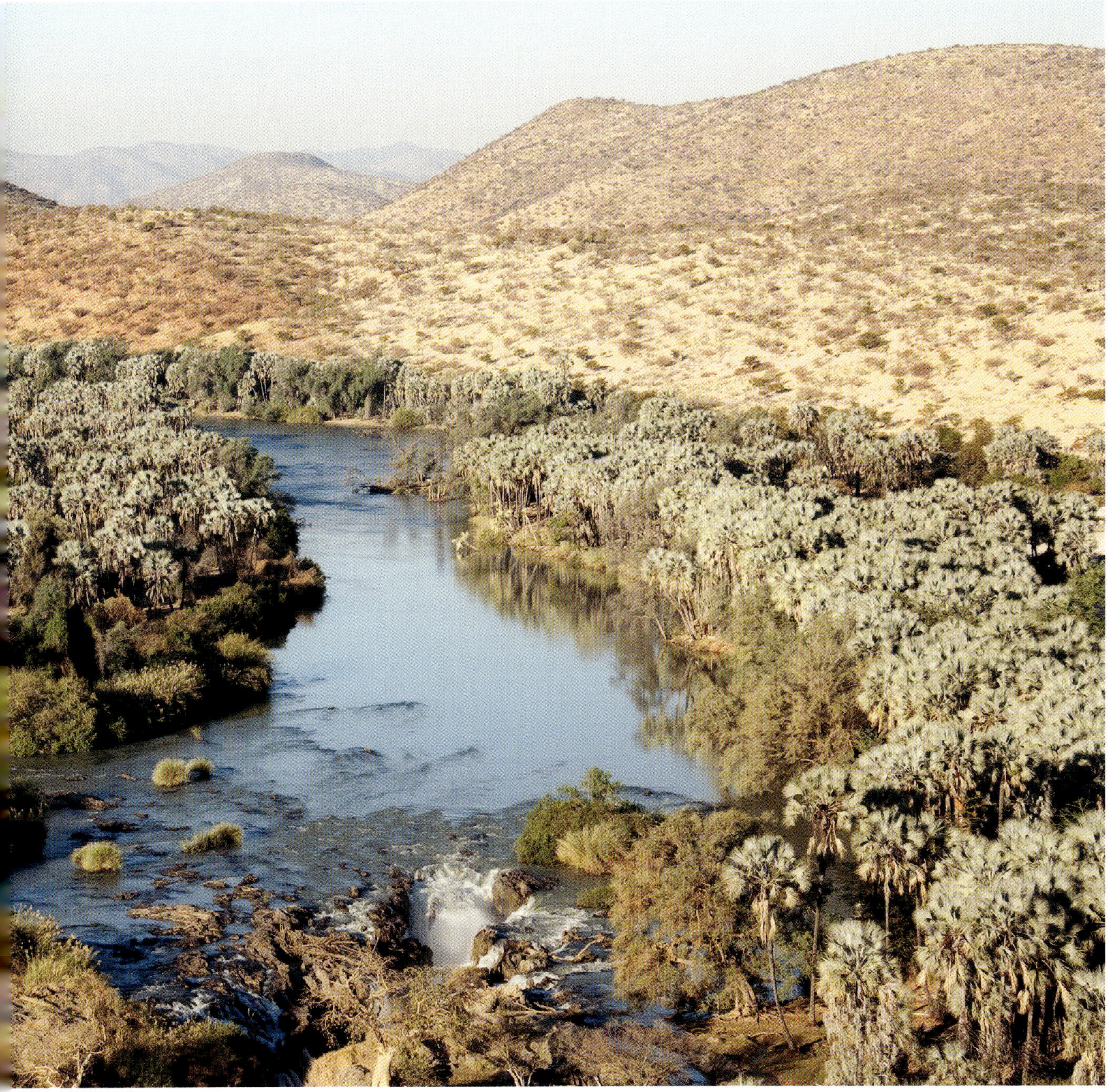

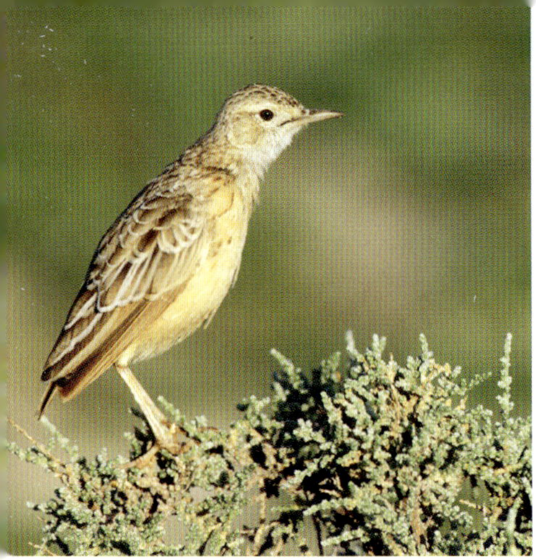
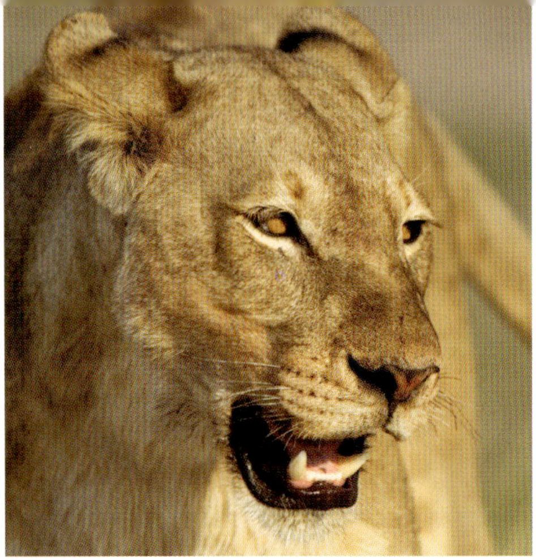
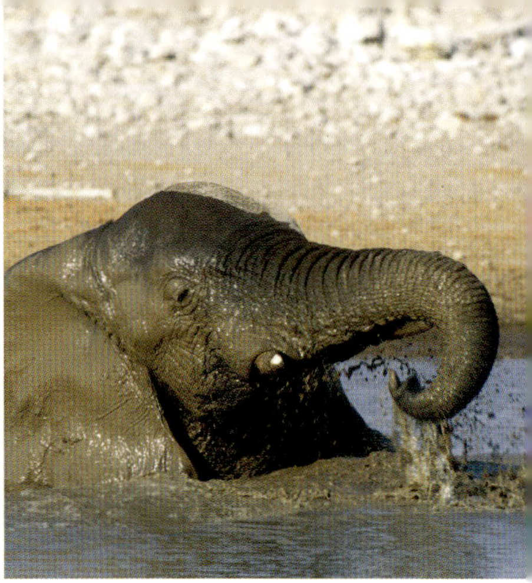
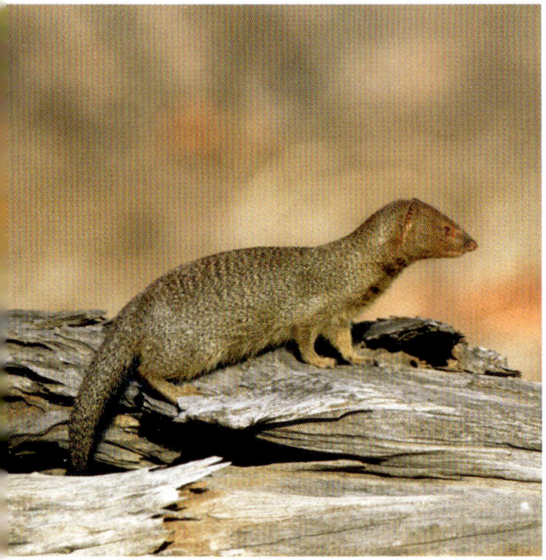
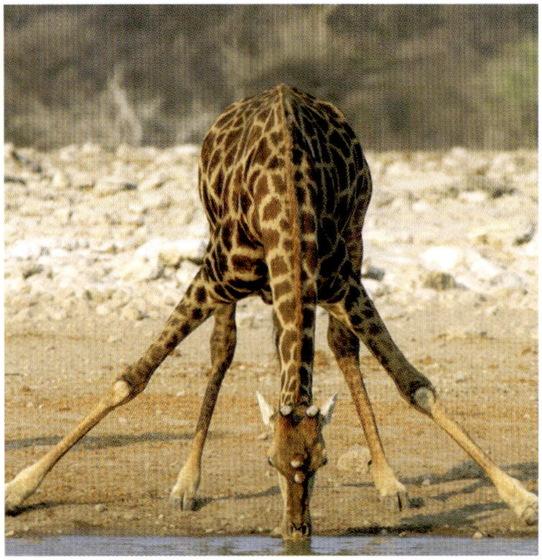
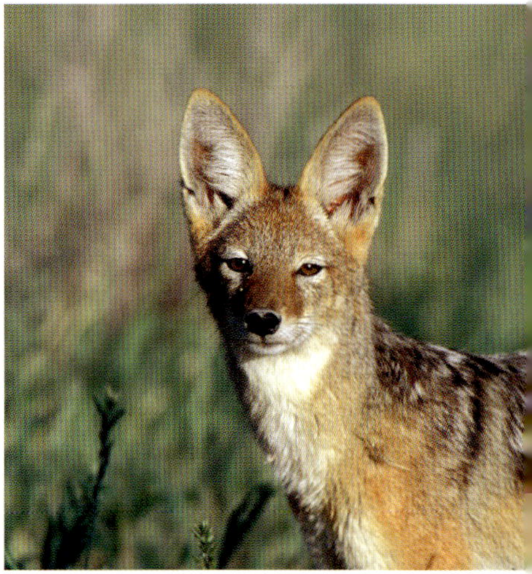
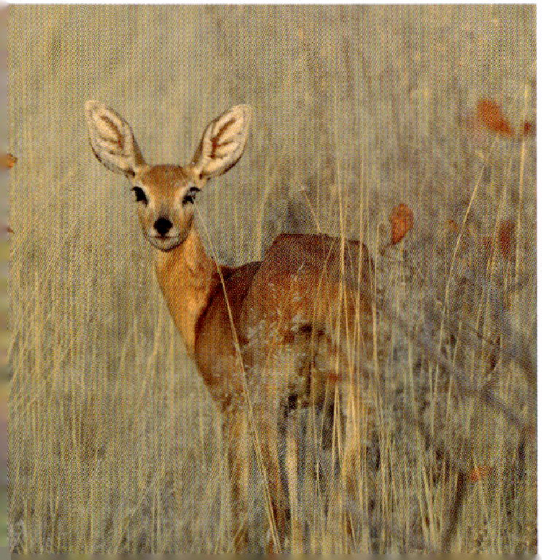
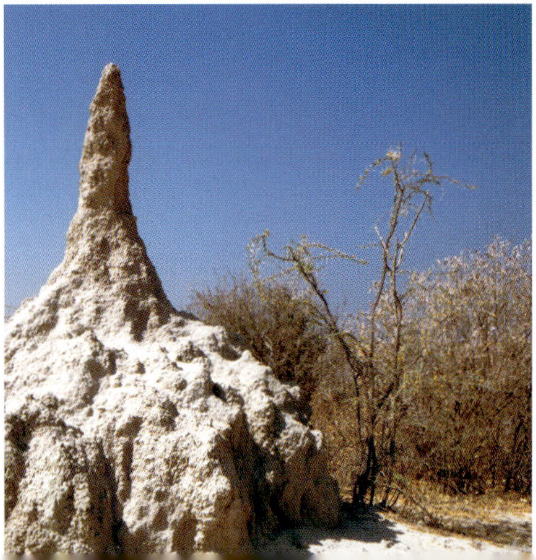
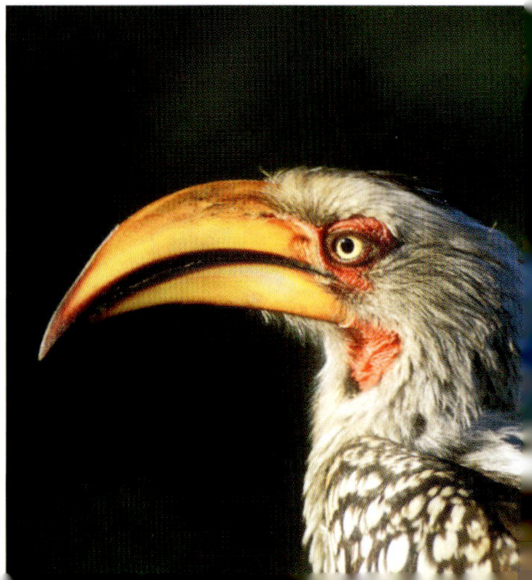

Etosha

Etosha National Park is the showcase of Namibia's wildlife heritage. It is a vast, untamed wilderness, one massive pan covering no less than 5 000 square kilometres of the arid northwest. Millennia ago, the entire area was a giant lake that sustained the abundant wildlife that made their home here. Today, despite the fact that this huge depression is for the most part no more than a semi-arid hollow in the ground, it remains pivotal to the survival of local species that congregate when it is filled by the seasonal rains. For much of the year, the 120-kilometre-wide Etosha Pan is a dry and somewhat desolate dust bowl, and yet it remains an all-important gathering place for an astonishing diversity of animal life. Many of these species – ranging from the diminutive Damara dik-dik and rare black-faced impala to black rhino, wildebeest and zebra – rely entirely on the generosity of the land, the forces of nature that bring them water and shelter and on the delicate balance between abundance and scarcity. During the dry season, many of these species move from one unreliable water source to another in a desperate fight for survival. But when the rains fall on this otherwise stark and unforgiving terrain, Etosha springs to life. Temporary pools, shallows and streams offer a welcome respite from the oppressive heat and aridity of this mighty sun-baked pan. Despite the apparent inhospitality of Etosha and its surrounds, it remains home to thriving populations of mammals, birds and reptiles that have earned it a reputation as one of the finest wildlife reserves in southern Africa.

OPPOSITE FROM LEFT TO RIGHT:

- A spike-heeled lark calls from its shrub perch in the heart of Etosha National Park, northern Namibia.
- This lioness, her jaw slightly agape, strikes a pose of aggression.
- Etosha has a healthy elephant population. Here a bull takes to water to cool down.
- The slender mongoose is one of a number of smaller mammal species at home in Etosha.
- A giraffe bull stops to drink at a water hole.
- The rainy season sees a black-backed jackal venture out in search of prey.
- Steenbok are one of the smaller antelope species resident at Etosha.
- Termite mounds in Etosha are whitish in colour due to bleached calcite soils.
- The southern yellow-billed hornbill is one of about 10 hornbill species occurring in Namibia.

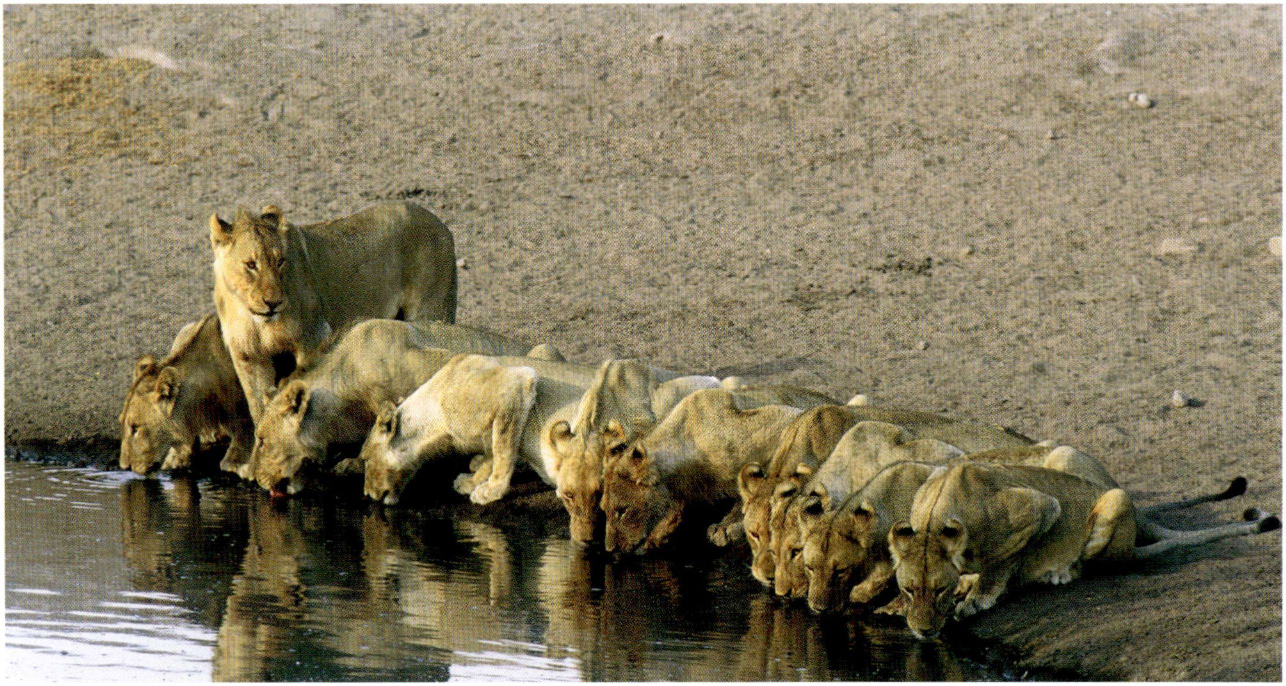

ABOVE: Etosha National Park is a wildlife paradise and Namibia's top wildlife destination. It is home to no fewer than 114 mammal species, including lion, but also cheetah, leopard and hyena.

OPPOSITE: The larger predators, notably the big cats, have a varied menu from which to choose. At some point, particularly during the dry season, prey species such as zebra, giraffe, wildebeest, eland, gemsbok, kudu and impala will inevitably make their way to the nearest water hole. Here a pair of Burchell's stallions fights for supremacy.

The waters of Etosha are the lifeblood of the wildlife that congregate around its shores. In fact, it is almost mythical in its attraction. In the twighlight, as either dusk or dawn settles, ancestral voices appear to call over the immeasurable space, summoning the herds to drink. This is where the rules of play are tested. It is where bulls and stallions stand their ground; where mothers bring their foals and calves. But, for Etosha, the circle of life can sometimes be cruel. It is often violent and bloody, occasionally gentle, and frequently fragile as witnessed in the dramatic fall of a zebra to the brutal power of a lioness; in the delicate unfolding of an insect's wings as it emerges from its cocoon.

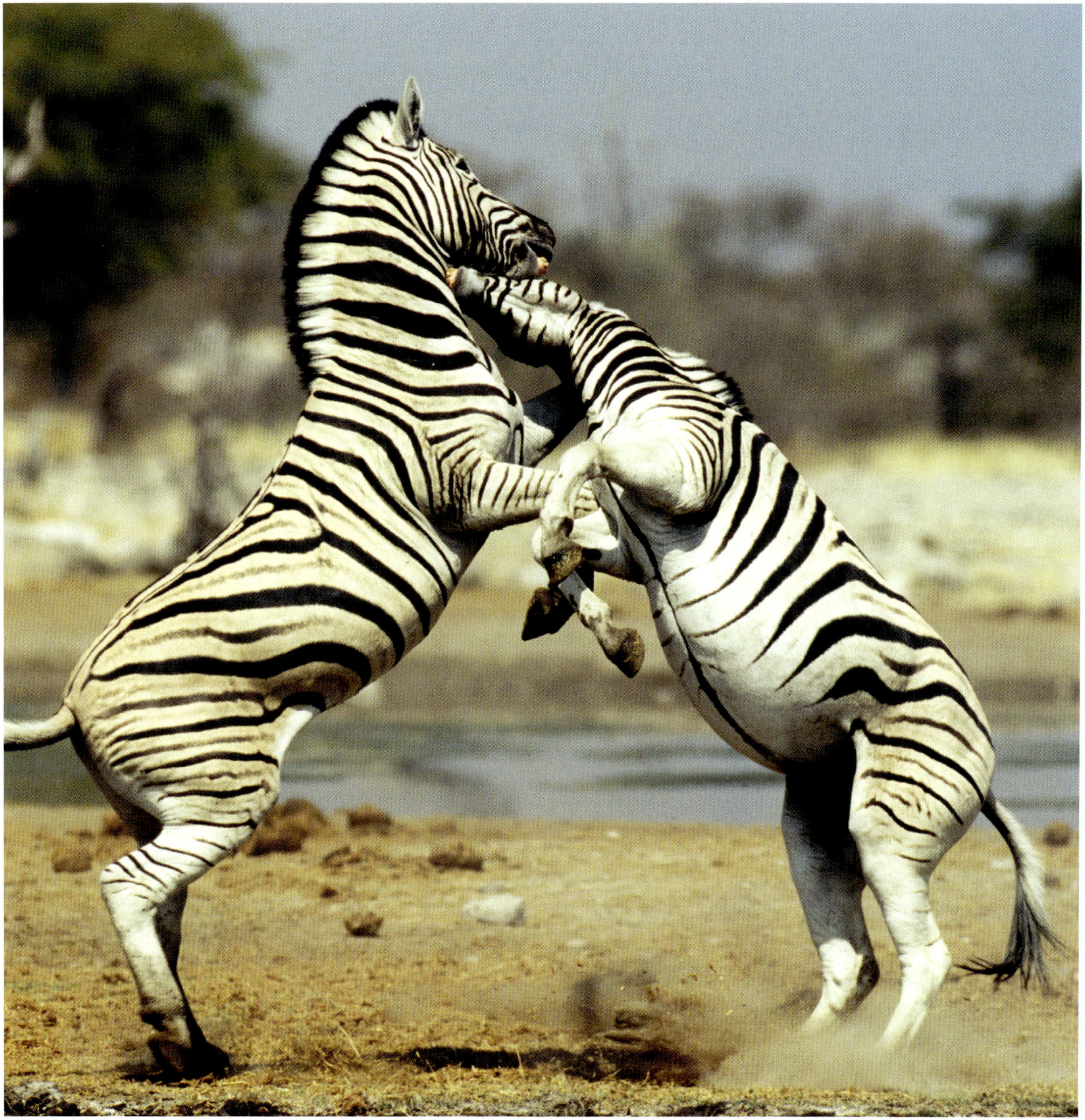

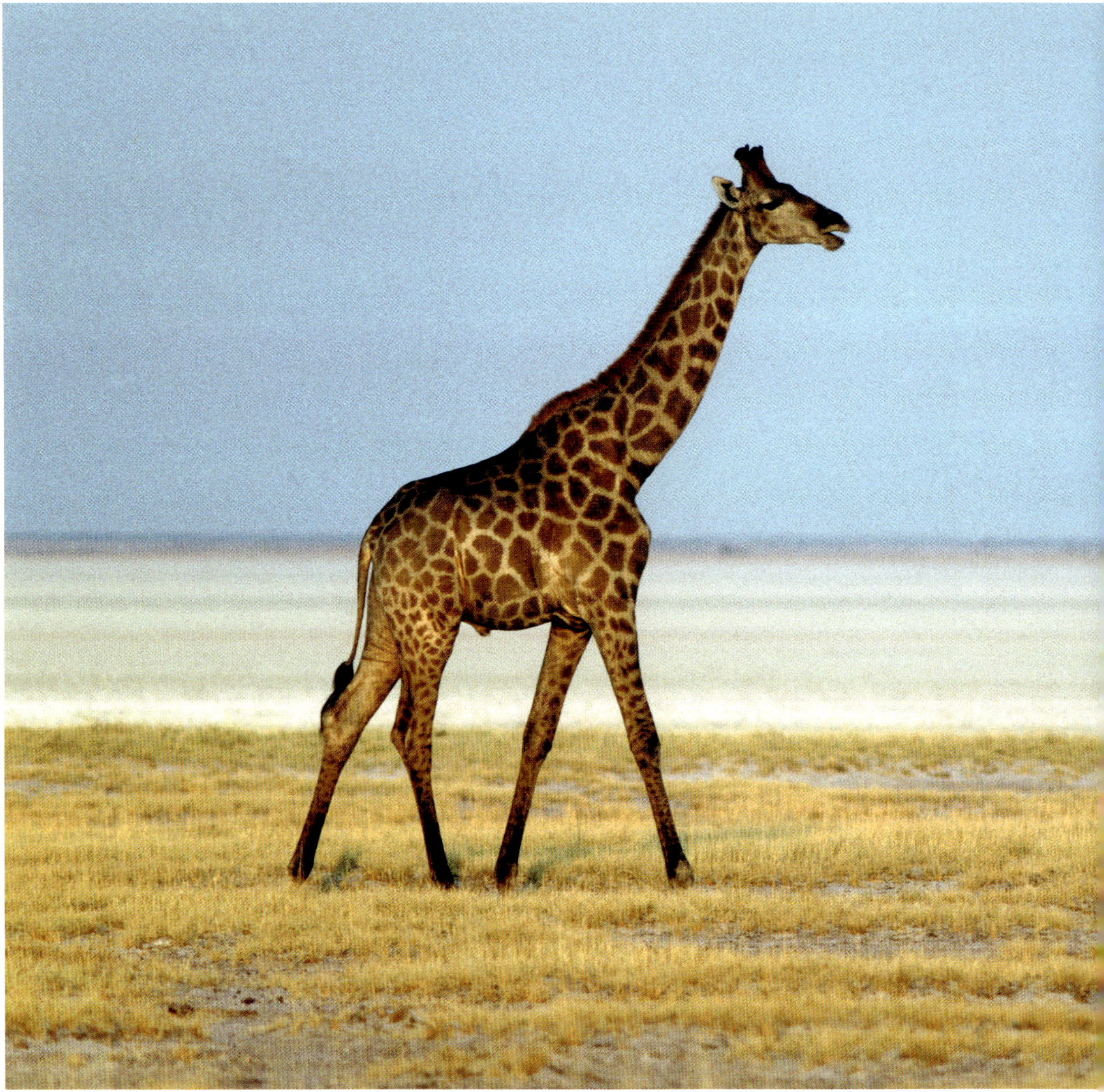

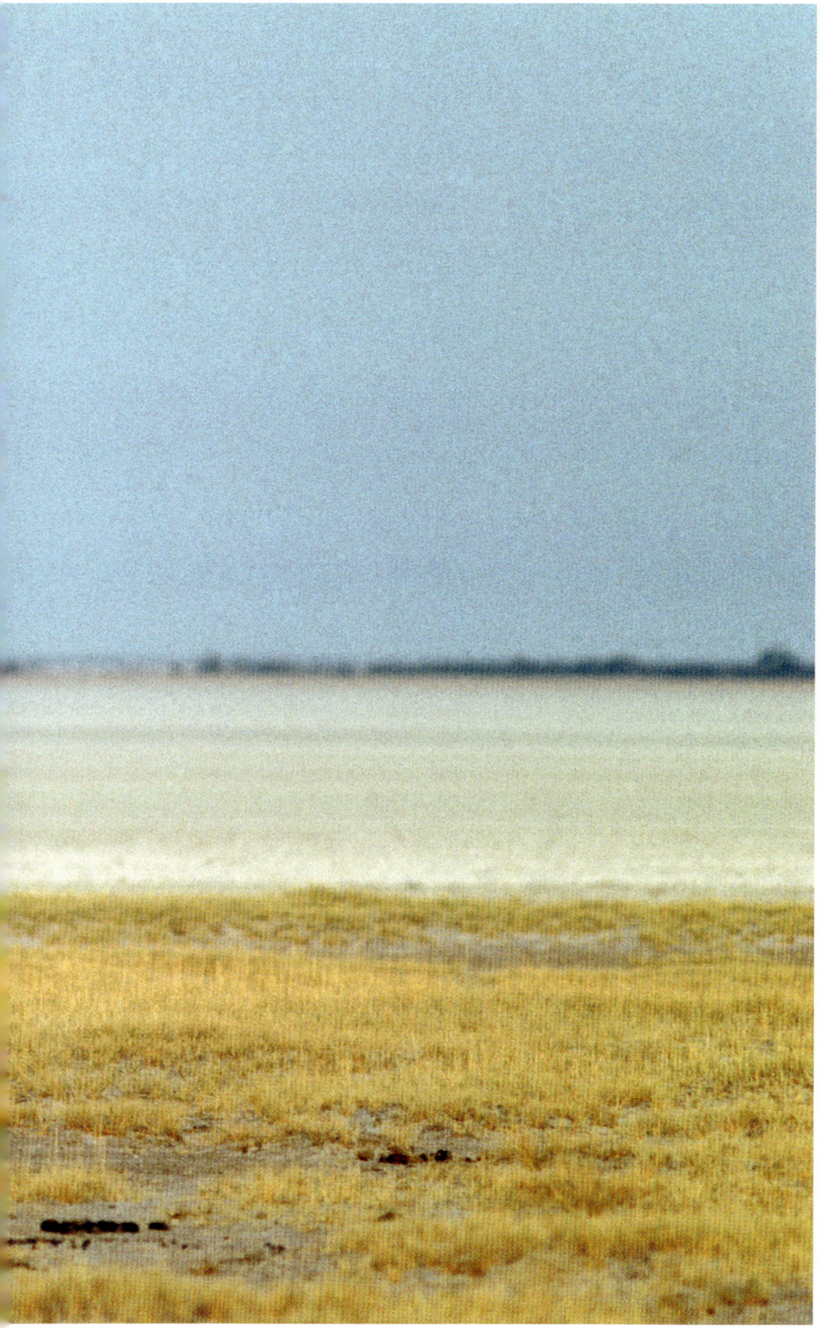

LEFT: During the dry months from May to about September, when water is scarce, Etosha's wildlife, such as this southern giraffe, tend to congregate near water holes, many of which are the only reliable source of water for kilometres. When the rains fall, the animals are more likely to scatter much further afield.

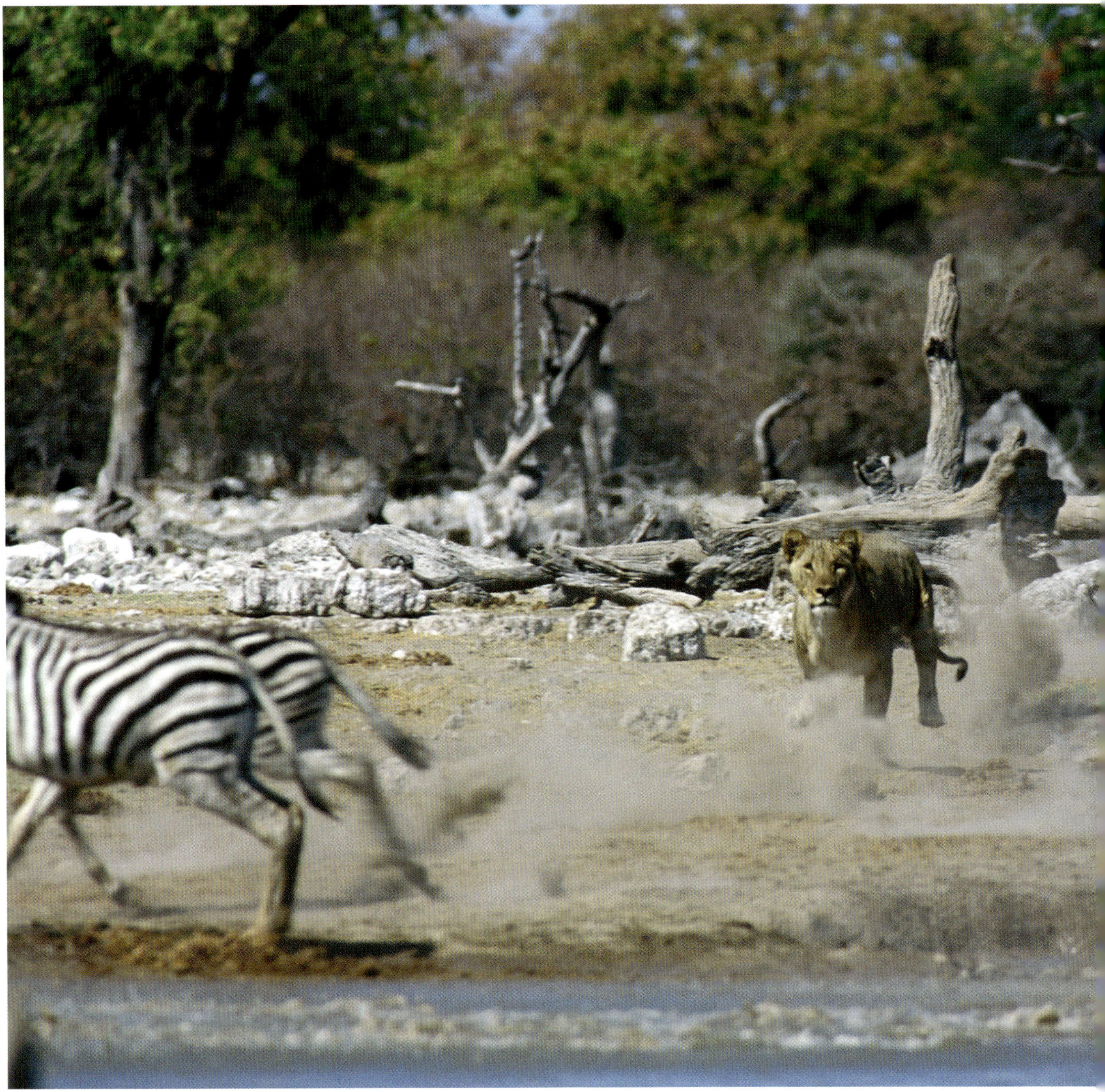

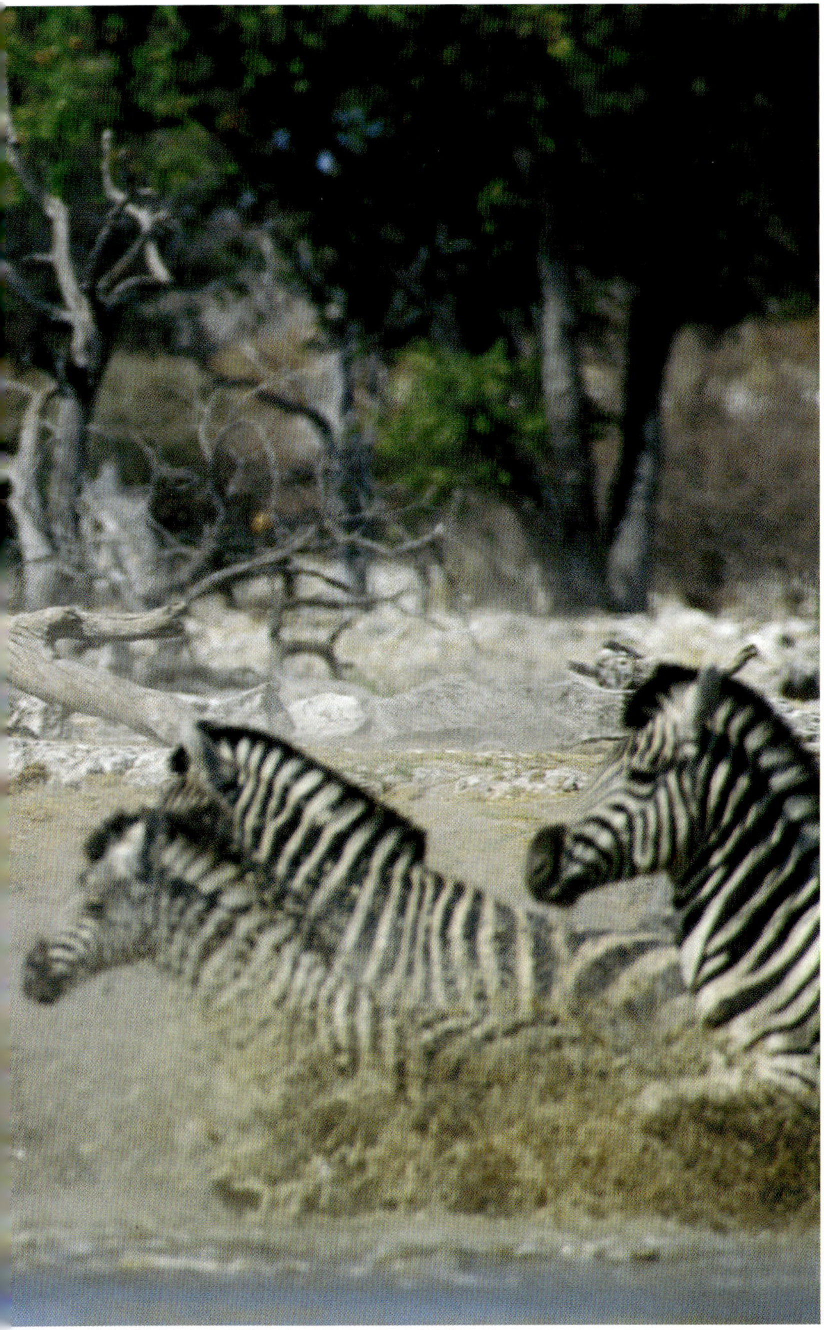

LEFT: The water hole is the focus of life. Animals great and small gather here to drink, usually in the dappled light of dusk or dawn, and predators take full advantage of the abundant prey.

OVERLEAF, LEFT: All prey species – except, perhaps, for elephant – are somewhat skittish at water holes. Inevitably, one of the big cats will be watching and waiting. Here a giraffe gives way to a herd of approaching elephant bulls.

OVERLEAF, RIGHT: Many bird species rely on the presence of water. To protect their eggs and young, male weaver birds craft their nests on branches overhanging the water.

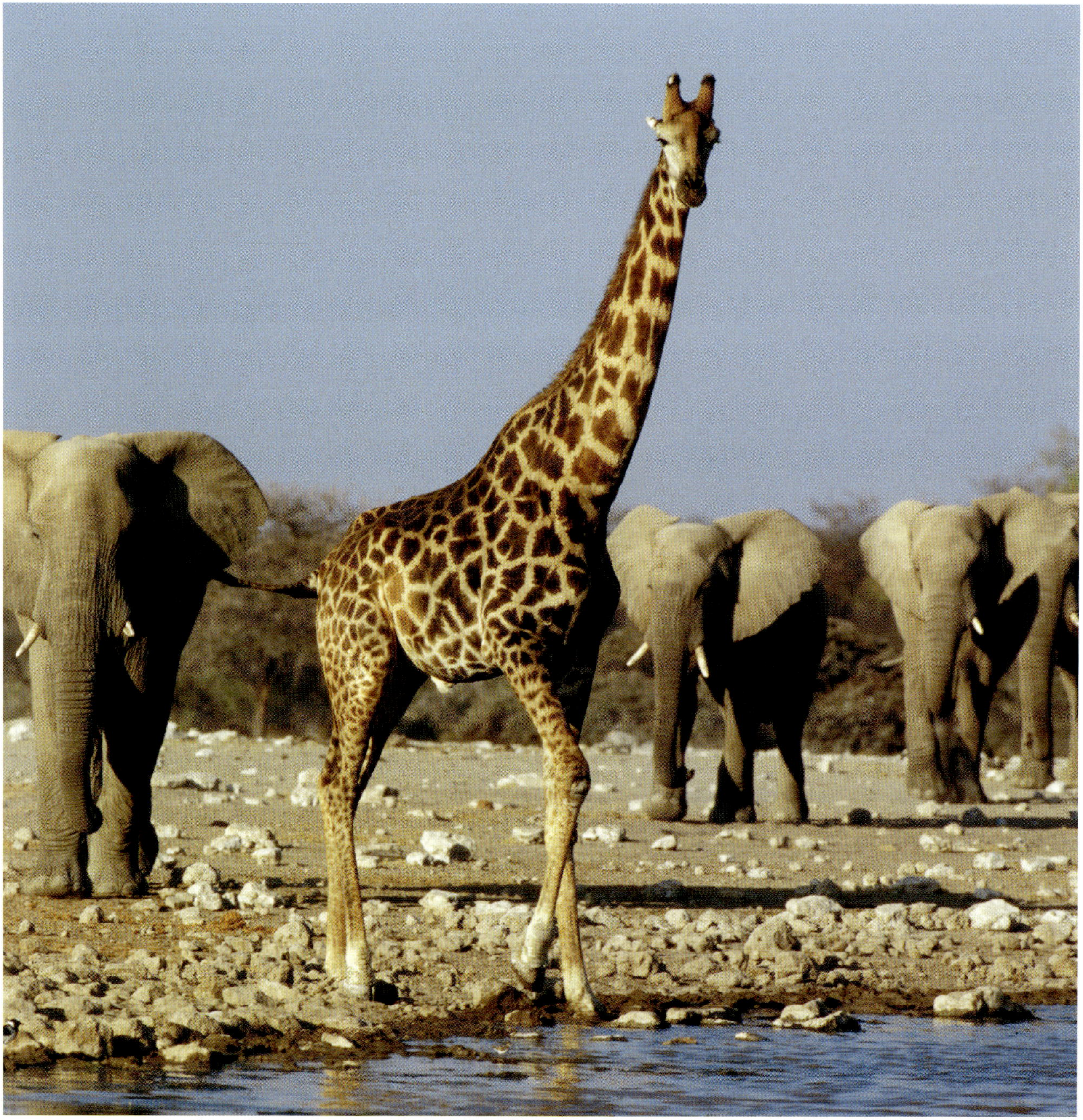

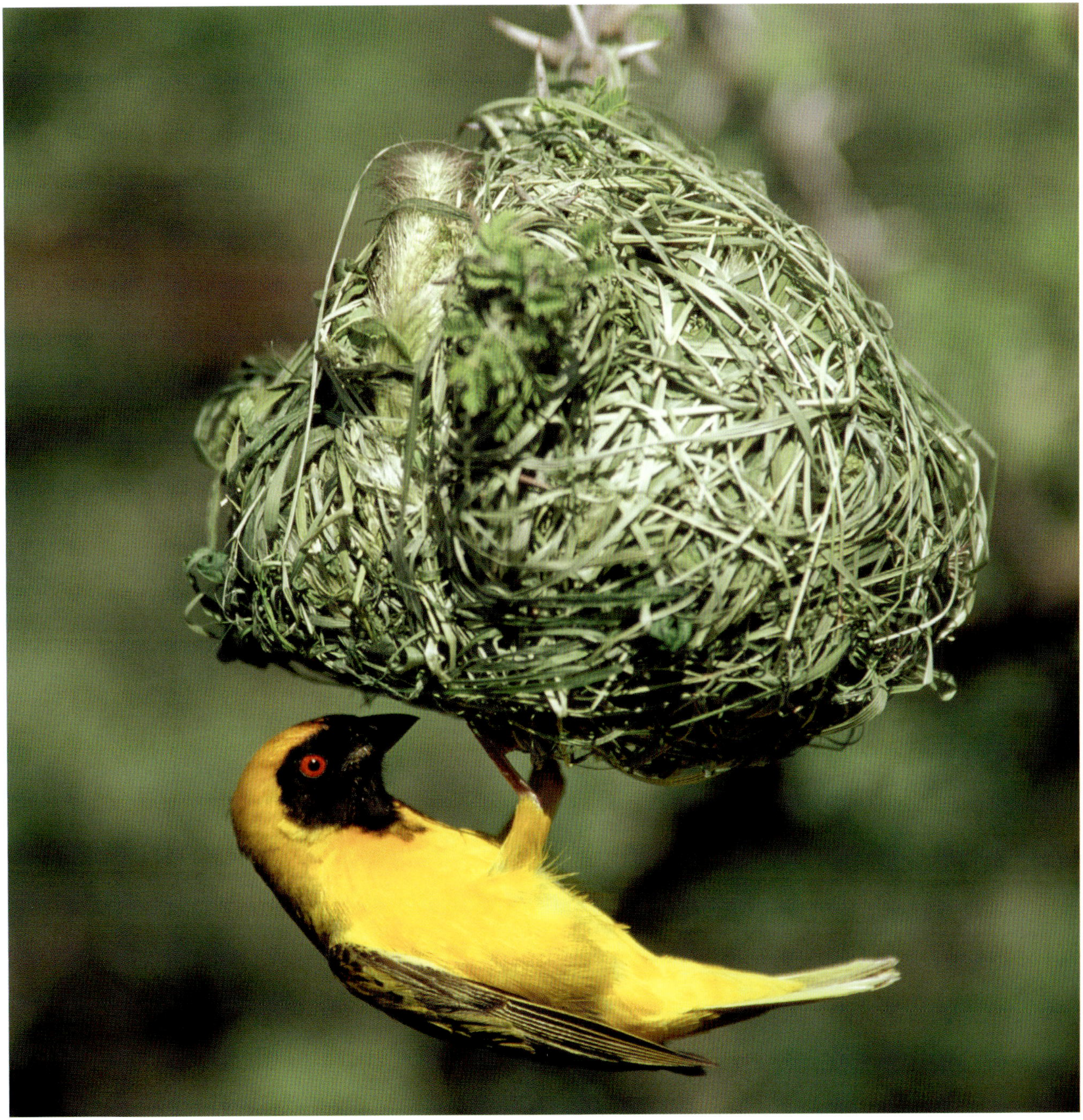

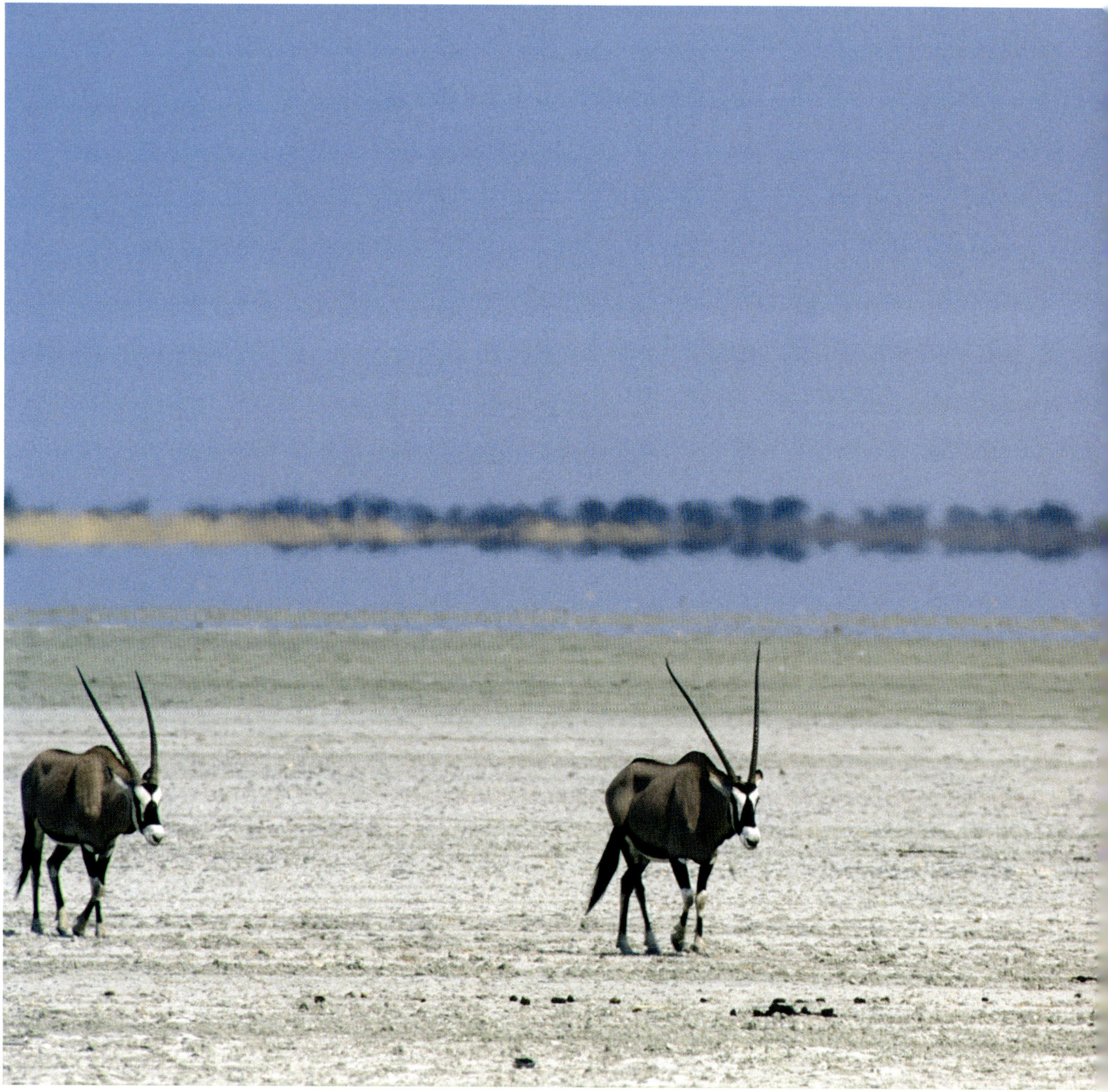

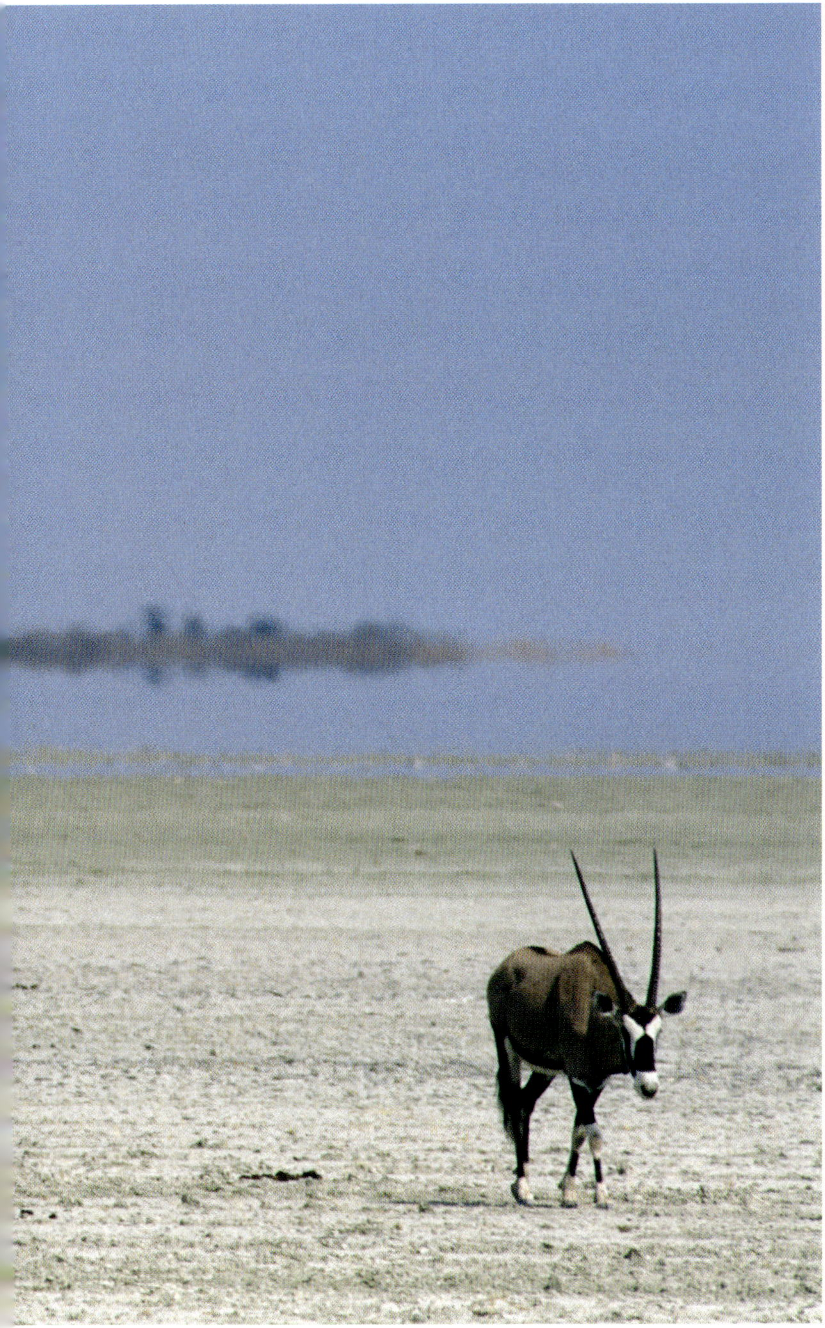

LEFT: The gemsbok, with its long arrow-straight horns and distinctive markings, is one of the larger antelopes of southern Africa. Many herds – which can number up to 40 individuals – cover terrain where water is limited and rainfall pitifully scarce. Gemsbok, however, are able to survive for extended periods without actually drinking.

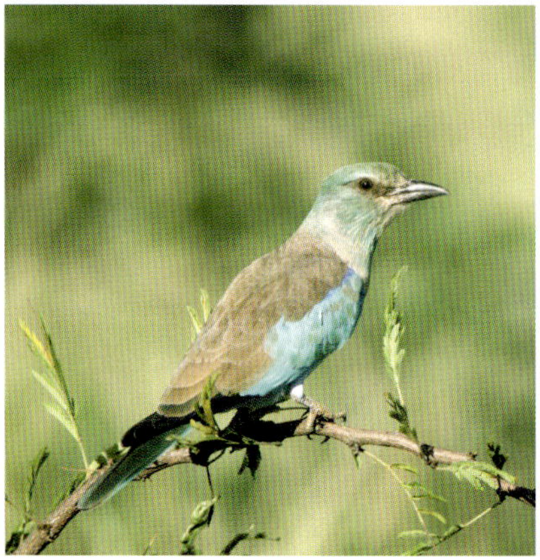

ABOVE: Despite the harsh conditions, Etosha boasts a rich and diverse birdlife. Here a European roller surveys the green countryside following the annual rains.

RIGHT: The scops owl emerges mostly as the light at Etosha begins to dwindle at sunset. Here one is perfectly camouflaged against the mottled bark of a mopane tree.

OPPOSITE: The Burchell's, or plains zebra which is found across the northern region of the country, is the most common of the two zebra species occurring within Etosha. The ears of the Burchell's zebra are slightly shorter than in other species, but coloration and pattern vary considerably.

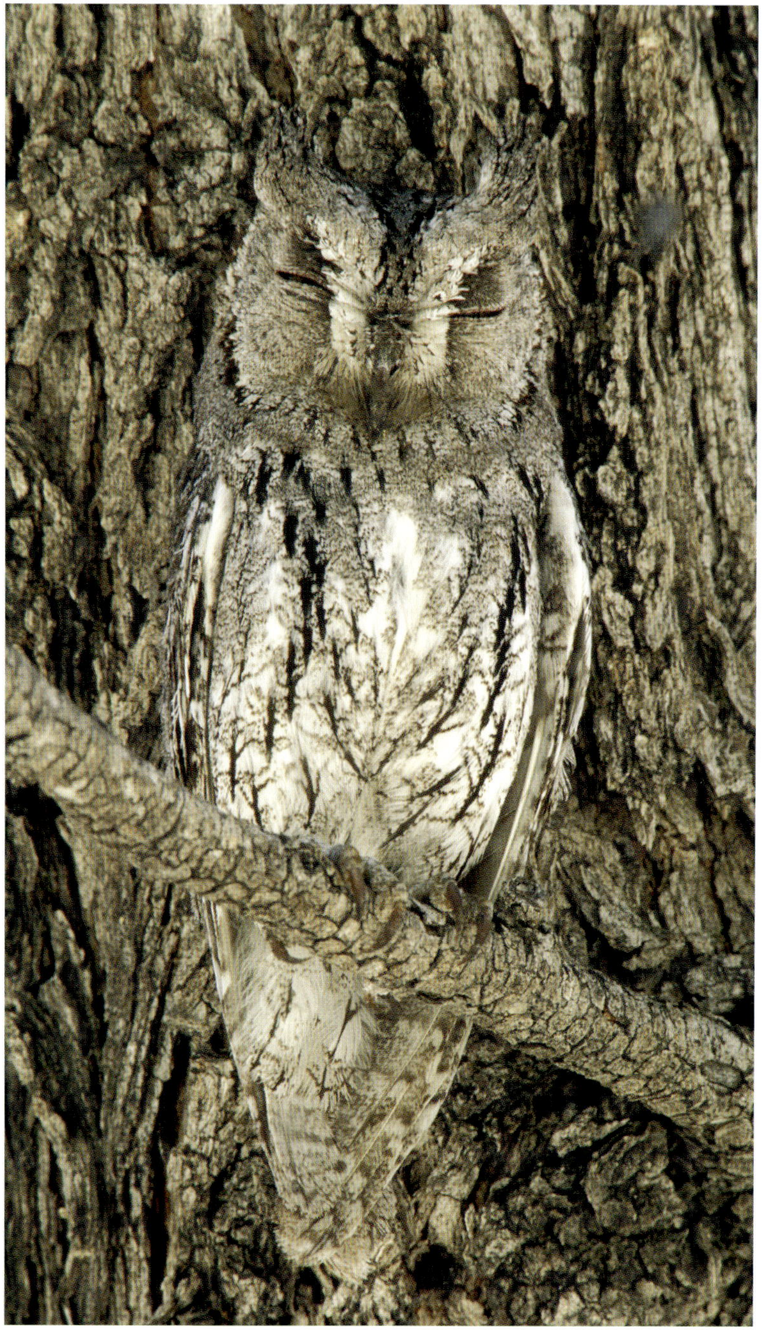

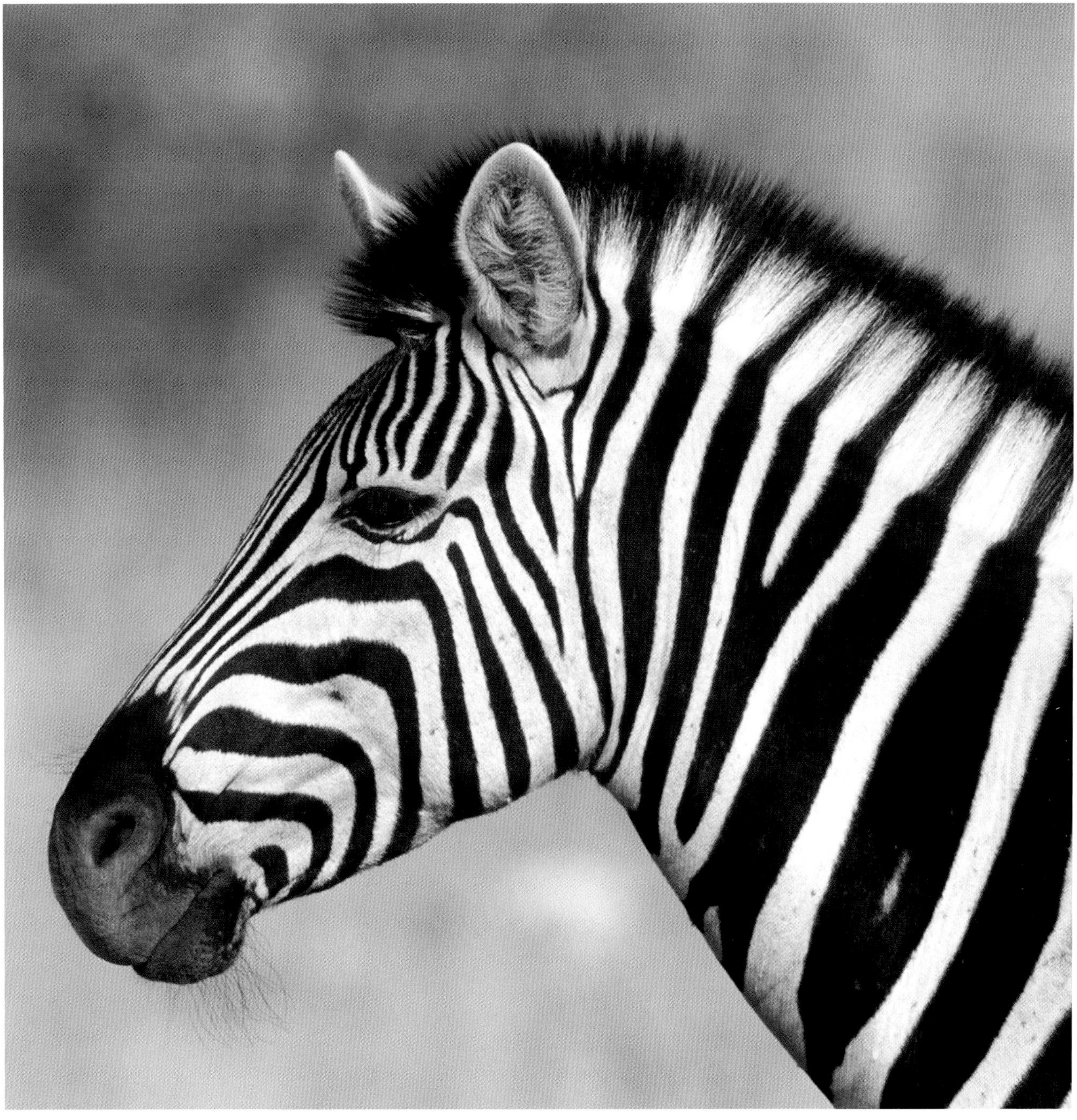

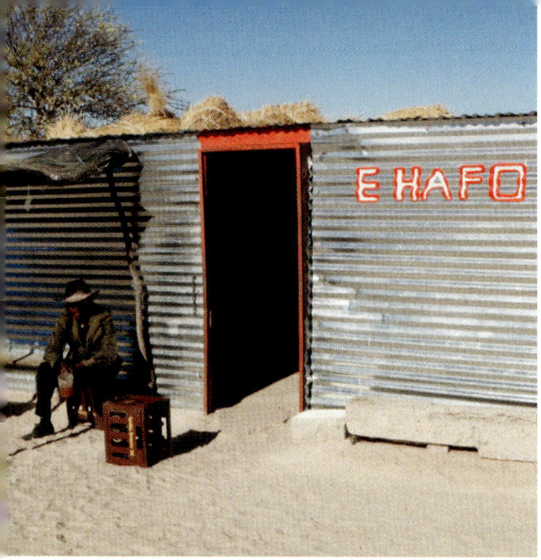
E HAFO
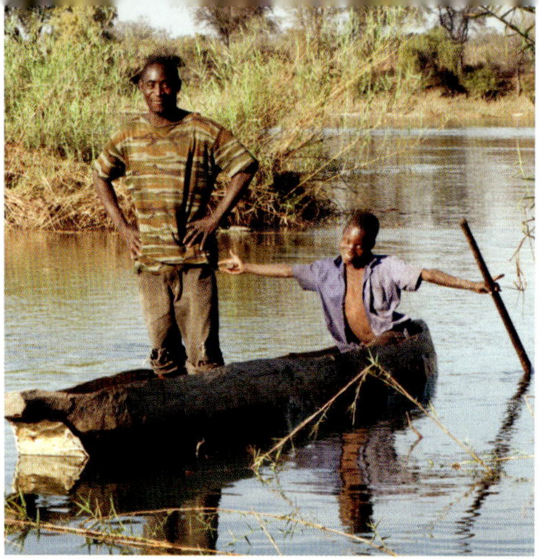
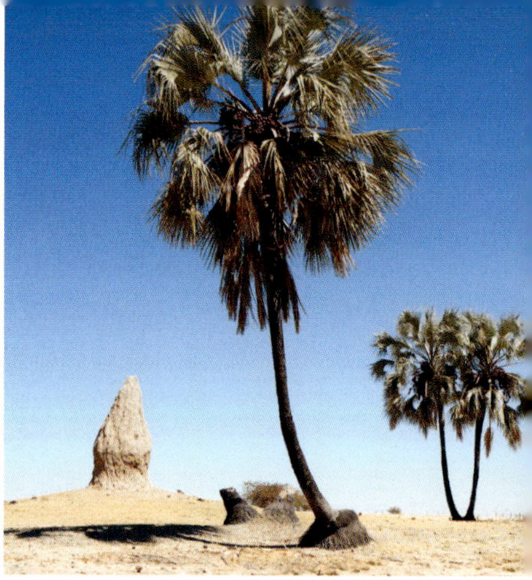
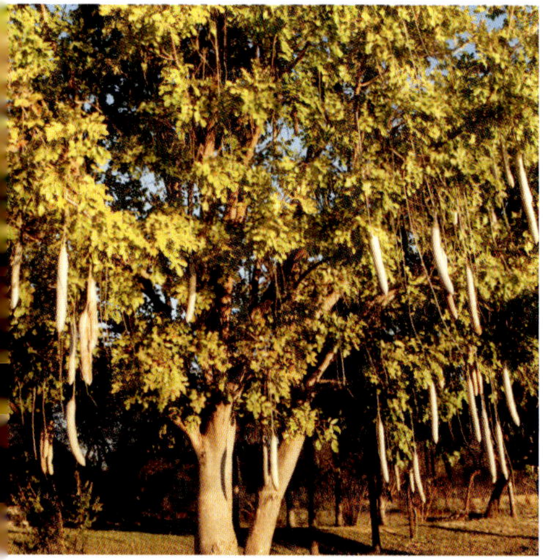
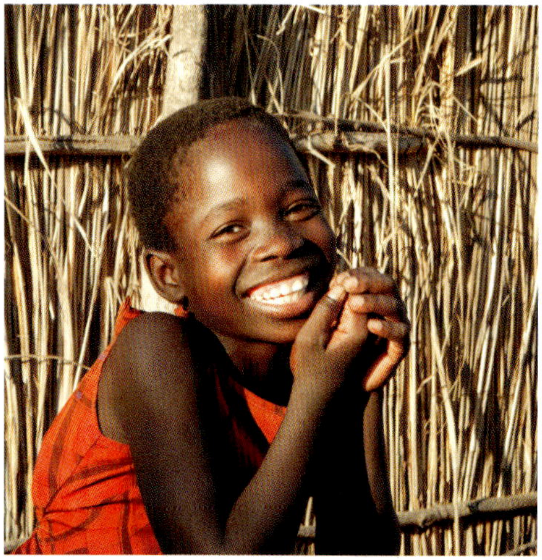
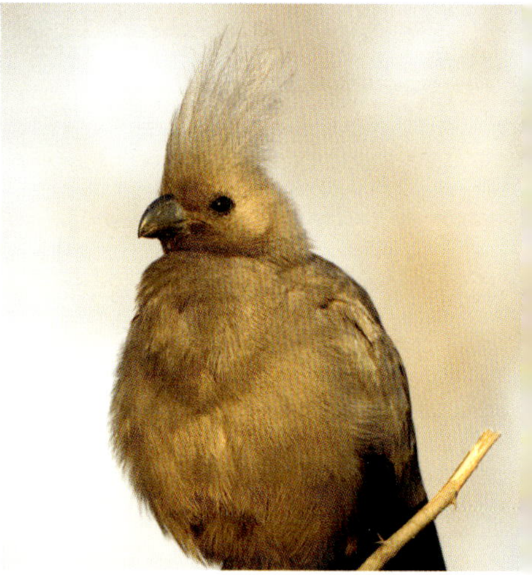
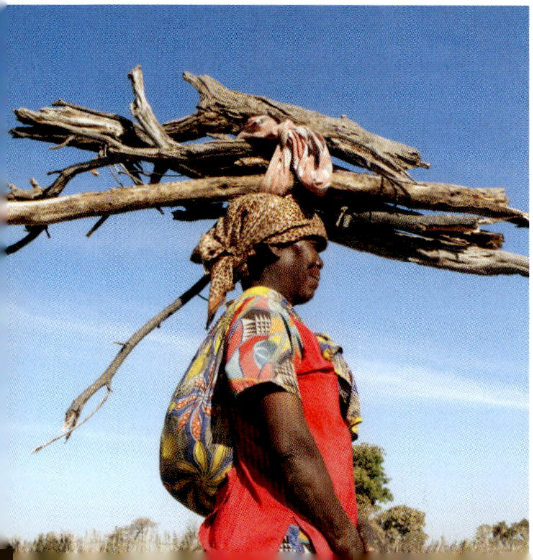
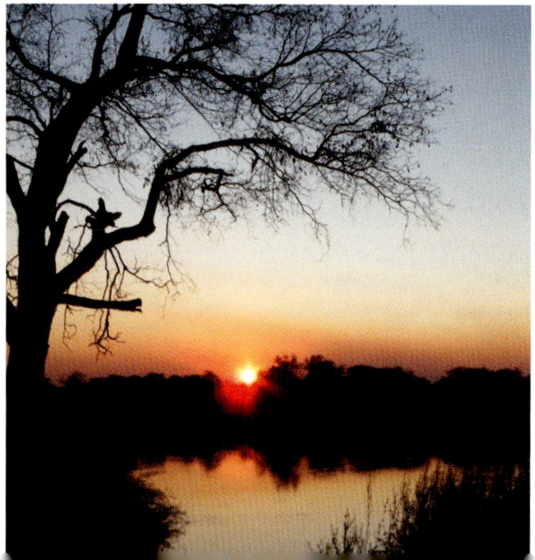
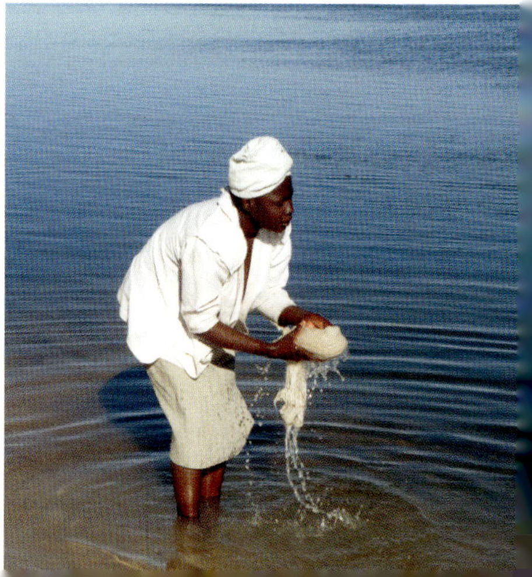

North

Northern Namibia – the region covered by what is traditionally known as Owamboland, Kaokoland and Caprivi – is characterised by wide, open spaces intermittently dotted by giant termite mounds, scatterings of small stands of trees and the occasional hill. These vistas stretch all the way from the west coast, across the Hartmann and Marienfluss valleys to Rundu and beyond into the Caprivi Strip, that small finger-like expanse of Namibia bordered by Angola, Zambia and Botswana at different points along its length.

Life is generally hard here. Both the air and the land are dry, and water is scarce. The area has been ravaged by drought over the years, most recently in the 1970s when its wildlife was all but decimated. Today, in order to monitor and protect the indigenous wildlife, two important conservation areas – apart from Etosha National Park to the south – have been established: the Khaudum and Caprivi game parks. Human activity is limited to mostly traditional Herero and Himba people, and village life tends to revolve around the water, particularly along the courses of the Kunene, Kavango and – deep into East Caprivi – even the Zambezi rivers. It's these mighty water courses, winding their way through the far north, that add colour to an otherwise parched landscape known for its reddish gneiss rocks formed over 2 000 million years ago. It is here, too, along the languid course of the Kunene, that the Ruacana and Epupa falls tumble and cascade, transforming the rugged wilderness into an astonishingly green and lush landscape.

OPPOSITE FROM LEFT TO RIGHT:

- Informal Cuca shop, an unlicensed bar named after a brand of Angolan beer typical of northern Namibia.
- Fishing on the Kwando River in Caprivi, in the far north of Namibia.
- Characteristic *oshana*, or shallow pool, with makalani palms and a termite mound on its banks.
- A sausage tree on the riverbank of the Kavango, east of Rundu.
- Caprivi is the traditional home of the Kavango people.
- Also known as the go-away bird, the grey lourie is at home in the Mahango Game Park.
- Life in the Caprivi is simple and often hard for local villagers.
- Dusk sees the sun settle over the still waters of the mighty Kavango River.
- For many rural Kavango people, many daily chores centre around the waters of the Kavango River.

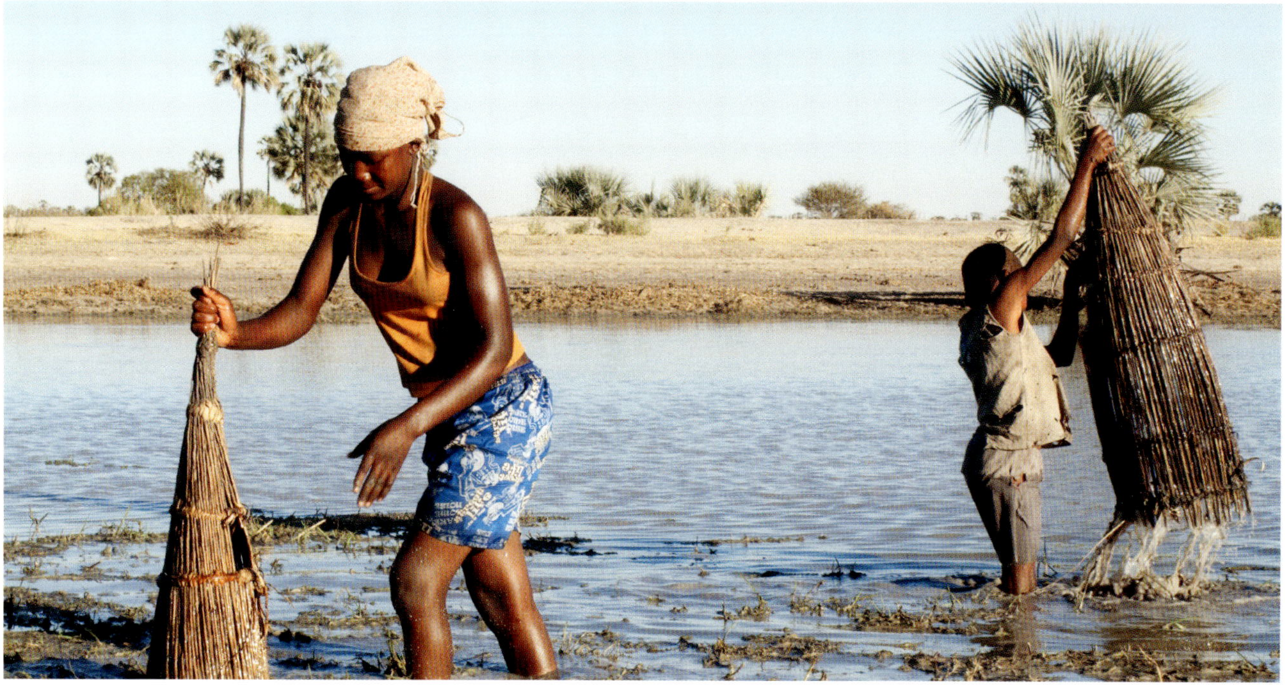

ABOVE: The traditional Owambo people in the Omusati region have devised an ingenious method by which to trap fish in thc shallow pools known locally as *oshana*.

OPPOSITE: The Owamboland landscape is dotted sporadically with trees, the most recognisable being the great icon of the southern subcontinent, the baobab. Shrouded in myth and mystery, these strange-looking trees – some said to be hundreds of years old – have a number of uses, both nutritional and medicinal.

Because the north of Namibia is in such close proximity to neighbouring Angola and Botswana, it is inevitable that subtle influences – on both the people and the landscape – have drifted across the borders. The interior remains dry, but by no means barren. Baobabs, so iconic of Botswana, stand tall and proud across the north, while palms and shallow pools lie scattered along the grassy banks of the Kunene and Kavango rivers. Like their neighbours, Namibians who have made their homes in these far-northern reaches of the country rely heavily on the bounty of nature. Isolated and far away from contemporary urban settlements, many rural Namibians still lead simple lives in traditional villages.

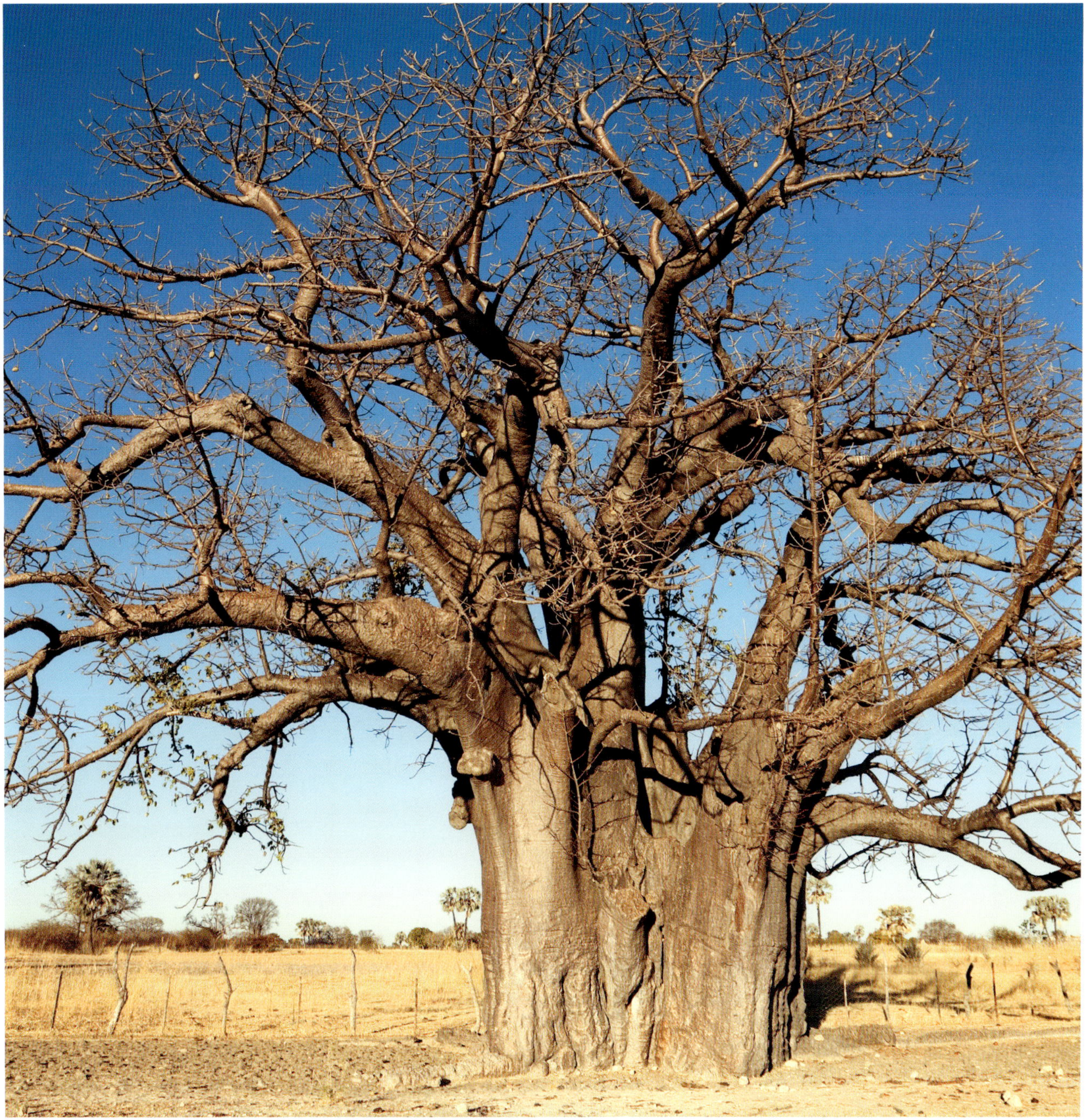

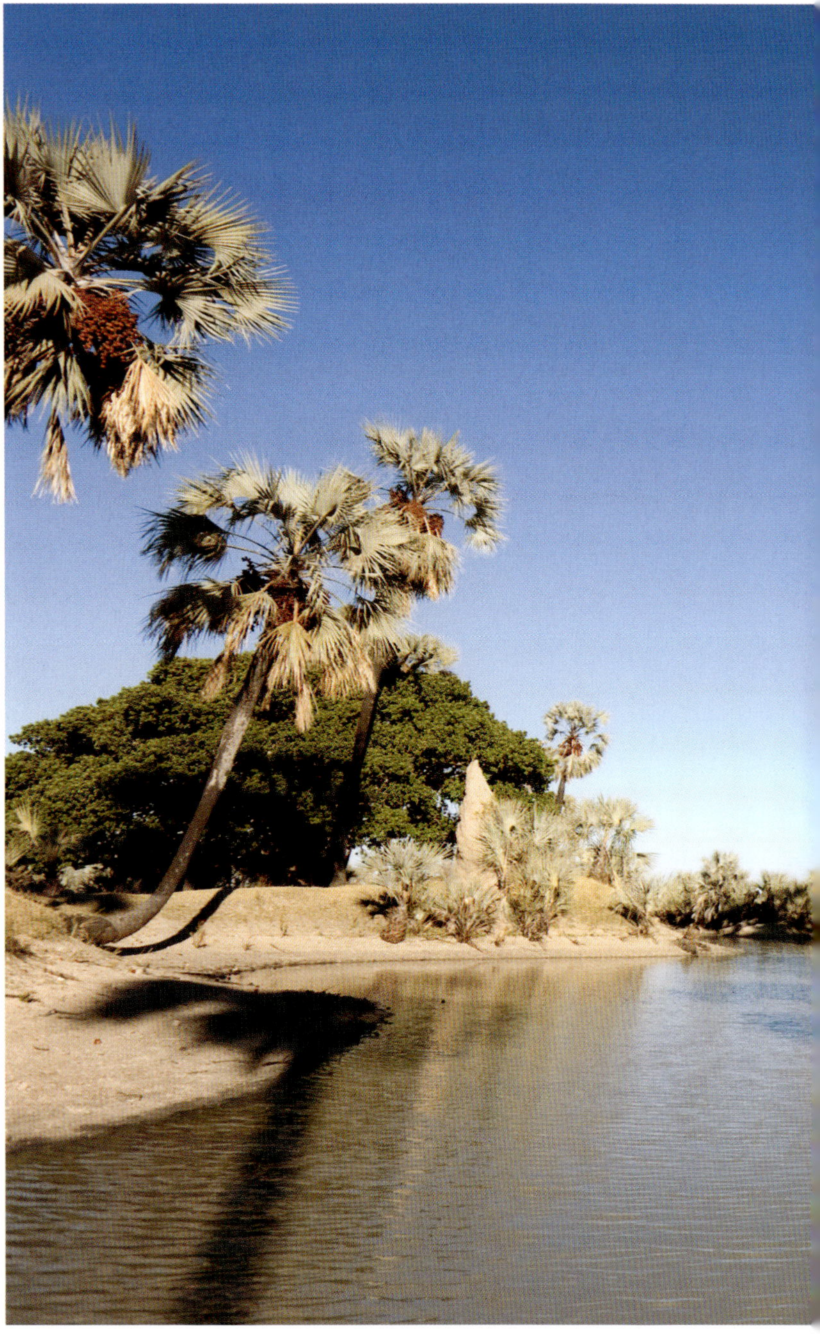

RIGHT: Like the baobab, the makalani palm, which lines many of the water courses here, is one of the most recognisable features of the northern Namibian landscape. Both the Himba and Owambo people make carvings from the tree's nut-like seeds.

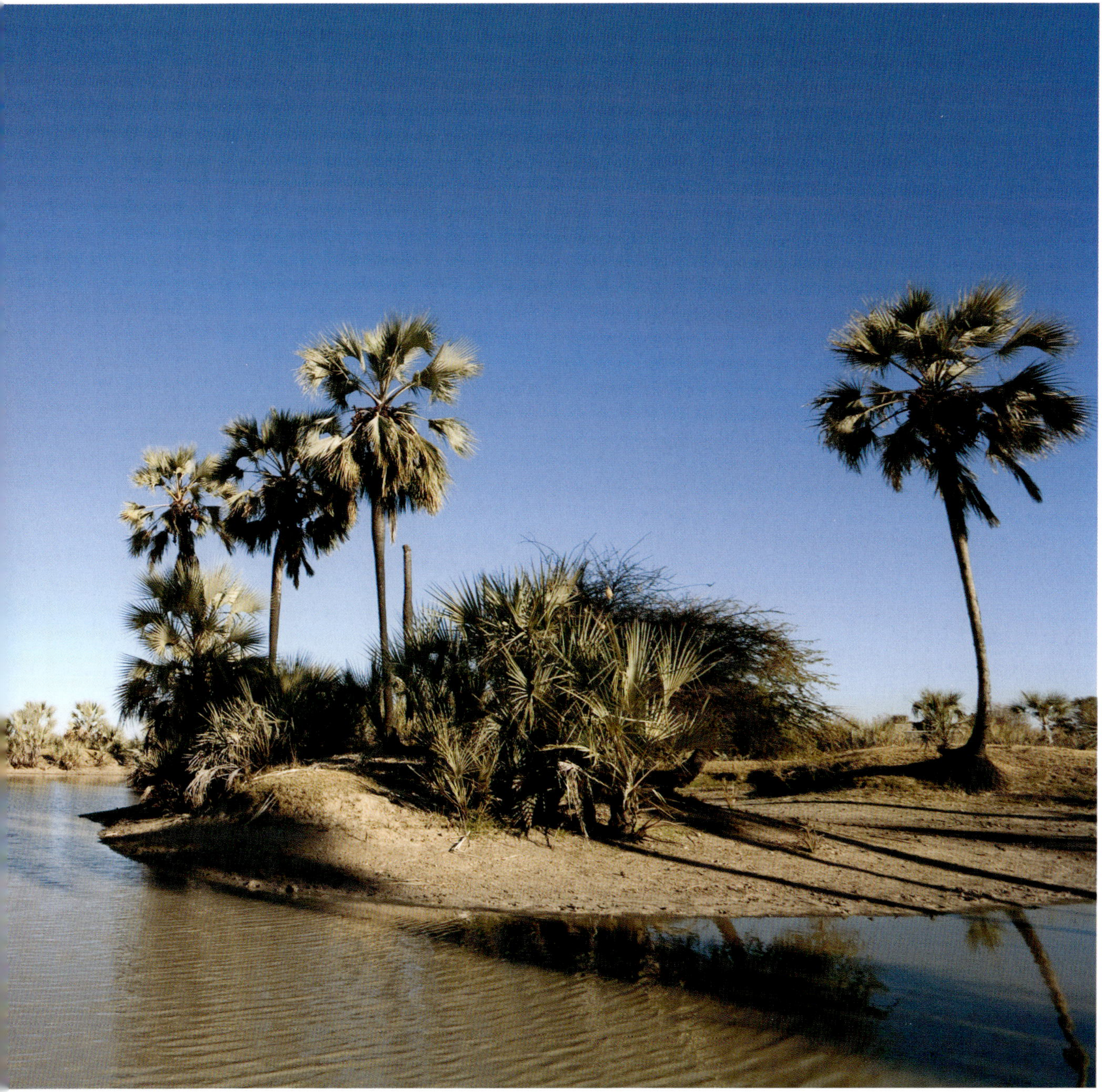

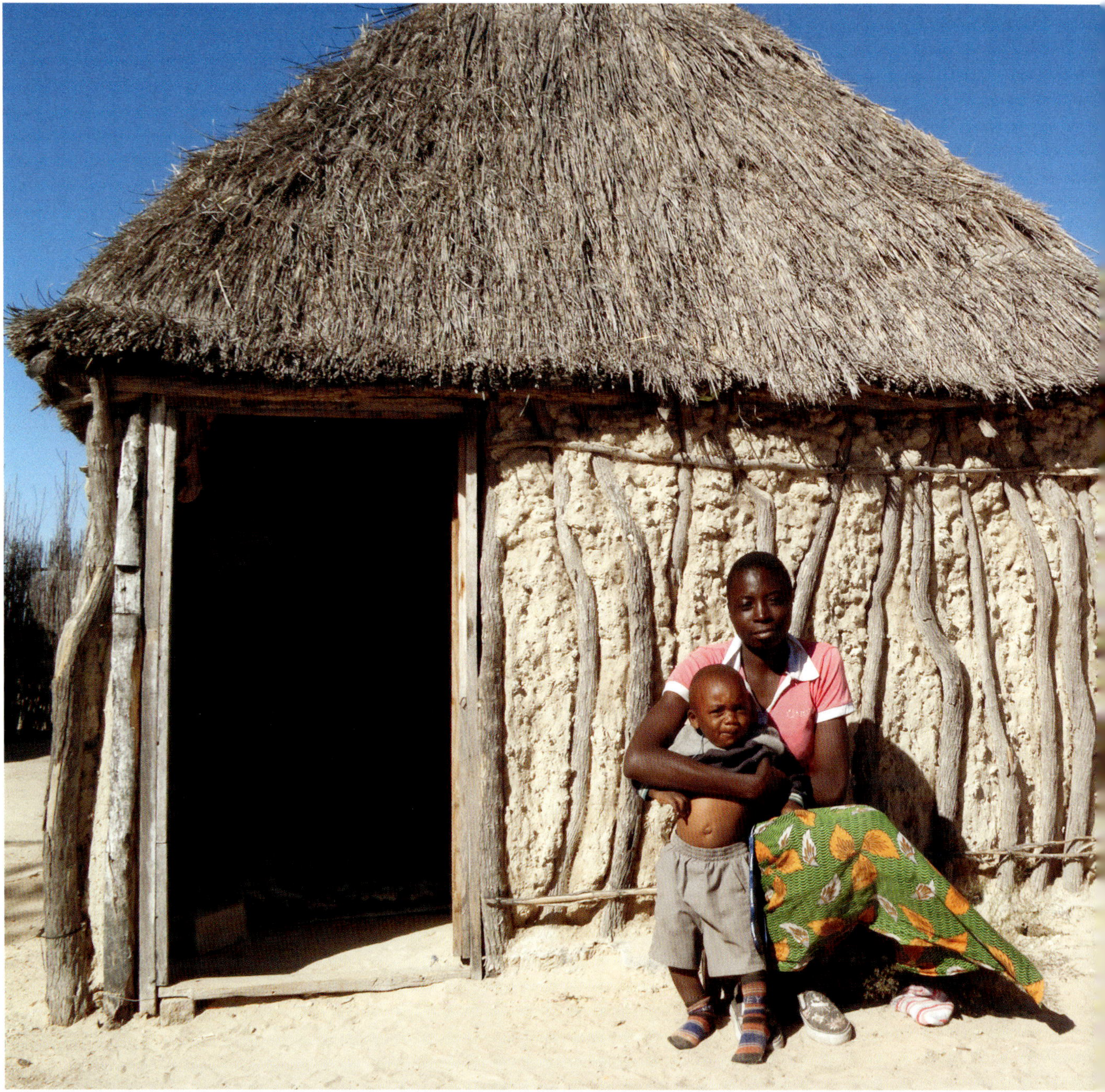

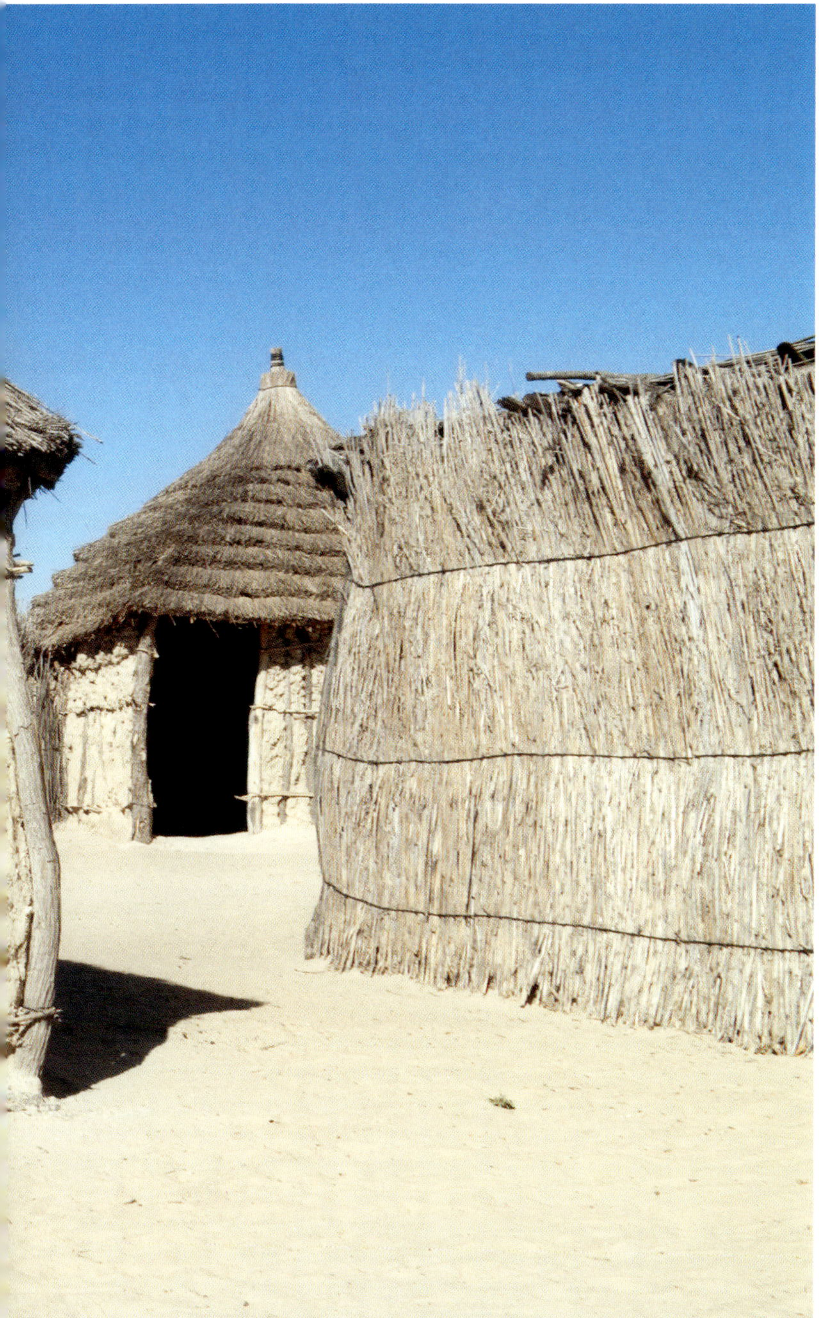

LEFT: The town of Rundu was established as a humble bus stop from which local labourers were ferried to nearby farms. Today the lively little settlement is the commercial and cultural capital of the Kavango region, but remains modest and populated mostly by local farm workers and their families.

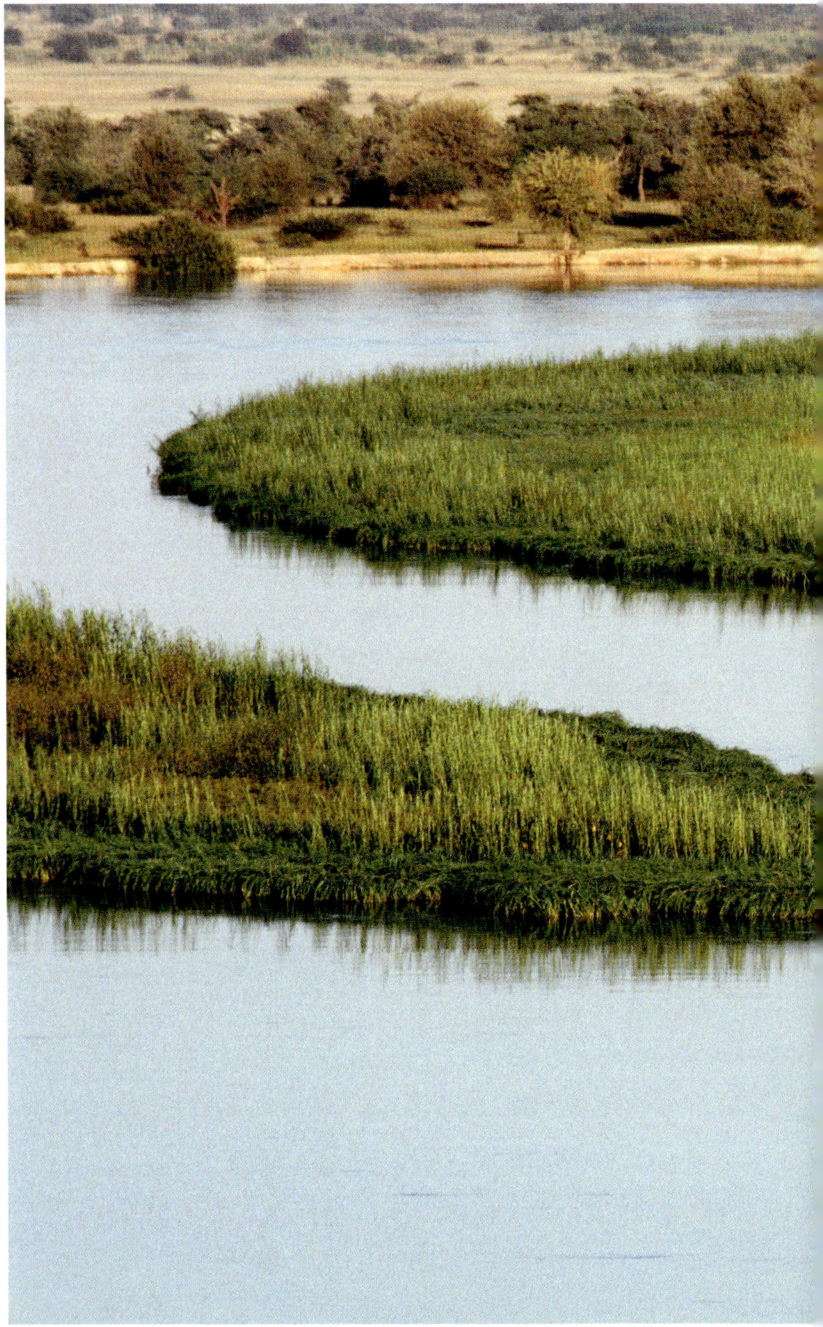

RIGHT: The Kavango River, also known as the Okavango, starts in Angola, where it is known as the Cubango River. On its winding course south, it forms the natural boundary between Angola and Namibia and finally empties in Botswana in what is known as the Okavango Delta, a wet and verdant swampland in stark contrast to the surrounding Kalahari plains.

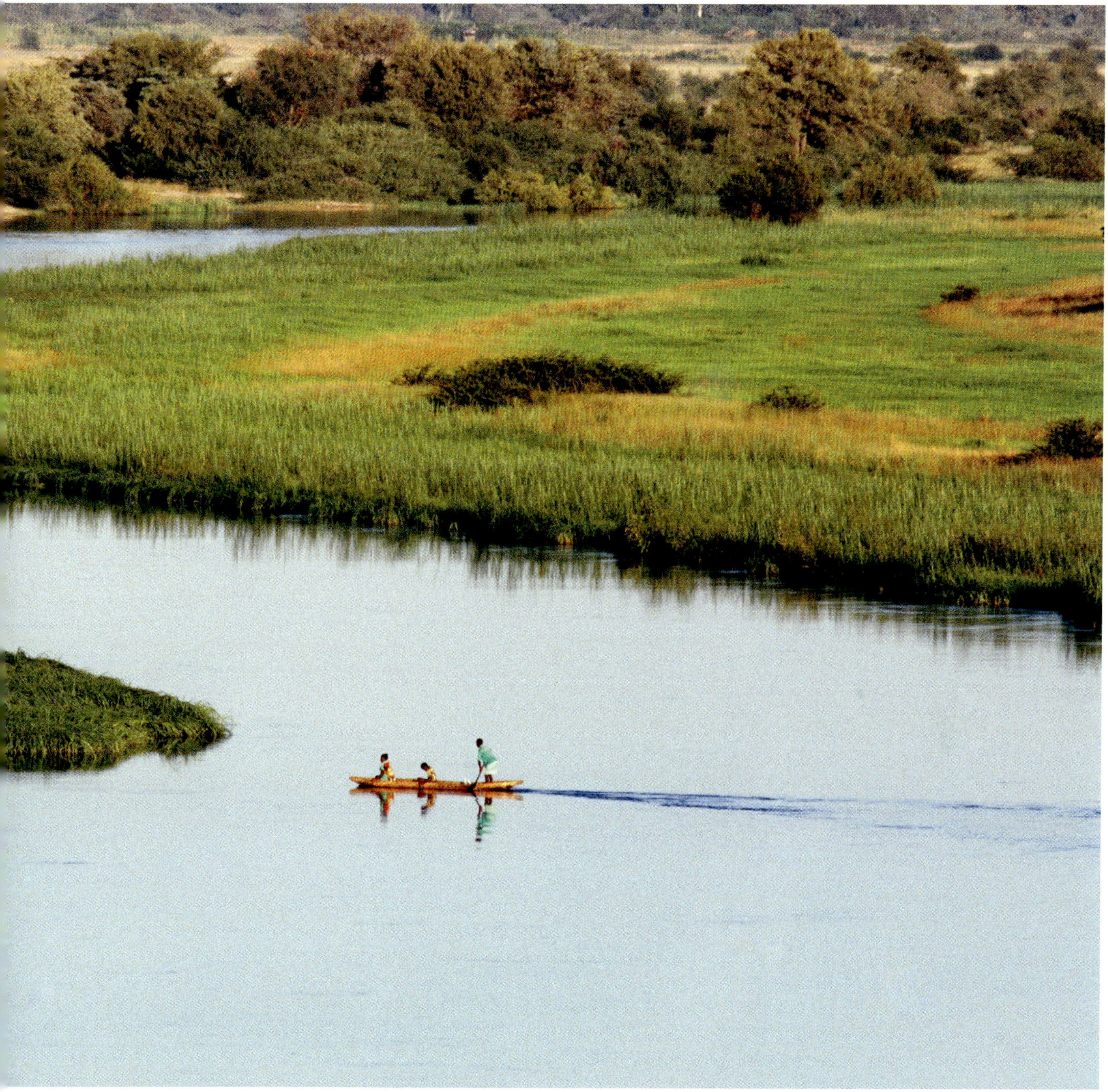

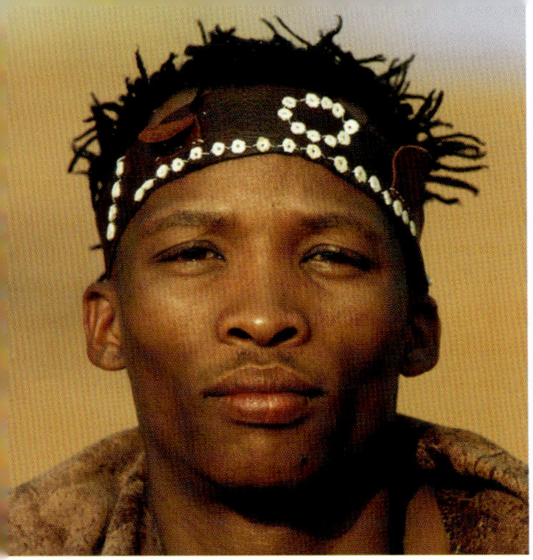
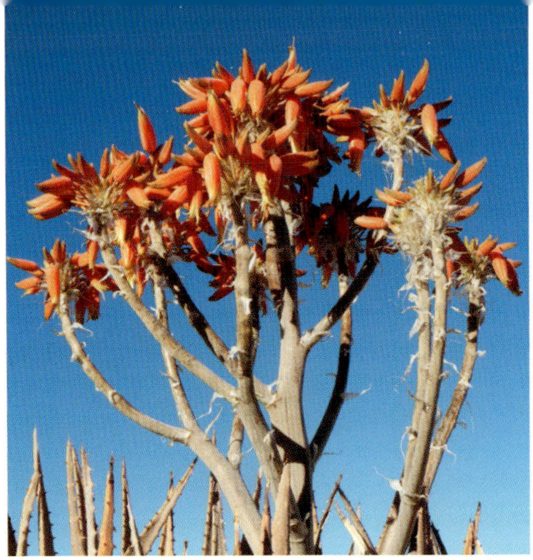
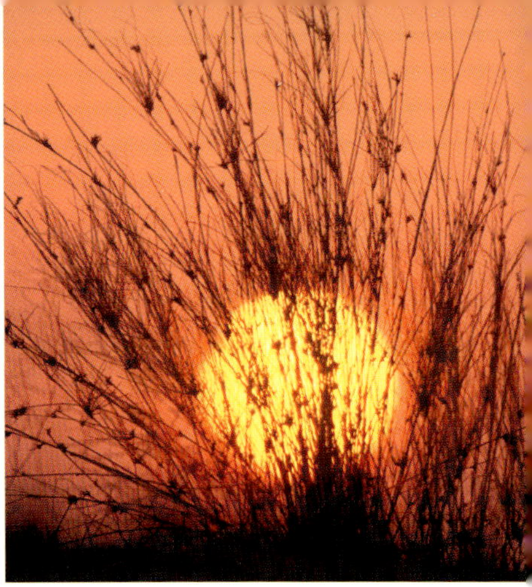
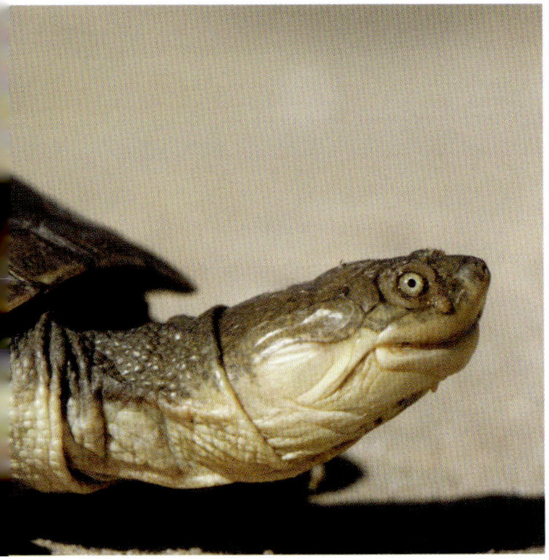
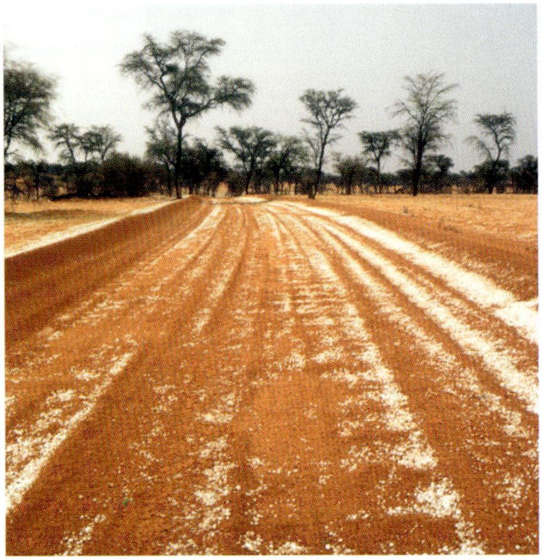
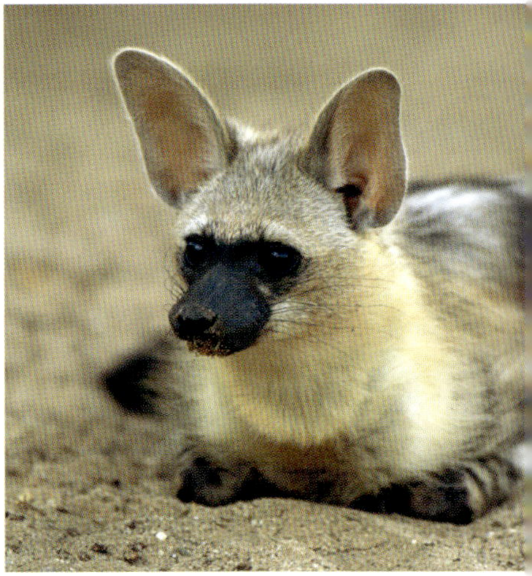
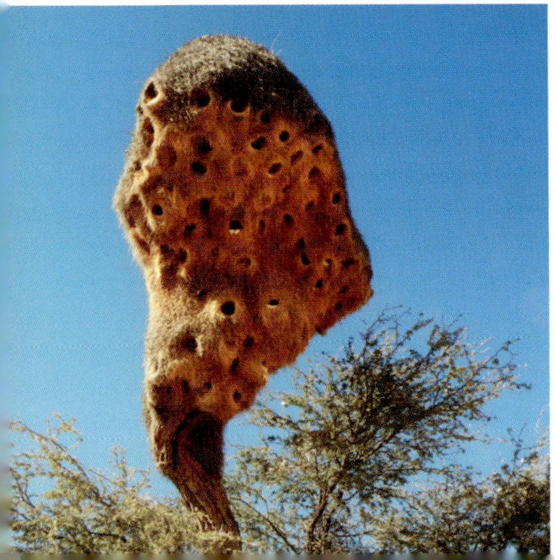
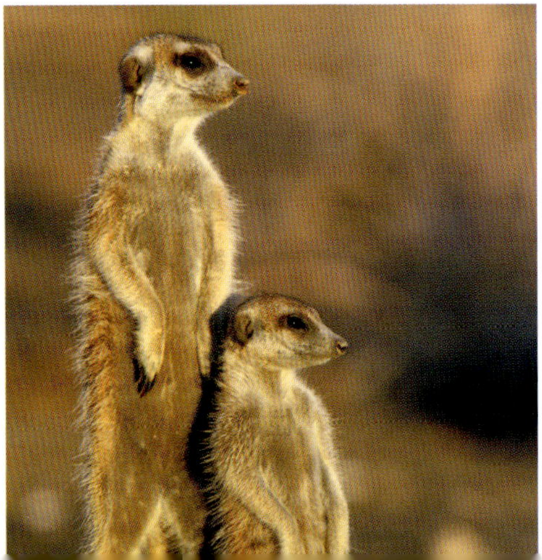
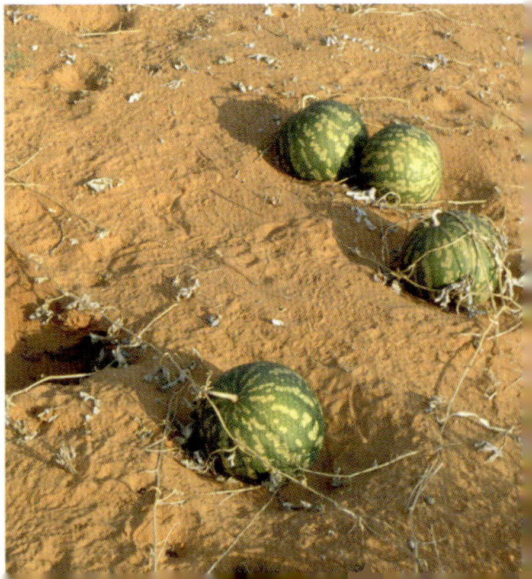

Kalahari

The Kalahari may not be a desert in the official sense of the word, but it is widely recognised as the largest continuous stretch of sand on the planet. Its vast, empty and dry plains are clearly visible even from space. Said to extend over 900 000 square kilometres, it covers a huge tract of southern Africa, including parts of Namibia, South Africa and approximately 80 percent of neighbouring Botswana – even spilling over into parts of Angola, Zambia and Zimbabwe. This wide, open expanse – lashed by clouds of dust, pummelled by summer rains and schorched by an unforgiving sun – stretches from about the Orange River right up to more equatorial regions in the north. Set on a solid foundation consisting of shale, sandstone and, in parts, coal laid down a phenomenal 300 million years ago, this massive sand bowl is approximately 200 million years old. It was formed at the time that the Gondwana supercontinent started to disintegrate and reform to make up the landmasses we recognise today as those of the southern hemisphere. Given the sparseness of its landscape and the searing heat of its semi-arid hinterland, it should come as no surprise that summer temperatures are high, reaching 45° Celsius in places, with almost insignificant rainfall, averaging about 130 millimetres a year over much of this apparent wasteland. The Kalahari, however, is not without its wildlife: from the majestic gemsbok to the curious suricate, more commonly referred to as the meerkat in this part of the world, to a number of reptile and bird species that populate a region mistakenly considered inhospitable to even the hardiest of life forms.

OPPOSITE FROM LEFT TO RIGHT:

- Family groups of the indigenous !Kung still live in the challenging environment of the Kalahari.
- Plant species, such as the aloe, have adapted well in order to survive the semi-arid conditions.
- Fine-leaved but extremely hardy grasses cover parts of the Kalahari dunes.
- The marsh, or helmeted terrapin, is one of more than 60 reptile species found within the geographical boundaries of the Kalahari.
- Despite its usually exceedingly dry conditions, the Kalahari does see the very occasional tumult of hailstones.
- Small mammals such as the aardwolf shelter in the scrub that covers parts of the Kalahari.
- Sociable weavers craft massive communal nests amid the hardy branches of camel-thorn trees.
- Meerkats, or suricates, live in small family groups burrowed into the hot sand.
- Tsama melons are a vital source of both food and water for animals at home in this harsh environment.

RIGHT: The Kalahari's !Kung people, who have formally condoned the use of the otherwise offensive word 'bushman', are a tight-knit community. Most have adopted elements of a Western lifestyle, such as informal schooling, and yet retain many traditional customs.

OPPOSITE: Many of the !Kung still follow at least some of the traditions of their forebears, gathering fruits and other edibles from the semi-arid landscape and hunting for meat and skins.

OVERLEAF, LEFT: Gemsbok are well suited to the Kalahari's dry conditions. They generally graze on the sparse grasses, but when these are not available, the herds readily browse on higher leaves.

OVERLEAF, RIGHT: To combat the threat of predators in this demanding landscape, meerkats post sentries that warn foraging family groups of imminent danger.

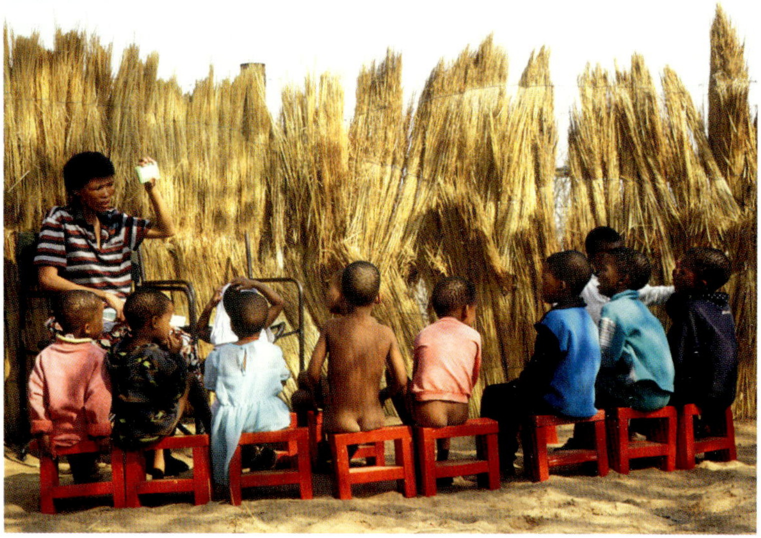

According to official census records, human settlements in the Namibian section of the Kalahari are limited to Gobabis and Mariental, with just four others in Botswana and two in South Africa, but there are nevertheless a number of tiny clusters of family groups and informal settlements dotted virtually throughout. Most significant of the Kalahari's population – at least for their cultural and historical reasons – are the hunter-gatherers commonly referred to as the San, whose ancestors settled here 20 000 years ago, bringing with them the clicking sounds that have infiltrated a number of Bantu languages since. While many have taken to a contemporary Western lifestyle, traditional family groups still hunt wild game with bows and arrows, gather edible plants and satisfy their water requirements from indigenous vegetation and underground sources, as surface water is virtually nonexistent.

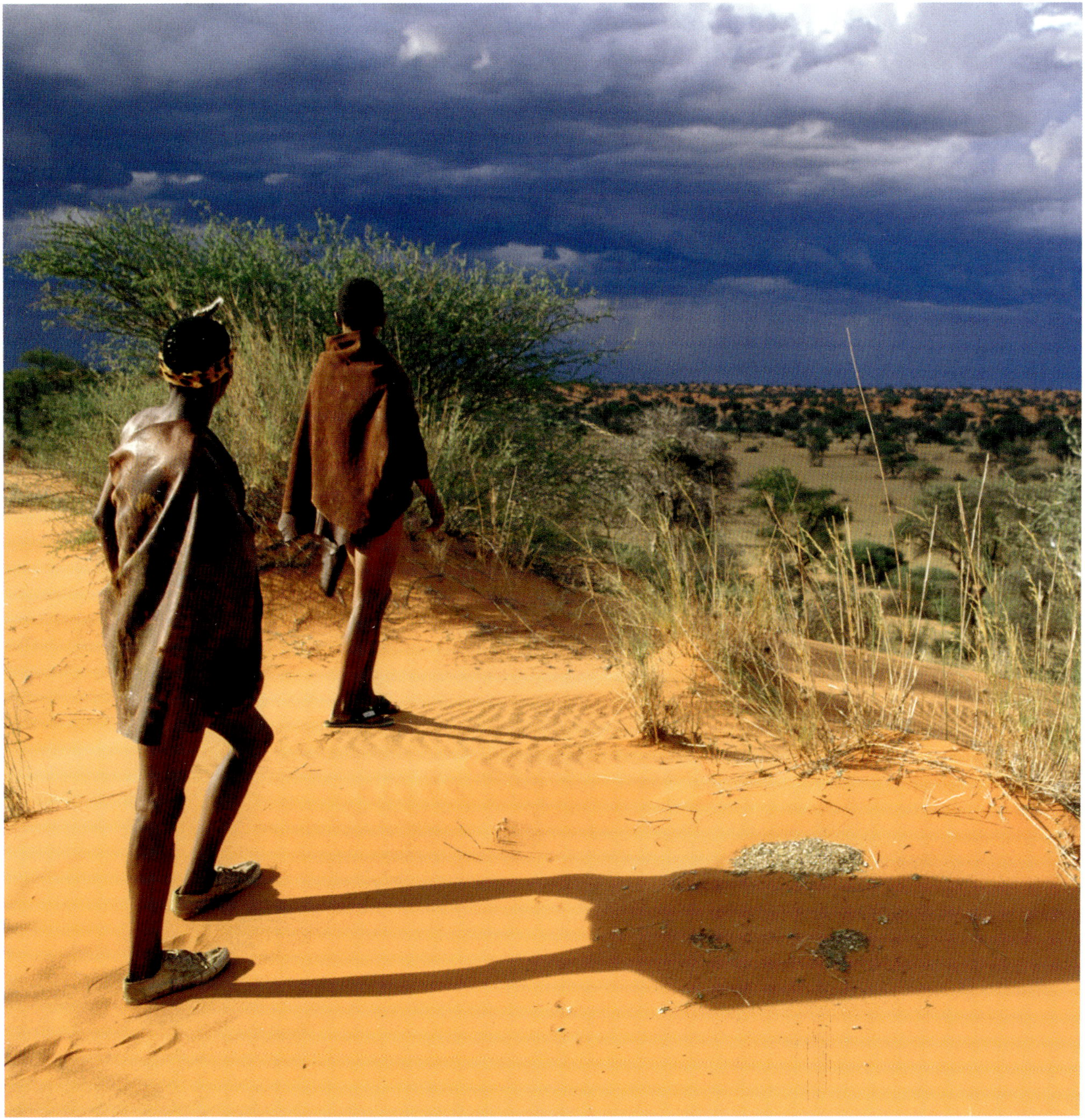

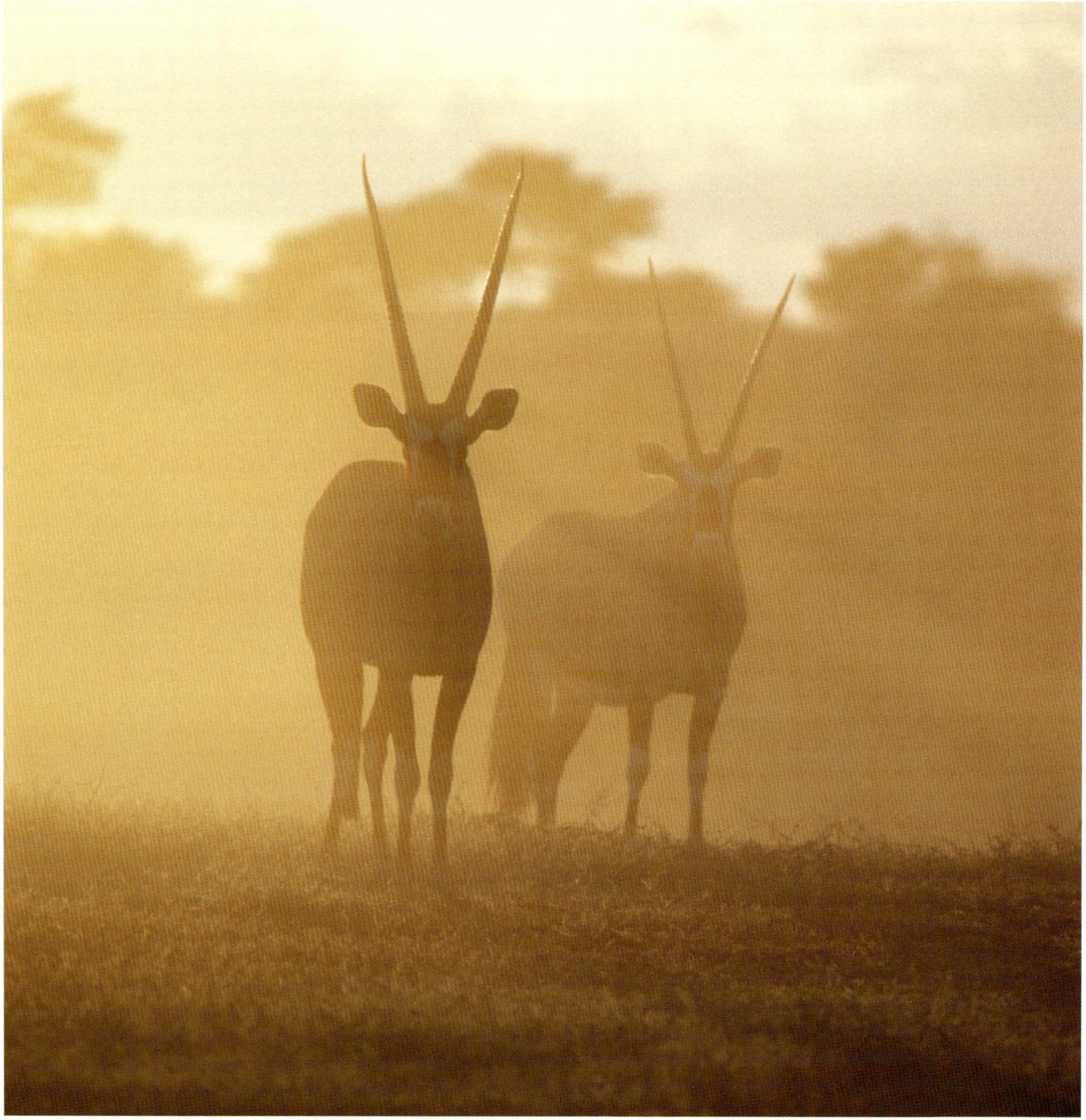

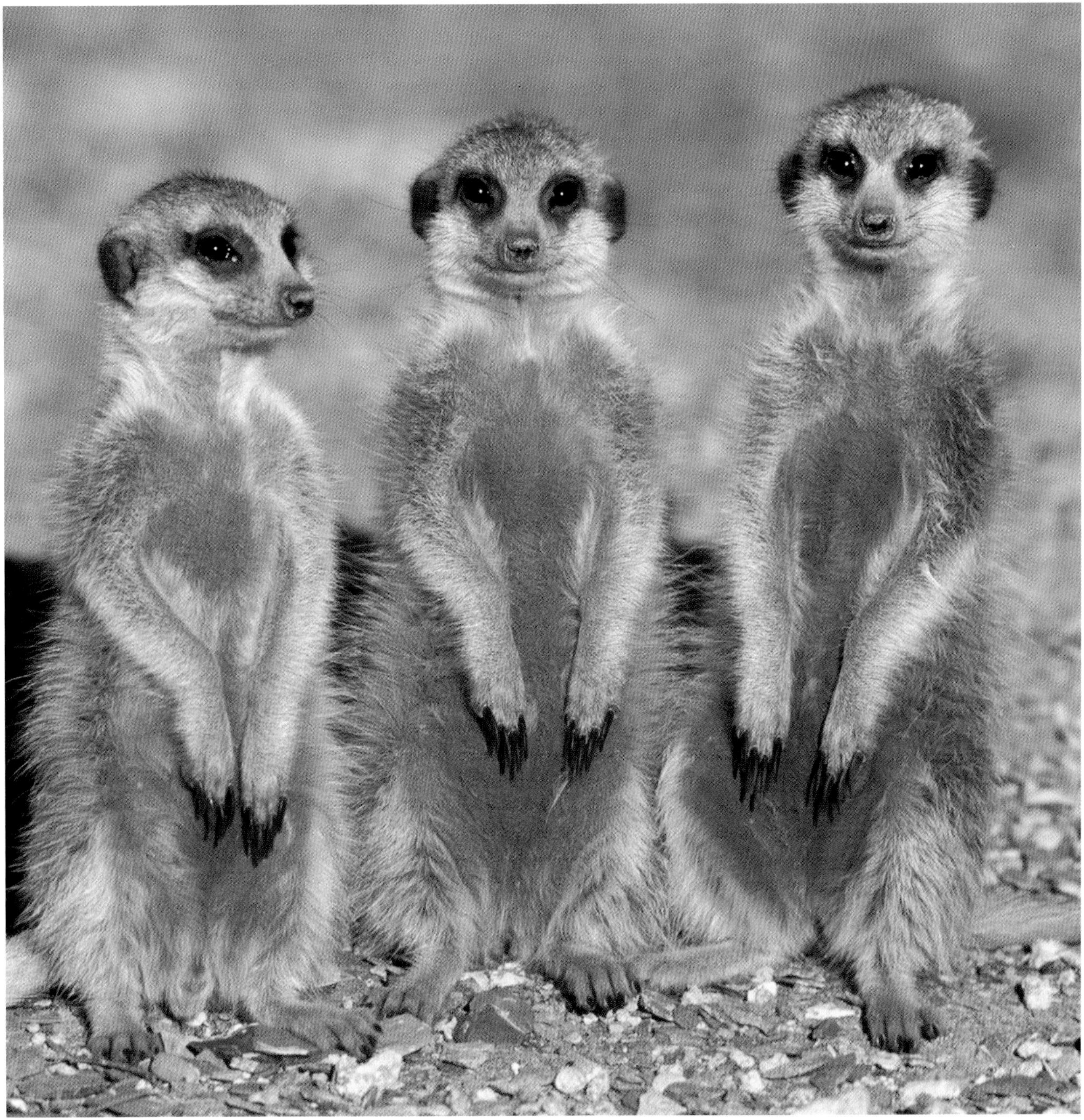

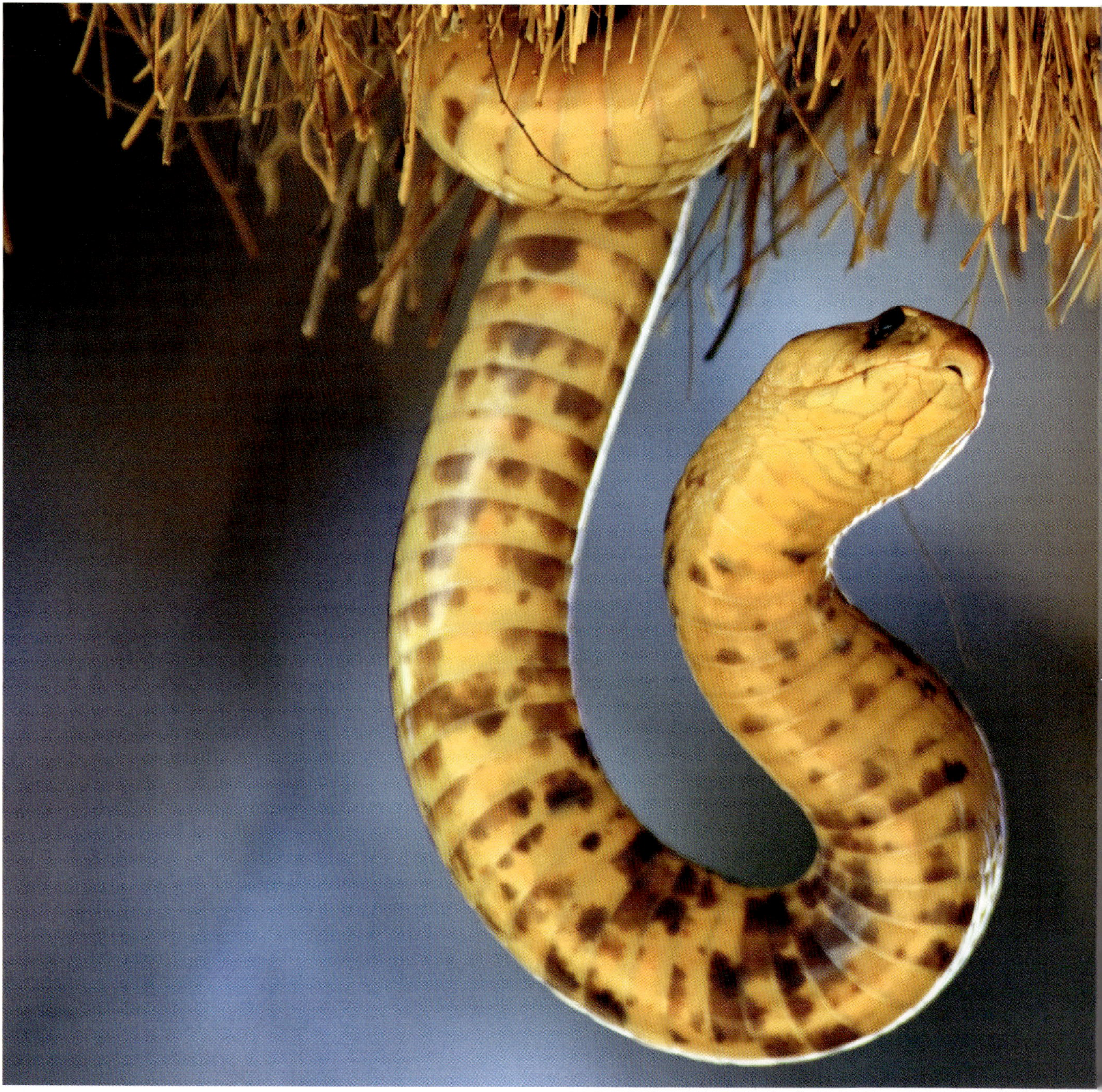

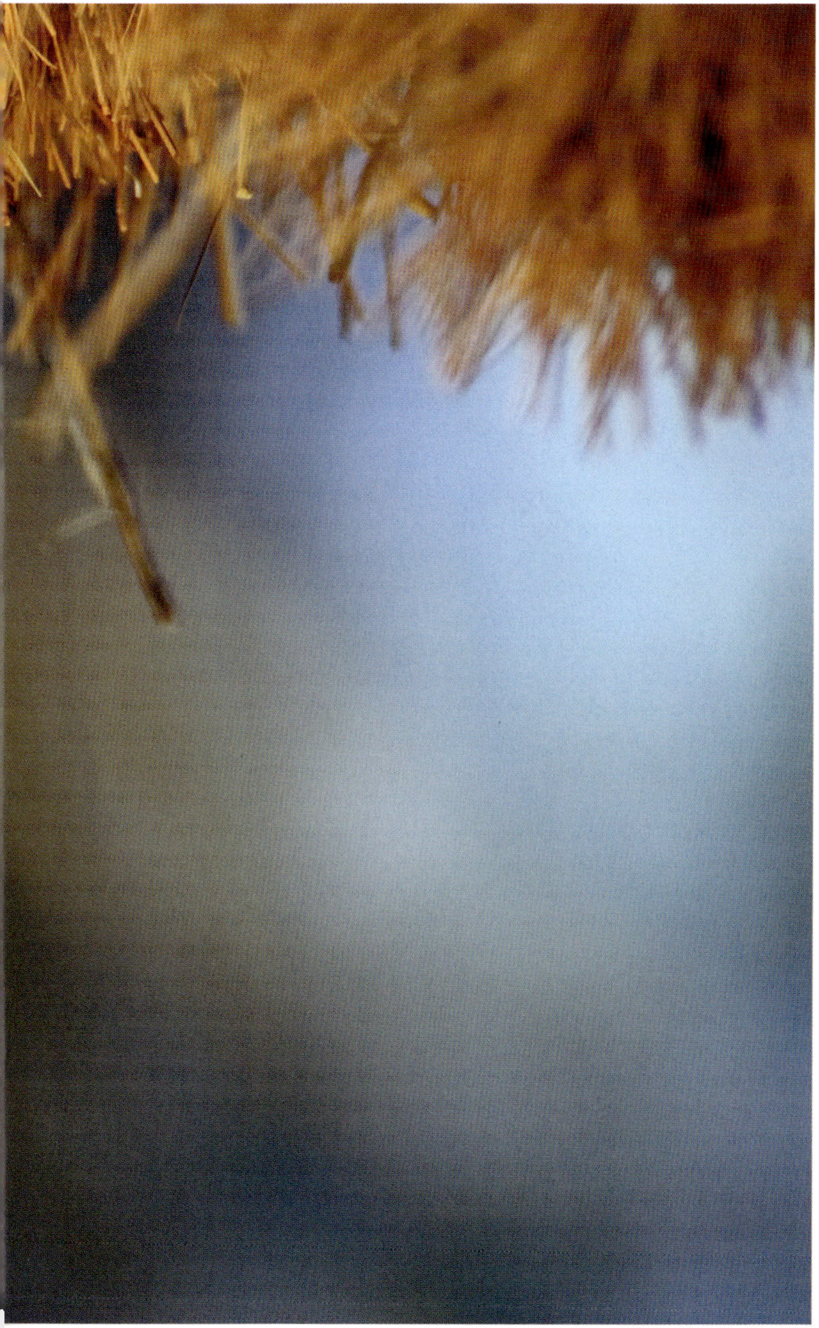

LEFT: The Kalahari can be merciless. Here a Cape cobra, whose neurotoxic venom is usually fatal for humans, raids the huge communal nest of sociable weavers. It is a rare opportunity to gather sustenance. It may be a long time until another find such as this.

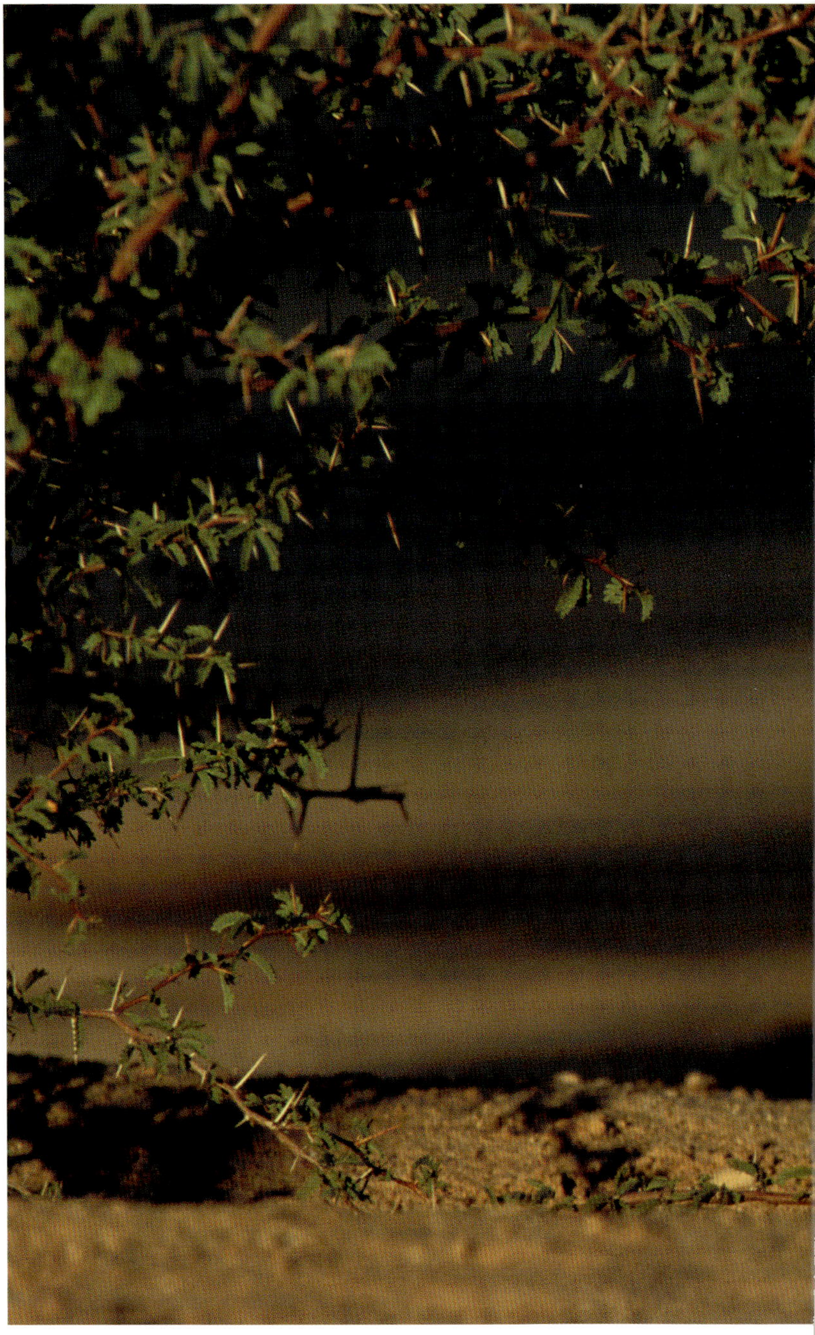

RIGHT: Even the most agile of its creatures take precautions against the dangers that lurk in the Kalahari. Here a feeding Cape ground squirrel senses its vulnerability and remains alert as it nibbles from the lower branches of a thornbush.

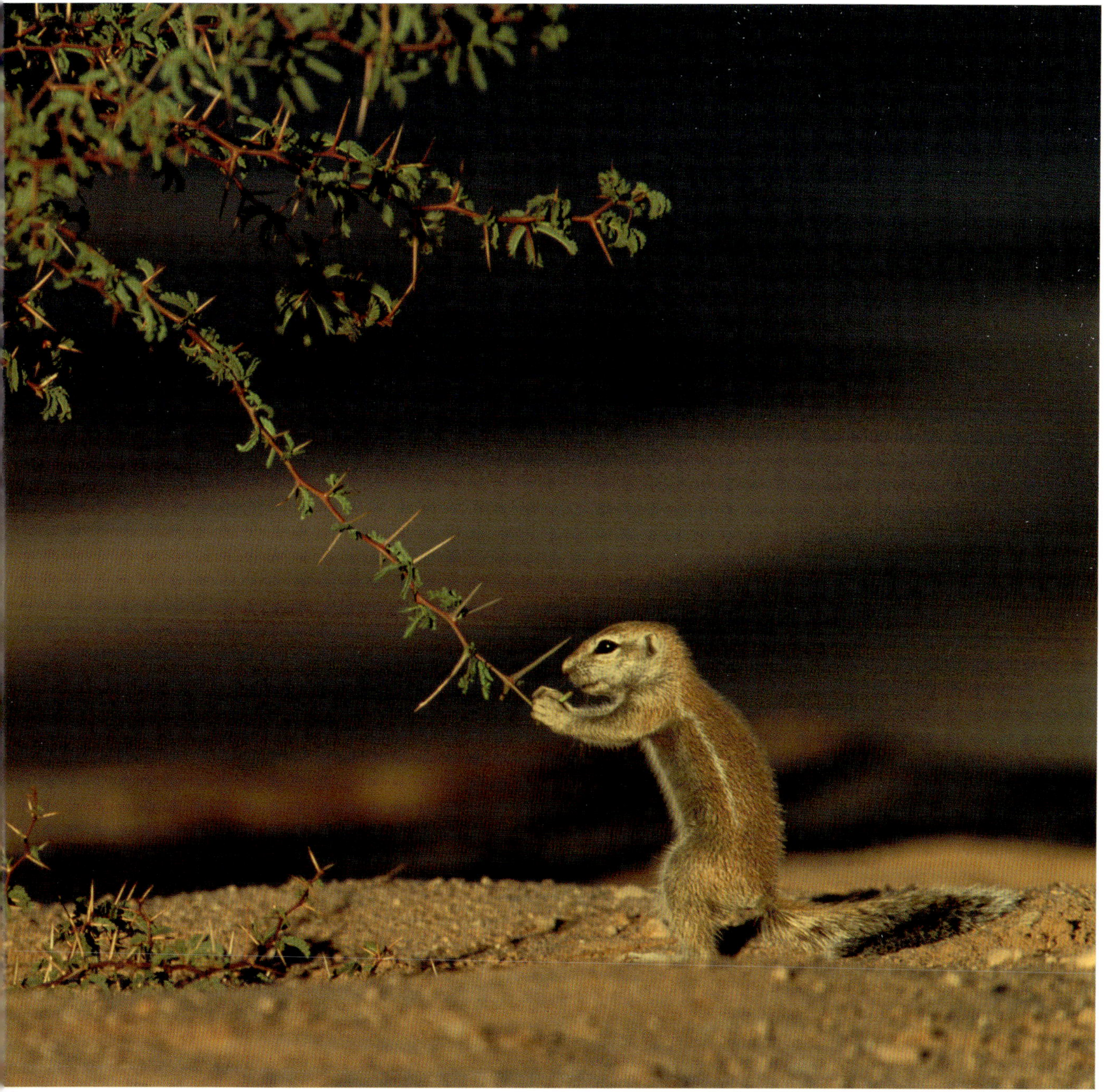

First published in 2010 by
Sunbird Publishers (Pty) Ltd
(an imprint of Jonathan Ball Publishers (Pty) Ltd)
Registration number: 1984/003543/07
PO Box 6836
Roggebaai 8012
Cape Town, South Africa

www.sunbirdpublishers.co.za

Publisher: Ceri Prenter
Cover, design and typesetting: MR Design
Reproduction: Resolution, Cape Town
Printed and bound by Tien Wah Press (Pte), Singapore

ISBN 978-1-92028-919-5

Photographic credits
Copyright in photographs remains with Thomas Dressler (www.thomasdressler.net) unless listed below.

Ariadne Van Zandbergen: 6f; 34b; 78–79
Garry Black/Masterfile/Great Stock!: 48–49
Frank Krahmer/Masterfile/Great Stock!: 62–63
The Hoberman Collection/Great Stock!: 68–69; 132–133 **Samantha Reinders:** 84; 85

FRONT COVER: African elephants head towards a water hole in Etosha National Park.

BACK COVER: A male lion in captivity at the Okonjima Lodge, home of the AfriCat Foundation.
The Evangelical Lutheran Church (*Felsenkirche*), a prominent landmark of the coastal town of Lüderitz, was consecrated in 1912.
A Himba girl in the Kaokoveld with a double plait hairstyle typical of pre-adolescent girls.
Dune grass on top of a sand dune in the Kalahari desert at sunset.